Stability, Sport and Performance Movement

GREAT TECHNIQUE WITHOUT INJURY

JOANNE ELPHINSTON

Lotus Publishing
Chichester, England

North Atlantic Books
Berkeley, California

First published in 2008 by
Lotus Publishing
Apple Tree Cottage, Inlands Road, Chichester, PO18 8RJ and
North Atlantic Books
P O Box 12327
Berkeley, California 94712

Illustrations Amanda Williams
Technique photographs Joanne Elphinston/CMD
Sportsperson photographs istock 47, 53; Sporting Heroes/George Herringshaw
(all cover photographs), 16, 20, 28, 29, 51; Scanpix 16, 17, 42, 43, 45, 48, 94
Text and Cover Design Richard Evans
Printed and Bound in the UK by Scotprint

Disclaimer

The information in this book has been presented with care on the basis of the author's professional experience and the available research. The programmes are designed for healthy individuals with normal levels of fitness unless under the supervision of a health professional. The author is not liable for misuse or misunderstanding of the material herein, nor any injury which may be incurred while pursuing the programmes provided.

Stability, Sport and Performance Movement is sponsored by the Society for the Study of Native Arts and Sciences, a nonprofit educational corporation whose goals are to develop an educational and cross-cultural perspective linking various scientific, social, and artistic fields; to nurture a holistic view of arts, sciences, humanities, and healing; and to publish and distribute literature on the relationship of mind, body, and nature.

British Library Cataloguing in Publication Data
A CIP record for this book is available from the British Library
ISBN 978 1 905367 09 2 (Lotus Publishing)
ISBN 978 1 55643 746 5 (North Atlantic Books)

Library of Congress Cataloguing-in-Publication Data
Elphinston, Joanne.
  Stability, sport, and performance movement: great technique without
injury / joanne elphinston.
  p. cm.
  Includes bibliographical references and index.
  ISBN 978-1-55643-746-5
  1. Sports--Physiological aspects. 2. Movement therapy. 3. Human
mechanics. 4. Sports injuries. I. Title.
RC1235.E47 2008
612'.044--dc22
                                                              2008013790

Contents

Preface

During the years that I have been sharing my work through teaching and consultancy, I have met hundreds of enthusiastic and committed people. Included amongst these are athletes, coaches, fitness professionals, sports medicine and sports science personnel. I have enjoyed the challenge of working with all of these groups, and greatly appreciate what I in turn have learned from them.

I have finally sat down and written this book because I am constantly being asked by participants during my seminars for a resource that can support and enhance their understanding of functional stability and its relationship to movement. They are often caught between the exercise books that present the "how" but not clearly the "when", the scientific papers that tell us the "what" but not necessarily the "how", and the anatomy books which tell us about body structures but not necessarily the relationships between those structures as they occur in movement. So, I have set about putting together the practical information that I've been developing, working with and teaching over the years.

Some of you will use all of it, and others will dip into certain chapters. Most things are best explained in simple terms, so I have tried to remove the language barrier between athlete, coach, and medical professional where possible in order help you to communicate with each other.

I believe that simple things done well win the day. I believe that we should use our common sense. I believe that we should know our bodies and respect them. We should also be kind to them and listen to them, even though at times we must push them to their limits. I also think that we can all move beautifully and effortlessly if we make it a priority.

Joanne Elphinston, Cardiff, 2008

Acknowledgments

Although I had intended to write this book at some stage, it may not have come about when it did had it not originally been commissioned by SISU Idrottsböcker of Stockholm, and guided into life by Catarina Arfwidsson for the Swedish sports community. For the first two years of its life it existed only in Swedish, until Jon Hutchings of Lotus Publishing had the vision to produce it in English.

There are many people without whom this book would never have been written. The athletes who have challenged me to look for solutions, and who have taken responsibility for themselves and their training; the coaches who have applied the principles with their athletes and upheld my belief in raising the bar for coach education; the sports scientists who have been willing to share in the multidisciplinary process, and the physiotherapists and other sports professionals who have so kindly shared their enthusiasm for simple specific concepts and who have spurred me on with their support.

There are some individuals who must be thanked personally. Sarah Hardman, Heather Watson, Jackie Zaslona, Susie Morel and Karen Fuller kindly shared their thoughts on the text. Karen's attention to detail led her to personally perform every exercise in the book: no author could hope for greater commitment to the cause!

Danielle Nichols, Rob Ahmun, Kent Fyrth, Nick Jones and Leah Cox gave their time to be models and for this I am very grateful. Jo Thomas-Kemp of Esporta Cardiff very kindly lent her support by making space available for photography.

Richard Evans was the most tolerant and good natured of book designers an author could hope for.

Finally, I must thank my husband, Kent Fyrth, without whose unfaltering support I could not do what I do.

Introduction

In every sport there are athletes who represent true technical excellence. We recognise them instinctively, as their efficiency is expressed through the beauty of their movement and the effortlessness with which they seem to perform. This technical mastery requires a physical structure that supports the sport's biomechanics, the neuromuscular coordination to correctly sequence the movement, the psychological skills to focus effort without unnecessary tension and the physiology to sustain the movement pattern until the event is completed.

With its ability to move through multiple planes in complex combinations, the body is capable of extraordinary movement diversity. This makes an enormous range of sporting endeavours possible, but this versatility can become our greatest challenge to technical proficiency. It permits unwanted movements, which then require increased muscle tension to try to control them. It allows deviation from the most effective line of motion, compromising efficiency. It allows variability in joint angles, timing and movement sequencing which gives us many movement options, but can also amplify control problems under conditions of increased complexity, fatigue, speed, agility, endurance or technical demand.

In closed skill sports such as swimming, pole vaulting or sprint kayak, performance depends upon an ability to accurately reproduce a movement with minimal variation. These athletes hone their movement skill to progressively narrow the window of variability. This does not limit their adaptability however. Their fundamental technical consistency allows them to make small but accurate adjustments if their environment requires it in order to deliver their best performance. In open skill sports such as tennis, football and alpine skiing, athletes must be able to move in a variety of ways and adapt to rapidly changing situations, but still produce accurate and effective movement by controlling the forces acting on them. Their challenge is to widen the diversity of their skills but to control their variability. They aim to develop more movement options with reliable results.

Even at world-class level we can observe differences in movement economy and control. Some athletes compensate for their technical limitations by maximising other assets, such as an astounding natural physiology or a combination of strength and determination. They may achieve success, but using this method is somewhat like taking a jigsaw puzzle with a missing piece and trying to make up for it by making the other pieces bigger. You may cover the space, but the picture will not be as coherent as it might have been with the missing piece in place. The question is not how athletic success was achieved, but how much more might have been possible with all systems optimised.

The building blocks of stability, mobility, posture, body awareness, symmetry and balance provide the foundation for sporting movement development and injury resistance. These elements work in combination to ensure that physical restrictions, imbalances and inefficient muscle recruitment patterns do not hold you back from meeting your technical movement goals. The right muscles firing at the right time in the right sequence can increase your chance of achieving your physical potential.

The purpose of this book is to promote effective movement, rather than to develop "core stability". "Core stability" has been defined as the capacity for the trunk to support, control and withstand the forces acting upon it, so that the body structures can perform in their "safest, strongest and most efficient positions"[24]. The core muscles are usually identified as those involved in force transfer between the limbs and trunk, as well as the muscles of the trunk itself.

Core stability has been transformed from a concept into an industry, and great claims are made for its potential effects despite a lack of consistent evidence in the scientific literature to support them. Part of the problem is that it has been taken out of context.

When stability is perceived to be a separate fitness marker like speed or power, athletes start to look for exercise regimens that activate "more core". Some professionals advocate instability activities such as Swiss Ball exercise and others argue in favour of Olympic lifts for developing "core stability". Both in fact stimulate the trunk in different ways and for different purposes. Research to determine the amount of trunk activity involved in different activities sometimes compares loaded with unloaded activities. Unsurprisingly, researchers find that there is more activity in the trunk when the body is loaded [37]. This is then taken as evidence that the loading approach is more effective.

If our objective is movement efficiency, then "more" is not necessarily desirable. Certainly if you are squatting with a heavy weight, you will require an increase in trunk activity to support your spine against that resistance. You will be training a response to a predictable, loaded, symmetrical movement, and this may be appropriate to certain specific sporting demands. However, you will not have trained for unpredictability, change of direction, control through different motions or at the low levels of continuous muscle activity needed to optimise whole body movement over extended periods. These conditions require a different set of neuromuscular responses. It is a matter of what is appropriate for your functional requirements.

Core stability cannot independently optimise movement availability and control. The moving body in sport requires a complex sequence of activation and timing appropriate to the activity that you are performing. This sequence is known as a *functional motor pattern*, and it requires an interplay between your musculo-skeletal system and your nervous system from the soles of your feet through your whole body to your head.

The programme presented in this book develops this interplay by integrating core stability concepts with posture, balance, mobility and neuromuscular control to provide you with a physical platform for fluent, trainable movement. Once you have this movement, you can train to make it faster, stronger and more powerful.

There are top athletes who have all of this working naturally. There are others who don't realise that there are elements which could improve, because no one has ever looked. There are many who are unaware that they have lost elements due to injury, and wonder why they just can't seem to make a successful comeback. Then there are those of us who are just trying to find the natural athlete within ourselves.

This book is for anyone interested in developing their own sporting movement, or who deals with athletes and athlete development at any age. It has been crafted in response to the needs of coaches, sports trainers, therapists and athletes who aim to develop sound, efficient movement in their sport, and is based on many years of experience in solving technique and injury problems across a wide variety of sports.

It is a practical resource, written as simply as possible in order to establish a common language between athletes, coaches, sports scientists and medical professionals working in sport. It was written to be a bridge so that we all can make ourselves understood.

The concept of functional stability for performance is explained, and how it contributes to the control and production of force and form in athletic movement. Once you are familiar with the anatomy and behaviour of some of the muscles which provide body control, we look at how to assess them and what to do when you find areas of weakness.

The exercise programme is presented in four phases which guide you in how to order and progress your programme. Many of the exercises will be familiar. Understanding why you are doing them, what they should look like, how they should progress and what you can use as alternatives is what makes the difference.

The principles are straightforward and relevant to most sports, and can be applied to children as well as adults. A chapter is dedicated to stability concepts for movement development in children, as many coaches work with athletes across a range of ages. I believe that the movement we have as adults starts a long time before we ever start training. I don't believe you can be too young to learn how to move beautifully, and in the computer game generation, the issue becomes ever more relevant.

This approach has been used with international-level athletes in disciplines as diverse as swimming, badminton, gymnastics, karate, judo, cycling, football, weight lifting, basketball, athletics, snow sports, golf, equestrian sports and tennis. However, it works just as well for weekend warriors and people who just want to enjoy their sport and enjoy their own movement.

Moving well doesn't have to be complicated. The principles are based in science, but in practice you need to know what to look for, what it means and how to fix it if it isn't what you are after. That is what this book is all about.

A note on language and expression
This resource is intended to be a bridge between athletes, coaches, and other sports professionals. Some readers will be testing and training themselves, and others will be supervising athletes. This is reflected in the language used throughout the book: mostly it is necessary to write for the person who is increasing their own awareness and capabilities, but in order for the processes described to be used in a team environment, some content is aimed at professionals trying to implement injury prevention or movement programmes with athletes. The different purposes would normally be presented in separate publications and it certainly would have been much easier for language consistency if this was the case, but it would have taken away the opportunity for those who are interested in a bigger picture to see how different perspectives fit together. As such, switches between the athlete's perspective and that of the medical, science or coaching professional will be recognisable in the book but should enhance rather than detract from its usefulness.

Chapter 1: What is Stability?

Pillars of Functional Stability
Functional Stability in Sport
How Can Functional Stability Influence Movement?
Optimal Performance Vs High Level Compensation
What Can Cause Movement Dysfunction?
Stability Principles in the Training Programme

The concept of "stability" can mean different things to the athlete, the coach, the sports scientist, and the sports medicine professional.

It may be used to describe how the whole body produces movement, directs force, or reacts to load challenges. This can be termed *functional stability*, and most simply put it is *your body's ability to meet the load and control demands of the required task*. It includes the controlled, sequenced relationships between moving body parts, and the planes and proportions in which they move. It also includes your neuromuscular responses and reactions, and overall movement efficiency. For the coach and the athlete, this meaning corresponds closely to sporting *technique*.

Core stability describes the ability of the trunk to support force production, and withstand the forces acting upon it [24]. For fitness professionals in many sporting programmes, this is addressed as part of athlete *conditioning*. Links between core stability deficits and increased risk of injury have been identified [67,116], but it is important to note that core stability contributes to but cannot fully account for overall functional stability, which is the result of multiple interrelated factors. This may be why research has found little direct correlation between core stability training and performance enhancement [106], but has found support for programmes which include core stability principles as part of a broader neuromuscular programme [86,107].

Core stability is sometimes confused with *core strength*, where these central muscles are addressed with high load exercises in order to produce and withstand large force demands safely. For some athletes, core strength is extremely important, but for others, this type of training will have little positive effect. A rugby player will need core strength as well as stability in order to withstand sudden impacts and the physical pressure of other players, whereas a triathlete will need a continuous but lower level of stabilising muscle activity to support optimal biomechanics for long periods.

Stability can also refer to the integrity of the joints, and the specific muscles which ensure that joint movement is controlled within safe structural limits. For physiotherapists and other sports medicine professionals, this meaning relates to *motor control*.

The term *stability* can be applied in all of these ways, and for injury prevention as well as performance in sporting movement they are all important and interrelated. If you are stable across all of the above categories, you will be firing the right muscles in the right sequence so that your forces are sent in the most efficient direction.

This is a *functional motor pattern*, which encompasses timing, proportion and sequencing of muscles in a chain of activation. Your joints are being moved in the appropriate order by the most suitable muscles. You can also optimally control the forces acting upon you.

The functional motor pattern is one of a collection of interdependent characteristics, which form the *pillars of functional stability*. These are the fundamental components, which must be in place in order to train for optimally efficient movement.

Pillars of Functional Stability

Functional mobility: the ability to move through the full necessary range of motion required by the sport under dynamic conditions.

Balance: the ability to organise the body over its support point quickly and accurately.

Posture: the neuro-musculo-skeletal relationships which optimise joint motion and muscular action, trigger automatic stabilising activity and minimise structural stress on the body.

Optimal functional motor pattern: the timing, proportion and sequencing of muscle activation.

Neuromuscular control: the unconscious, automatic activation of joint stabilising muscles to prepare for the impulse to move, or respond to rapid, sudden or unexpected body control challenges or loading (Louw, 2006).

Movement symmetry: the balance of movement and counter movement around a controlled central axis in the body.

Learning about these pillars can help you to structure your programme in a way that ensures that you have the motion and control necessary to move well. They prepare the foundations from which you can safely and effectively develop:

- Speed
- Power
- Strength
- Agility
- Flexibility
- Injury resistance

The entire training programme is therefore influenced by functional stability.

To better understand the role of functional stability in sport, this chapter outlines the principle of stability as it relates to movement.

Functional Stability in Sport

In the human body, the term stability describes how effectively a body manages forces. The body must *produce* force in order to move, and therefore must manage the biomechanical stresses it produces within itself. A footballer must balance himself perfectly over his stance limb, and maintain a firm and supportive hip and trunk in order to strike the ball accurately and powerfully with his other leg. Without this stable foundation, the force generated by the kicking leg affects the positioning of the player's pelvis and spine, causing stress on his groin muscles and on joints of the lower back, as well as decreasing power and accuracy. Similarly, a tennis player with a weak trunk will compensate for the loss of this firm supportive foundation when playing a forehand by overusing their shoulder muscles, affecting their timing and movement patterns, losing power and risking injury.

The body must also *withstand* forces imposed on it by its environment. A good swimmer tries to use the resistance of the water to generate an effective pull, but without sufficient trunk and shoulder stability, that same resistance can force the shoulder into a poor position, leading to biomechanical inefficiency and often shoulder injury. The ground reaction forces pushing up through the foot of a runner as he strikes the ground should help to propel him forward, but without a stable pelvis these forces can instead cause a vertical collapse in joints from the foot to the hip. An ice hockey player must withstand a direct blow from an opponent, and a shot putter must overcome gravity in order to project his shot up and away. All of these external elements exert forces upon the body and will require an athlete to respond and adapt to control them.

> **A useful definition for stability is, "the ability to utilise the body's structures in the safest, most efficient positional relationships for the functional demands imposed upon them".**

The key words here are *efficiency* and *safety*. The concept of *efficiency* sits at the heart of sports training. Ideally, an athlete should be able to produce the best result for his or her effort investment. For example, when novice golfers try to drive the ball, they generate a great deal of muscle activity but are unable to consistently focus the forces that they generate into the most effective pattern of movement. The relationship between effort and outcome is skewed towards effort. This is inefficiency. When professionals perform the same activity, their greater skill results in a longer, straighter drive, but the level of muscular activity, or effort investment, is less. They do not use what they don't need. The professional is more efficient.

The same effect can be observed in any sport. Those who truly excel manage to minimise the impression of effort when compared to their result or outcome. They are able to channel their effort into the most effective line of force. They are *efficient*. In simple terms, champions are not people who make difficult things look difficult. They are people who make difficult things look easy.

Functional stability can influence technical performance by increasing biomechanical efficiency. By increasing biomechanical efficiency, we can achieve better results for our effort. In certain circumstances, this may influence physiological efficiency, although the precise relationship is yet to be clearly defined [3,59].

The other key word in our definition is safety. Insufficient stability alters biomechanics, which can lead to injury for a variety of reasons. Athletes in multidirectional sports can sustain acute injuries because they are unable to balance and control their body mass in response to sudden acceleration, deceleration or change of direction [6]. Endurance athletes with biomechanical inefficiency can develop overuse injuries as they try to overcome a performance plateau by training harder and longer to compensate for it. There is a limit to how far determination and training volume can compensate for functional inefficiency without the body breaking down.

Functional stability can reduce injury risk by minimising musculo-skeletal stress, managing forces, and increasing balance and control.

How Can Functional Stability Influence Movement?

Directional Limitation

The principle of movement direction limitation is at the heart of technical training, and functional stability training directly targets this.

To actively move a limb a muscle must contract, and there must be a fixed or stable point for that muscle to pull from if it is to fulfil its function effectively. If it does not have a stable point to pull from, it will lose efficiency, i.e. it takes more effort to achieve the same outcome.

For example, in the diagram below, we can see that if a force is applied to a fixed point, it is likely that the person will produce a result that corresponds to his effort, and the skateboard will speed away from the wall. The only direction of movement in the system is away from the wall.

If the person tries to exert similar effort against a semi-stable surface, the result will obviously not be so positive: the effort is the same but force is lost as the surface "gives" against his pressure. There are two directions of movement involved: each in opposite directions. Applying this knowledge, if you wanted to push another person over, you would want to make yourself into a fixed point, so that the force of your push went entirely forward.

If you are unbalanced, part of your effort would go forward, but the resistance you encounter in the other person's weight will push you slightly backward. If the fixed point is lost, an extra direction of movement is introduced into the system and force is lost. In a contact sport such as ice hockey, this is an important principle to know.

Now imagine two pulley systems. The first has a pulley fixed to a wooden ceiling beam. The second has a pulley attached to a firm bungee cord instead of the horizontal beam. Both offer some level of fixation for the pulley. However, pulling the weight over the fixed beam involves one direction of movement: the weight towards the beam. When pulling against the bungee cord, two directions are involved: the weight towards the bungee and the bungee towards the weight. The bungee cord cannot provide sufficient stability for the force to be efficiently transferred to the weight.

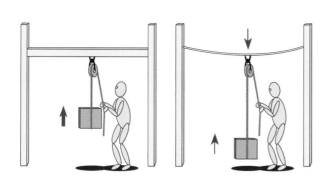

Secure shoulder bicep curl.

Loss of shoulder as fixed point.

If we apply this understanding to the body, imagine the action of muscle pulling on bone. If the origin of the muscle is fixed, or stable, the muscle shortens to pull the bone towards it. The insertion of the muscle moves towards the origin. There is one direction of movement in the system.

If the fixed point is not quite secure, it "gives" under the load of the muscle pulling, just like the bungee cord. Instead of one direction of movement, we now have two: the origin of the muscle moving towards the insertion, and the insertion towards the origin. The bone will still move, and the muscle is working just as hard, but the result is a weaker movement. By losing stability, efficiency is lost. There are many people wasting time in gyms because they don't apply this principle to lifting weights.

A secure foundation is therefore needed to support an efficient muscle contraction. This principle applies whether you are moving your thumb or your whole body. The control of each segment of the body builds upon the stability of the next in the chain, so the hand's stability depends on a stable wrist, elbow, then shoulder, then shoulder blade, then trunk. The trunk is supporting the entire chain, and is responsible for the greatest proportion of stability. The trunk must in turn be supported by a stable pelvis in order to cope with this demand. If any one of the links in the chain is weak, an additional and unwanted direction of movement can appear.

In summary, to benefit most from a muscle contraction, you must create a fixed point for the muscle to pull from. In a dynamic movement, the fixed point may move relative to other body parts, but should not collapse towards the insertion of the contracting muscle.

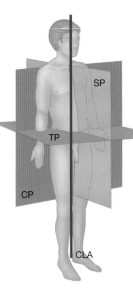

Securing the Planes of Movement

Efficient movement maintains motion in the most direct plane for the required task. Some sports, such as sprinting, weight lifting and cycling are predominantly uniplanar, i.e. they are most effective when the gross movement is limited to one plane. Multidirectional sports such as tennis and football require control in multiple planes.

The *sagittal* plane (SP) is the forward and backward plane. Running, classic Nordic skiing and cycling represent sagittal limb movement. Allowing the spine to absorb the motion of a horse when sitting to the trot, or performing a series of back flips as a gymnast, demonstrates spinal sagittal motion. The movements of the sagittal plane are flexion (forward motion in the trunk, bending in the limbs) and extension (backward motion in the trunk, straightening in the limbs).

The *coronal* plane (CP) is the side movement plane. A gymnast's spine must side bend to allow his legs to swing over the pommel, and a volleyball player may need to adjust her arms sideways to block a spike effectively. A defensive player in handball may have his arms out from his sides to block a pass, or he may need to change direction sideways quickly, moving his legs apart. The movements of the coronal plane are abduction (moving limbs away from the body), adduction (moving the limbs towards the body) and side bending (in the spine or pelvis).

The *transverse* plane (TP) is the rotational movement plane. The rotation of the pelvis and trunk in a golf swing or a tennis forehand occur within this plane, as does a sprint canoe paddler's stroke or a discus thrower's wind-up.

Whether they are mostly sagittal, coronal, rotational or multidirectional, all sports require control of a *central longitudinal axis* (CLA) to achieve their most efficient movement. In practice this central axis is not a rigid position: it is the sense of a firm but flexible central reference point, which supports movement of the torso and limbs. Imagine a firm, thick metal cable passing vertically through the top of your head and down through the middle of your body. This cable would form an axis for your shoulders, thorax and pelvis to smoothly rotate around, but still enable you to move easily in all directions.

To achieve a stable central longitudinal axis, the pelvic stabiliser muscles must provide a secure platform to support the trunk, and a deep stabilising muscle system works to support each segment of the spine. If this central longitudinal axis is not stable it will buckle under load in a forward, backward or sideways direction, causing postural and movement deviations and control problems.

If the axis buckles in the sagittal plane, the pelvis tilts either forward or backward and the trunk is placed in a position of weakness.

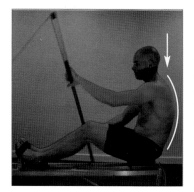

Collapse of the central axis in the sagittal plane. The slumped posture demonstrates a collapse into spinal flexion. The spine appears bowed. This is a poor position to generate rotational force.

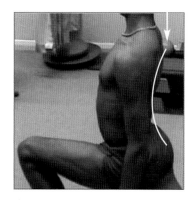

The arched position of the spine in this lunge demonstrates a collapse into spinal extension.

Collapse of the central axis in the coronal plane. One hip is higher and the spine is buckled sideways, concave on the left.

If the axis buckles in the coronal plane, the pelvis and trunk will tilt sideways, once again placing their supporting musculature in a position of weakness and compressing the joints on one side.

The central axis must stay firm whether or not the trunk is vertical. For example, the ice hockey player shown has a firm central axis, forward tilted but not bent. He then rotates around this axis.

If the central axis collapses, rotational movement will be restricted due to joint compression on the concave side of the collapse, and soft tissue tension on the convex side. **Performing stretches to increase trunk rotation will not transfer effectively to sporting movement unless you work on stabilising your central axis.**

Introducing Unnecessary Planes

Technical errors are often spotted as unwanted movements, but we can be more specific by identifying unwanted planes. The most common occurrences of unwanted planar movement occur when the central axis collapses sideways into the coronal plane. For example, running is primarily a sagittal and transverse plane activity (the legs move in a forward-backward direction while the shoulders and pelvis rotate around the central axis), but athletes can be observed diverting

forces into the coronal plane when their feet hit the ground, collapsing at the pelvis so that it tilts sideways on impact, allowing their knee to deviate inwards, rolling their foot and ankle into excessive pronation or tipping their shoulders from side to side. Forces which should be directed at moving forward are seeping sideways costing the runner propulsive potential and ultimately speed.

The sprint kayak paddler who does not have sufficient pelvic rotation will divert their movement into the coronal plane, causing the boat to tip from side to side and demonstrating excessive side bending motion in the spine.

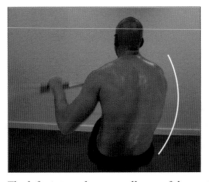

The left picture shows a collapse of the central axis into the coronal plane. Side to side movement will be greater than rotational movement. The right picture demonstrates a firmer central axis, with rotation as the primary motion.

A golfer with poor rotational mobility or inadequate trunk and pelvic control will try to gain swing motion by shifting their weight sideways into the coronal plane as they take their club head back.

The left photograph shows the golfer rotating his pelvis and shoulders. In the right photograph, he fails to rotate adequately. He must find another plane to move in, and shifts his hips sideways into the coronal plane.

The planar concept of motion occurs at two levels: local (individual joint motion) and global (total direction of motion). We will be working mainly with the global concept within this book; however it is useful to be aware that small joint movements contribute to the efficiency of global movements.

Rotating Through the Kinetic Chain

The *kinetic chain* is the series of joint relationships that make up a movement. From a global perspective, walking and running are largely sagittal movements, with the arms and legs moving in a forward and backward direction for a total movement direction objective of forward motion. However, if we take a more mechanical perspective, walking and running are in fact rotational activities. As you take weight onto one leg, the bones of your ankles, shins and thighs rotate to lock the joints in order to support weight, and then unlock as the leg swings through for another step. There is therefore a continuous alternating locking and unlocking action going on.

There is also a continuous rotation/counter rotation action occurring. As you step forward with your left foot, your pelvis on the left also moves forward. In doing this, your pelvis is effectively rotating to the right relative to your shoulders. This motion drives rotation of the spine. As your pelvis moves forward on the left, your chest moves forward on the right, bringing your right shoulder forward. Your spine is *counter rotating* so that the shoulders and pelvis move in opposite directions. This natural motion allows us to use the impulse created when our feet strike the ground to propel us forward, driving smooth, efficient gait[21]. It is so critical to walking and running efficiency that is has been called the *spinal engine*[32]. Degree and speed of pelvic and shoulder rotation are among the factors that have been linked to running economy[3].

This counter rotation action also dissipates the load on your spine as your foot strikes the ground. In doing so it can reduce joint stress. From a mechanical perspective, it also changes the demands on the leg and abdominal muscles. Some distance running coaches have misunderstood the "core stability" concept and train their runners to keep their pelvis and shoulders parallel and facing forward as they run. In doing so, they increase load on the propulsive leg muscles, decrease stride length and compromise shock absorption in the athlete's joints.

If you don't have counter rotation of the pelvis and shoulders (or more accurately, the chest) in both directions, your body will find another plane in which to move. This is most commonly the coronal plane. Instead of the shoulders and hips looking relatively level and the head position reasonably consistent, they appear to tip or rock from side to side in response to leg movement. From a global perspective, instead of energy being directed forward, it is being dissipated sideways.

Athletes with rotational restrictions can complain of movement limitations which don't immediately seem to be related. Runners who have stride length differences try to increase their hamstring flexibility to improve the short side, but often need to focus on allowing their pelvis to move forward sufficiently on that side as the foot swings through. Another example would be runners who complain that one shoulder is stiff or that an arm doesn't seem to swing freely, but no reason for this can be found when the shoulder is tested. When observed carefully, they don't rotate their chest evenly in both directions. They tend to pull the shoulder down instead of letting it move backward with trunk rotation, so the elbow does not seem to move as far despite the availability of joint movement.

Becoming more aware of your natural rotational movement can improve your symmetry, but specific movements can also help to pinpoint specific areas of decreased rotation. In later stages of the book we will look at rotational exercises for the foot and lower leg, hip, pelvis, and trunk.

Jonathan Edwards demonstrating counter body rotation.
Notice the degree of trunk rotation around his central longitudinal axis.

Key Concepts

If you do not have sufficient joint movement in one plane, your body will try to make up the difference by moving in another, usually unwanted plane. You need enough *movement* in all involved joints to perform your technique effectively.

If your body does not have sufficient stability in one plane, it will permit unwanted movement in another plane. You need sufficient *control* of all involved joints.

Personal Investigation

Which is your predominant walking plane? We often don't notice how we walk, but we are aware that some people are more efficient walkers than others. Some people can walk quickly with little effort, but some of us tire after a short period of walking faster than we normally do.

Observation exercise
Start by walking normally.

- Look at yourself as you walk towards a mirror: does your head stay balanced in the centre of your movement or does it move from side to side?

- Look at your shoulders: do they stay level or do they tip from side to side?
  They may only tip to one side.

- Is your stride length the same on both sides?

Awareness exercise

Start by walking normally. If there is visible side to side movement, your global objective of forward (sagittal) motion is being compromised by diverting movement into the coronal plane. Your effort is not going in the direction you want it to! This is usually caused by decreased rotation of the pelvis and shoulders, which you can investigate as follows.

Place your hands on your pelvis and note that as your foot moves forward, so does the pelvis on that side. Does your pelvis move forward the same distance on both sides? Take some time to examine this, especially if running is part of your sport.

Allow your arms to swing freely now, and notice that your shoulders move forward and backward as you walk. If you imagine a line across your chest from shoulder to shoulder, you will notice that it is not just your shoulders, but your whole chest and rib complex rotating from left to right. Do you rotate the same distance in both directions?

Did you notice that as your pelvis rotates forward on one side, the shoulder moves forward on the opposite side? This is called *counter body rotation*, and it is the driving force for efficient walking and running.

If you have found a difference between the sides, can you make it more even just by focusing on it? Rather than forcing one side to move more, think about relaxing to *allow* it to move more. As your pelvic rotation becomes more even, does your stride length change?

Collapse Within the Same Plane

Functional stability problems can also appear as collapse within the same plane. This occurs most commonly when the central axis collapses into the sagittal plane. A footballer throwing in from the sideline can collapse within the sagittal plane by taking his trunk into an excessive backward bend as he moves the ball over his head, losing control of his lower back and decreasing the power of his throw. A volleyball player landing from a jump may fail to absorb the landing force through his hips and knees, causing his lower back to buckle under the impact. A cross-country skier may not have sufficient stability to maintain a consistent trunk position against the strong movement of his arms as he pulls through with them, and this shows up as a wave like up and down motion in the spine.

In the lower body, collapse within the same plane leads to longer foot contact times on the ground and decreased power. Endurance runners or sprinters who appear to "sit down" as they foot strike, or jumpers who drop their hips too far on take off will find their performance reduced if this happens.

Imagine your legs are filled with pressurised air. You will bounce off the ground each time your foot hits it. However, if a small puncture appears, air starts to escape and your leg starts to buckle on impact with the ground. It may buckle in the same plane, or it may buckle sideways. The more it buckles, the more effort it is to push off again. In your legs, your muscles work in partnership to provide the same support as the imaginary air. If the muscles supporting your joints react too slowly, or are in fact the wrong ones for the job, they will permit too much bending in response to load, increasing foot contact times. The most likely area to have a "puncture" is at the pelvis and hip.

Investigation

For most sports, there is a predominant plane and possibly a number of plane variations in the limbs at different times. In your sport, which are the main planes of movement? They could be forward-backward (sagittal), side movements (coronal) or rotational. For many sports a number of planes will be used.

To work the planes out for a movement, first identify a start position for the trunk and legs. From that point, work out which direction the legs will move, which way the pelvis will move, and which way the trunk will move.

Example

- To kick a football, an axis is formed from the stance foot up through the trunk. Once this axis is secure, the trunk movement is largely rotational, with the pelvis and shoulders rotating in opposite directions.

- In freestyle swimming, the whole body should rotate cleanly around the central axis so the positional relationship between the chest and the pelvis will not markedly change. The major rotation does not occur within the body itself. The motion of the kick is sagittal. The arm motion combines all three planes.

- In skiing, the hips and knees must absorb landings in the sagittal plane, but the trunk and pelvis use rotation and side bending on turns.

Specific Example

A road racing cyclist finds that his right knee always seems closer to the cross bar of his bike as he rides. His leg action is deviating from the straight sagittal plane to the coronal plane. It is altering the angle of pressure through his pedal and putting the muscles of his hip at a disadvantage. This makes driving off a left hand curve less powerful, and also puts more stress on his lower back.

Think of something about your technique that you would like to improve. Is there a plane that you are not controlling? Are you dropping into a less effective plane?

Securing Your Limbs

Your arms and legs do not attach directly to your trunk. Instead, they attach to bony "girdles", and it is through these girdles that forces transfer between limbs and trunk. For forces to transfer between the limbs and the trunk, they must pass through the shoulder girdle or pelvic girdle. The only bony attachment securing the shoulder girdle and therefore the arm to the skeleton is where your clavicle (collarbone) attaches to your sternum (breastbone). This is a tiny attachment when you consider the loads that we expect our arms to tolerate. Similarly, the pelvic girdle, which connects the leg to the trunk, is only connected by bony attachment at the base of the spine. Once again, considering the forces that we expect the legs to produce, this is a very small attachment. Clearly, bony attachments alone cannot secure the limbs. There must be a high degree of muscular support to enable us to function.

For the greatest amount of support, the forces from the limbs are ideally transferred through the girdles to the trunk over *large* surface areas via multiple muscular attachments to the skeleton. The broad structure and interconnections of the stabilising muscles make them perfectly suited to the job. However, due to a variety of reasons you may use alternative strategies to secure your arms and legs. Unfortunately these alternative patterns use muscles which are not suited to stabilising and controlling joints. They may transfer the forces to small surface areas, which focuses the loads on body tissues which are not designed to tolerate them repeatedly or for extended periods of time. Their action may also pull their attachment points towards each other, changing the body's posture and compromising breathing patterns and muscular lines of pull.

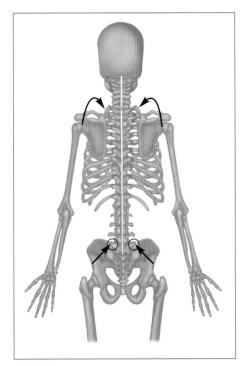

Skeleton, posterior view. The shoulder girdle comprises the scapula (shoulder blade) and the clavicle (collar bone). The shoulder girdle's only direct attachment to the main skeleton is at the small junction of the clavicle with the sternum (breastbone) at the sternoclavicular joint. The pelvic girdle is made up of the triangular shaped sacrum at the bottom of the spine, with an ilium either side. The pelvic girdle's only direct attachment to the main skeleton is at the small joint between the fifth lumbar vertebra and the sacrum. Note how small these attachment points are, and then consider the size of the muscles acting on the girdles and the forces that athletes will need to transfer through these girdles to the trunk. A considerable muscular network will be necessary to secure and support the pelvis and scapula.

Prone hamstring curl. (A) If the broad, corset-like deep abdominals work in partnership with the large gluteal muscles, the pelvis is stabilised by spreading the load of the weight across a large surface area of the trunk. (B) If the hip flexors and back extensor muscles are used to stabilise the pelvis, it is being held in place with relatively narrow muscles which attach directly to the spine, and the load of the weight is focused on a smaller more vulnerable area.

Stability provides secure attachments for contracting muscles to pull from, eliminates unnecessary movements so that force is focused in the most effective direction, and activates muscles which are physiologically designed to work at low cost for long periods. In doing these things it can influence speed, power, strength, flexibility and agility. *Functional stability* combines stability concepts with functional mobility, balance, posture and symmetry to provide movement control relevant to the requirements of an individual sport.

Optimal Performance Vs High Level Compensation

"The human being has a particularly deep attachment to his movement habits since he created them himself" [2]

Every athlete has a movement objective. Whether it is to move faster, jump higher, or even just lift a heavier weight in training, they will try to find a way to meet that objective. If an athlete has a deficit in strength, flexibility, coordination, balance, stability or perception, they will unconsciously try to find a way to achieve their movement objective even if their method is not biomechanically ideal. This is known as *compensating.*

Compensating will cause deviation from a technical "ideal", and can be dramatically obvious or very subtle. It is an attempt to find a solution to make up for a weakness or control problem. Even high performance athletes compensate, and it is challenging for the coach to evaluate the root cause of the compensation and formulate a strategy to overcome it.

The problem with compensating is that while it initially appears to allow the athlete to perform a certain skill, it rarely yields optimally efficient performance over time. This is seen even in high performance athletes. Many athletic performance plateaus are associated with compensatory movement strategies that cannot support further development. The athlete may have demonstrated great potential or even achieved success at an early stage, but a loss of form or persistent barrier to improvement is eventually reached if the compensatory strategies are not addressed.

Compensating can alter the stress ratios on different body structures. This can lead to overuse injuries, such as tendonitis, or even contribute to traumatic injuries where the athlete has been unable to control the forces, which are acting on his or her body.

An athlete can cope quite successfully by compensating as long as their ability to compensate always meets or exceeds the degree or duration of physical loading upon their body.

Ability to compensate > physical/functional loading ➤ trainable system is intact

If the functional loading on the body exceeds its ability to compensate, injury can occur. Increasing the training load, setting new goals or trying to find that extra tiny percentage when it counts in a competition can be just enough to overload the system.

Physical/functional load > ability to compensate ➤ trainable system is impaired (injury/plateau)

Being injury-free in the present doesn't guarantee that all is well for the future. Sometimes it seems that the body is coping well, but after years of unbalanced forces, a body structure breaks down and resists healing. Basic testing as outlined in Chapter 4 can help to identify the control problem that led to the breakdown. If the issue is not addressed, the injury tends to recur or persist.

Compensating alters the movement pattern of the athlete away from the ideal movement strategy for his or her structure and sport. Compensating for a physical shortcoming causes a movement *dysfunction.* A movement dysfunction is an inefficient strategy to meet a physical demand. *In coaching language, a movement dysfunction is synonymous with poor technique.*

Sometimes compensating is confused with "personal style". We all have different physical characteristics, and this can produce variations in the overall appearance of a movement. Many athletes with highly distinctive movement are successful, as they use the movement strategies which best suit their physical make up. Despite this, the successful athlete who is relatively injury resistant will demonstrate fundamentally sound movement and control strategies, which are consistent with normal biomechanics, joint control and muscular patterning.

Differentiating personal style from compensating is not easy when looking at the athlete performing their sport. Isolating and examining the elements of control can help to make that distinction. The testing section in Chapter 4 of this book focuses on the fundamental building blocks of control which support efficient movement. These should be consistent from athlete to athlete. There is no personal style involved.

Notes from the Clipboard: Movement Dysfunction

An elite male triathlete returned from an international championship with a right quadriceps injury which was failing to heal. When examined, he displayed exceptionally poor trunk and pelvic control, poor balance, and "fixing" patterns of excessive muscular activity from his feet to his neck during all movements. On the treadmill, he ran with his trunk tipped to one side, and when asked to perform a simple knee lift in sitting or standing, he used so much extra trunk muscle activity to stabilise himself that he could not inflate his lungs fully. Technically, he had made few improvements over the previous years, but had nevertheless enjoyed success at national level.

The athlete was overusing his right quadriceps as part of a compensation pattern for poor stability and balance. He used them even in movements where the quadriceps would not normally play a major role. It could not heal as it was being constantly overused. The stability and balance deficits also prevented him from improving his running technique.

This athlete needed to:
1. Secure his central longitudinal axis in order to maintain symmetry and decrease uneven loading.
2. Integrate better trunk and pelvic stability into his movement.
3. Re-establish normal breathing mechanics.
4. Re-establish normal balance reactions.

The athlete was given remedial exercises to address the problems, but needed to start at extremely low levels in order to activate the correct neuromuscular patterns. This is common in elite athletes who have repeated their existing movement patterns many thousands of times. Gradually the athlete was able to progress, and was able to detect a difference in his running technique. A session on transference of the new principles and patterns to cycling demonstrated that with correct patterning, his power output could be maintained with far less effort. On physiological testing, it was found that greater speeds were achieved at lower heart rates, demonstrating a relationship between his physiology and his biomechanics.

Stability is often implicated when movement dysfunctions appear, but stability problems can be the result of other movement altering issues, not just the cause.

What Can Cause Movement Dysfunction?

Primary Loss of Stability

Stability can be divided into structural and functional categories.

Structural instability occurs when a body structure fails, usually as a result of direct trauma. An anterior cruciate ligament rupture in the knee, or lateral ligament rupture in the ankle are common examples. In the presence of structural instability, control of the injured joint itself is affected, but balance, stability, muscle patterning and control are also usually altered. Even if the athlete has surgery, a functional stability programme will therefore have an important role to play in the athlete's rehabilitation.

In the case of *functional instability*, the structures are sound but the athlete is unable to consistently control and produce forces without compensating. Functional stability training will incorporate balance, proprioception, muscle patterning and control to address this type of problem. Any athlete who is repetitively injured should be screened for functional instability to identify control problems affecting the area of injury. Control problems are rarely confined to one body area, so whole body movements should be examined.

Poor Postural Awareness

Stability can help maintain an efficient posture, but paradoxically, poor posture can make it hard to activate the stabilisers. Some athletes do not understand what an efficient postural position feels like, as it does not come naturally to them. There may be several reasons for an athlete to adopt a less than ideal posture:

1 They may not have the flexibility to achieve the best position. An example of this may be a young sprint kayak paddler whose tight hamstrings pull his back into a slumped position.

2 They may not have the right muscles activating to maintain their posture. An example of this may be a swimmer who has only trained her abdominals with trunk curls, but has not trained the abdominal muscles which maintain a secure posture in the water when the trunk is straight.

3 They may have insufficient body awareness. Even if they are corrected, they cannot feel when they change their position and return to their normal posture.

If an athlete cannot change their posture while actually performing their sport, they need to be trained in less complex ways first. It may be that they need to practice postural awareness in simple tasks such as those provided in Chapter 5, or that joint mobility and control needs to be restored to make it possible to change posture when the body is moving. The tests in Chapter 4 should help to identify these issues. Reinforcing postural principles in all aspects of training including flexibility and strength and conditioning will help to develop postural awareness.

Loss of Range of Motion

If range of motion (ROM) is restricted, whether because of joint stiffness, muscle tightness, or motor patterning, it is likely that the body will have to compensate to try to fulfil performance objectives. For example, a common response to restricted shoulder flexion is hyperextension of the lumbar spine, which gives the false impression that the limb is achieving adequate range.

This can be seen in many young swimmers and gymnasts as they perform their warm-up and stretches, and if the coach is not attentive to form, this pattern will persist. If not corrected, this movement dysfunction will be very difficult to dislodge as it becomes integrated into the nervous system of the athlete. Coaches in charge of young athletes should be aware that loss of specific flexibility can occur during growth spurts, and this range of motion can be very difficult to recover. This particular pattern is often associated with lower back pain in sports which require good shoulder flexibility. Trunk stability training will not relieve lower back pain in this athlete nor will it improve their form unless it is combined with techniques to restore normal shoulder joint motion.

The concept of *relative flexibility* explains this phenomenon [101]. For most of us, some structures in our bodies have more "give" than others, that is, they are more flexible. This is not always a good thing – structures which tend to move more readily become vulnerable to increased strain and eventual injury, especially when their contribution is not part of the normal movement pattern for the activity.

Gymnast demonstrating poor shoulder mobility with her lumbar spine in a neutral position. In her sport, she must be able to hold another gymnast over her head. To do this, the load must be supported directly over her body. Due to her poor shoulder mobility, the only way that she can bring her arms directly over her head is to move her spine into a deep extension curve. This resulted in spinal stress fractures. Stability training will only prevent further injury if the shoulder mobility is restored.

Functional Rigidity

If an athlete's joints move normally when tested passively but they don't use that available motion as part of their technique, it may be that they are displaying *functional rigidity*. This often develops as an athlete tries to cope with a higher balance or stability challenge than they can adequately control. Instead of using functional stability, which allows them to move fluently while still in control, the athlete creates a false stability by increasing their general muscle activity to partially immobilise a series of joints. This locks body parts into place, but doesn't allow the athlete to move freely and subtly. This will be a big disadvantage in sports where swift reactions and fine adjustments are necessary, such as in alpine skiing or equestrian events. In sports which require larger movements of the limbs like tennis, it will cause difficulties in movement sequencing, changes in joint alignment or loss of balance. If the situation is allowed to continue, the athlete loses body awareness in the area, making technical improvement extremely difficult.

Example

A junior alpine skiing squad was functionally assessed to establish whether there were links between technical problems on the slopes and their physical characteristics. In all of the skiers who had difficulty in making right turns, functional rigidity of the left foot was found, along with left pelvic stability problems and decreased ability to actively change the pressure under the sole of the left foot with subtlety. The body depends upon accurate information coming from the foot in order to know how to balance itself. A rigid foot cannot feed back accurately, as it is effectively immobilised. In order to cope on the slopes without having good quality information coming from the foot, the skiers were using a compensatory but inefficient technique to keep their balance and control. They made their leg more rigid and did not transfer their weight effectively.

In this situation, the first priority is to establish the athlete's ability to create and detect small pressure changes. Restoration of awareness in the area is a part of this process. Stability activities which link the foot to the hip, and activate the pelvic stabilisers in response to weight transference can then be added, in combination with balance training. Finally, sports specific warm-up drills involving foot pressure changes and weight transference are performed on skis prior to hitting the slopes.

Personal Investigation

Stand on both feet, and feel the surface of the floor under your soles. Now stand on one leg: has the muscle tension in the foot you are standing on changed? Now try closing your eyes while standing on that foot, and to challenge you more, move your arms in any direction. Do you feel the tension in your foot increase as the balance challenge increases? Some people increase it so much that the foot becomes completely rigid, which means that it is not in such good contact with the floor. When this happens, the foot cannot transmit accurate information to you to help you to balance.

Insufficient Control of Momentum

Speed is sometimes developed without attention to whether the athlete can control their own momentum. If the athlete can't control momentum, their change of direction will be clumsy and slow, or they will be poorly balanced to perform an action. Depending upon the sport, forward, backward, sideways or rotational momentum may need to be controlled. A tennis player may be very quick to accelerate to a drop shot over the net, but will need to control his forward momentum to set up the shot. A footballer may be quick off his right foot to move left, but when he tries to move right off his left foot, his trunk momentarily continues to tip away from the new direction of movement, slowing him down. A basketball player may receive a ball in the air and turn his body to land facing a different direction, but injures his knee as he fails to control his rotation.

Poor Balance

Poor balance is surprisingly common even in elite athletes. Routine functional testing of international sprinters, badminton players, golfers and contemporary dancers revealed that most of them could not control simple balance tasks.

Balance requires an interplay between your vision, your inner ear and your body's feedback. Many of these athletes were unable to complete even simple balance tasks with their eyes distracted. To compensate, they increased the muscle tension in their body, which decreased their mobility and affected their technique.

Balance is not only a problem in standing: in dressage riders and kayak paddlers, significant differences in balance between left and right sides have been noted to correlate with technical problems.

Poor Coordination – Movement Patterning

The sequencing of movement may cause a movement dysfunction. This can be seen in any dynamic sport, but very obvious examples can be found in sports such as tennis, hammer throw, judo or golf where coordination and timing of pelvic and shoulder rotational movement is critical for force production.

Perception is linked to patterning problems. In all of these sports the athlete may perceive that the most important element is the arm movement. They therefore focus on this body part, and it is moved earlier in the sequence than it should be, closing down the real source of power generation, which is in the pelvis and trunk.

Champion hammer thrower demonstrating perfect trunk and pelvic alignment. Her power is produced with rapid whole body rotation, and the arms are used only as the end of the movement chain.

Timing

Sometimes poor stability is associated with timing problems or slow reaction times as demonstrated above. If this is the case, stability training needs to be done in conjunction with technical modification.

Two netball players demonstrating jumps. Their sport requires that they must catch overhead, be able to turn in the air and pass the ball before landing. In (A), the player is taking off too late, and is therefore having to catch the ball behind her head, causing the weak spinal position. In (B), this player has good timing and takes off earlier, allowing her to achieve a stronger spinal position.

Poor Understanding of the Movement Required

This is a communication issue between the coach and the athlete. It is not unusual for the athlete to be instructed to perform a movement or skill in a certain way, but the cue that makes sense to the coach may be understood to mean something different by the athlete. The athlete therefore performs the skill as best he or she can, but may choose movement strategies which resemble but do not replicate the skill. This is often seen when athletes are trying to learn weight lifting. The stabiliser system may not be working effectively in the pattern due to a misunderstanding regarding body position and muscle action.

Example

A power lifter injured his back while attempting a dead lift. When questioned on what he thought the movement should be, he said that he'd been told to push his hips out as he lifted. He therefore tried to quickly thrust his pelvis forward and throw his shoulders backward, loading the spinal structures maximally.

Once the athlete understood the role of the gluteal muscles in straightening his hip, he was able to activate them along with his deep spinal stabilisers as part of the movement. His lifting action changed from a forward thrust of the pelvis under the spine to a strong hip extension movement. Both techniques straightened the hip, but the new technique increased the action of the powerful gluteal muscles and decreased the pressure on the small spinal structures. The athlete began lifting safely and powerfully, moving past his performance plateau and regularly improving his personal bests.

Poor Training Design

Injuries and performance plateaus may arise from training practices that are unsuitable for the capabilities of the athlete. There are many training programmes devised on what the athlete *should* be able to achieve, rather than what they actually can achieve under control. When this disparity occurs, the athlete must compensate to manage the training demands, and this leads to tissue breakdown or failure to progress. Monitoring *how* an athlete performs a task rather than just whether he or she completes it will help to prevent errors like this.

Example

A high jumper was experiencing performance deterioration, and although her coach had worked out a periodised programme based on her competition schedule, nothing seemed to be working. Observation of the athlete performing bounding drills explained the problem. This athlete demonstrated poor pelvic stability even in static drills. The overload of bounding was causing a collapse of her joints, and was switching off the very muscles that she was trying to train. The problem was easily overcome. The high jumper's programme was modified so that power work was initially done off both legs while her pelvic stability developed adequately to cope with single leg work. The correct muscle pathways were activated so that she could start to absorb and produce forces more effectively. The performance plateau was overcome by focusing on the quality of the athlete's movement, and this was achieved by initially reducing the level of training difficulty instead of increasing it.

Stress

Although stress might originate in the mind, it is immediately reflected in the body. Stress induced changes in muscle activation can appear as extremely subtle movement dysfunction, and it may take a highly skilled evaluation to detect it.

It may compromise shock absorption, available range of motion, movement patterning and fluency, and under the demand of high level training and competition, can lead to pain and compromised performance. The diaphragm is a key part of the trunk stability mechanism [44], so stress induced changes in breathing pattern can influence trunk stability.

An athlete can "tighten up" under pressure, or unconsciously guard their movement as a result of a past injury. They might feel insufficiently physically prepared, or overthink their technique, knowing exactly what should be happening as if in a textbook, but lacking the insight to tell if it is actually happening in their own bodies. It may appear that stability may be the primary problem, and indirectly it may be. However, if stress is the trigger mechanism for the breakdown in the movement pattern, remedial stability work must be combined with management of environmental factors, stress management techniques, and establishing awareness in the athlete of the link between their tension and their movement.

Stability Principles in the Training Programme

For stability training to have an impact upon athletic performance, several steps should be implemented.

1 An assessment of stability and body control should be made to establish a baseline from which to work. By doing this you can identify specific weaknesses and structure a programme to accurately target problems. This is more effective than performing general "core" exercises which may miss the main issues. Assessment methods are provided in Chapter 4.

2 Relate the test findings to technique. Test findings usually relate to technical problems, and this establishes the relevance of the stability training. What needs to improve? It could be any number of things including the ability to remain uninjured, body alignment and dynamic posture, foot contact times, ability to turn quickly, ability to resist an opponent, coordination of the upper and lower body or the ability to be balanced but mobile. If you or the athlete you are working with has a technical problem, ask yourself what they would need to make improvement possible. Examples of this could be better leg alignment, more body rotation, improved weight transference, a more strongly connected arm, greater hip strength or improved flexibility.

3 Involve any professionals who provide coaching, conditioning or health care, as the findings will be relevant to all of them. The findings will influence design of the strength and conditioning programme, give the coach a new approach to improving technique and help the sports medicine team to understand possible mechanisms of injury.

4 Relate the demands of the sport to the level of stability training that needs to be achieved. For example, which planes of movement are involved, what are the speed and endurance demands, is it a contact sport, and is it an open or closed skill sport?

5 Be systematic. You need to activate the correct muscle groups to gain basic stability and gradually increase the complexity, coordination and load until you meet the demands of the sport. To gain maximum transference, the same principles should be emphasised in all aspects of training, including the warm-up, strength and agility training, sports specific drills and the sports movement itself.

The next chapter will explain the basic anatomy of stability so that you can familiarise yourself with the muscles you will be using and their relevance to sporting performance.

Chapter Summary

- Stability helps you to create and control force.
- Body awareness, balance, breathing, posture and mobility all contribute to stability.
- We have choices in the muscle patterns that we use, but our habits are not necessarily the most efficient option.
- Stability can limit unwanted movements.
- Without stability, the joints can buckle within the same plane, or into another plane.
- Poor stability can contribute to movement dysfunctions, but it may not be the primary issue. Sometimes stability issues are an effect rather than a cause.
- If our movement habits can't meet the demands of training, we compensate. Compensating is often associated with poor technique.

Chapter 2: The Anatomy of Stability

Stabilisers and Mobilisers
The Central Control Zone: the Trunk
The Lower Control Zone: the Pelvis
The Upper Control Zone: the Shoulder Girdle
A Whole Body Approach

This chapter deals with the behaviour of muscles in functional and dysfunctional stability chains. A deeper understanding of the anatomy and relationships of the muscles you will be activating may help you to interpret your own observations and assess movement with greater insight. Depending upon your interests and level of involvement in sport, you may wish to pursue the subject in greater depth, or you may feel that this is a chapter to dip into when a question arises.

Stabilisers and Mobilisers

To produce a movement, muscles must work in coordinated patterns or chains. Within these patterns some muscles are ideally designed to provide support, and others to produce force. They have specific physiological and neuromuscular characteristics and therefore different roles. To better understand the roles of different muscles within a functional movement pattern, muscles can be grouped according to their behaviour and structure. These groupings provide general guidelines which help to interpret movement and plan training programmes. The most basic model is that of stabilisers and mobilisers [5,14], which is summarised in the diagram below.

A movement needs a firm foundation, and a muscle group called the *local stabilisers* provides the most fundamental of joint support. Think of these as **joint controllers**. The *global stabilisers* provide control of the moving parts throughout the motion and also produce force. Think of these as **movement controllers**. The *global mobilisers* are the **movement producers**. This grouping does not exclude mobilisers from having a stabilising role, however based on structural characteristics and behaviour their movement-producing role is most relevant when considering training implications.

The bottom of the pyramid supports the other muscular actions, yet it is least attended to in training. When considering the different behaviour of the muscles of the body, we realise that any movement will involve the interplay of stabilisers and mobilisers. It is therefore important to train patterns rather than muscles. However, if a muscle is not activating correctly, the pattern will be distorted. If this is the case, it is most likely to be a stabiliser, which is the missing link. If it is not firing as part of the pattern, it must be stimulated to activate and then reintegrated into the pattern. Trying to compensate with other muscles will not promote smooth, efficient movement.

Global mobilisers
Movement

Global stabilisers
Force production/control through motion

Local stabilisers
Joint control (foundations)

33

The Local System

Much of the current research on this group of muscles has been done with respect to control of the lower spine, however a growing body of research is building to investigate the behaviour of local stabilisers in the knee [7,78], shoulder [72,81] and neck [58]. In the public domain, the most familiar of the local stabilisers is transversus abdominis, a deep abdominal muscle.

These muscles provide a foundation for movement in the same way that you build a foundation for a house. When you have the impulse to move, they become active just prior to the movement occurring in order to support the body's structures and provide a stable platform for the movement. This is called a *feedforward* response.

When functioning normally, they activate in this way regardless of the direction in which you want to move [41], and they continue to work throughout the whole movement. This steady continuous behaviour is known as *tonic* activity. Local stabilisers do not change length greatly when they contract and are usually positioned to spread closely over a joint, so they are ideally suited to controlling joint position but not for producing a range of motion. Because of these characteristics, the local stabilisers maintain joints in the safest and most suitable position to support muscular forces, and provide a secure axis for movement.

Despite their crucial role in efficient movement and joint protection, the local stabilisers can switch off for a variety of reasons. Pain can inhibit the function of these muscles, and even if the pain resolves, they can remain switched off [43,39]. Even fear of pain can alter the function of these muscles [82]. Without these local stabilisers functioning as part of the normal neuromuscular pattern for movement, other muscles in the system alter their roles to compensate for them. These larger *global* muscles normally produce force or movement and are not positioned well to maintain safe and secure joint position, nor are they physiologically suited to the sustained activity required in a stabilising role. The ongoing inhibition of the local stabilisers therefore leads to chronic biomechanical problems, and an athlete can end up in a frustrating injury cycle or performance plateau as a result.

Even without injury, the local stabilisers can switch off. Athletes will commonly use the movement and force producing global muscles as stabilisers in order to cope with a training demand which is beyond their true biomechanical and neuromuscular capabilities. This can occur in response to excessive loading, skill demand or training volume. The underlying reason for this altered pattern may be neuromuscular, physiological or psychological, but it can be avoided if sound sports specific profiling is provided and good communication between coach, sports science and medical personnel is established.

Notes from the Clipboard

A female judo athlete arrived at the clinic with instability and pain in her right knee. She had undergone surgical reconstruction of the knee several years previously and continued to struggle with it. She was in full training and had been given a heavy resistance programme in order to gain the necessary weight to fight in her chosen category. Despite adherence to the resistance programme provided by sports science personnel, the quadriceps on the painful side did not respond with hypertrophy.

The local stabiliser for the knee is the medial quadricep, vastus medialis, which in this athlete was inhibited, or "switched off". She had poor pelvic control, and she could not prevent her knee from falling out of the sagittal and into the coronal plane. Her stabilisation strategy was global muscle dominant, not just in her lower limb, but also in her trunk and upper body. Her pectorals, upper trapezius, rectus abdominis, hip flexors, superficial spinal muscles and hamstrings were all working constantly to stabilise as well create movement as, but her local stabiliser system, including her lower abdominals, deep spinal muscles, scapular stabilising muscles and deep neck muscles, were all underactive.

The athlete's resistance programme was aimed at hypertrophy, so the athlete was using poor patterns to push heavy weights. This reinforced the patterns, and the athlete started to experience neck and lower back pain in addition to her knee problems due to her inability to manage forces efficiently.

The athlete's weights programme was temporarily suspended in order to activate her local stability system, and then reintroduced as quickly as possible with modifications to enable her to learn more efficient technical patterns. To the athlete's surprise, low load partial bodyweight activities for her quadriceps activated her inhibited medial quadricep muscles, and her thigh circumference increased. Slightly lower resistance with better patterning throughout her programme reduced musculo-skeletal stress and increased functional strength.

Throughout the programme the amount of resistance was monitored against the athlete's ability to use her entire system without compensating. Instead of focusing on strength in individual muscles, it prioritised strengthening muscle chains to develop effective force production.

Despite a structural instability in the knee, the athlete's functional stability improved and she was able to compete and secure a medal at international tournament level.

The Global System

The global system can be divided into the global stabilisers and the global mobilisers. *Global stabilisers* usually have broad attachments and are suited to controlling joints throughout a movement. Unlike local stabilisers they do change length and therefore can create force. If working in their correct role in the neuromuscular pattern, these muscles can be very powerful. Muscles such as gluteus maximus and the external oblique abdominals are examples of global stabilisers.

The global *mobilisers* have a predominance of fast twitch fibres and are designed to produce movement. The local muscles activate tonically to provide continuous support, but the global mobilisers behave *phasically*, that is their activity, being task and movement dependent, is an on/off behaviour. As more research is published, muscles in this category are being found to have specific stabiliser roles, however with their relatively long muscle fibres, superficial placement, ability to build tension quickly and greater susceptibility to fatigue the mobilisers are considered to be *action muscles*.

Models for Muscles

Despite the best efforts of scientists, the body resists most attempts to definitively categorise its systems. The stabiliser/mobiliser model is helpful to understand broad movement control principles, but in practice, some muscles defy categorisation by having dual roles, acting as mobilisers and stabilisers under different conditions.

For many years, muscles have been grouped according to their predominant fibre type. Muscles which behave tonically have a larger proportion of slow twitch, or Type I fibres. They are fatigue resistant and work at low load and so are suited to supporting the body against gravity. Muscles with greater proportions of fast twitch, or Type II fibres are considered to be phasic, although this is further classified into whether the fibres are Type IIa, which are less fatigueable and have aerobic properties, or Type IIb, which are more fatigueable and have anaerobic properties.

As research progresses, it is becoming clearer that muscles do not always behave in such clearly defined ways. Muscles which have been thought of as operating exclusively tonically have been found to modulate their activity phasically under certain conditions. Transversus abdominis and the diaphragm, both predominantly tonic muscles, have been found to display phasic characteristics at faster running speeds [103].

Due to this shifting of boundaries with new discoveries about the behaviour and physiology of muscles, the model we will use is based on movement. For practical purposes in most training environments, remember that each movement is made up of muscles that *create motion* and muscles that *control motion*. To allow smooth, powerful movement there needs to be a balance between the local and global systems. Positioned closely over joints, the local stabilisers have short lines of pull, which are ideal for controlling joints, but produce insufficient force to create and control movement. Global stabilisers have long lines of pull over more than one joint, so they are effective for producing and controlling movement. When both sets of muscles are working together, stability and mobility are possible.

An athlete with *stability dysfunction* may try to achieve joint control by using large global muscles such as the external abdominal obliques, rectus abdominis, latissimus dorsi, the erector spinae and hamstrings. Because these muscles cross more than one joint, their line of pull produces a compressive force which can be helpful to stabilise against high forces when contracting in partnership with other muscles. However, if the local stabiliser system is not working effectively to secure each joint segment against the next, this long line of pull can contribute to joint buckling. This buckling produces unwanted and poorly controlled joint motion, leading to technical control problems and eventually injury (see diagram opposite).

As the global muscles commonly cross more than one joint, an increase in their stabilising activity causes problems differentiating movement from one body part to another. The ability to move body parts independently of one another is called *dissociation*, and every sport needs this to some degree. For example, to hit an effective drive, a golfer must be able to rotate his pelvis slightly before his trunk begins to rotate in order to effectively use his trunk muscles to create power in his swing through. If he is unable to separate the motion of his pelvis from the motion in his thorax because he is bracing his trunk using his global abdominal muscles, he will either lose power or start overusing another body part, such as the arms.

Imagine a flat water kayak paddler overusing his external oblique abdominals to stabilise his trunk and maintain his posture as he paddles. The primary trunk action for this sport is thoracic and pelvic rotation. He needs the obliques to be able to lengthen and shorten alternately as they produce torque, but instead they are working continuously in the same range to keep his trunk secure. The continuous action of these global muscles impairs the paddler's breathing by pulling on his lower ribs and decreasing his rib expansion. His trunk mobility is also decreased as is the power in his stroke. The paddler needs to re-establish a pattern where his local stabilisers secure his central longitudinal axis (CLA) and his external obliques produce force.

The global stabiliser muscles do not always overactivate. Sometimes their activity is poorly timed or inadequate for the task, leading to a failure to control a joint through motion. This can easily be observed watching people climb the stairs. Without the gluteal group controlling the femur, the knee moves inwards as the person transfers their weight onto that leg.

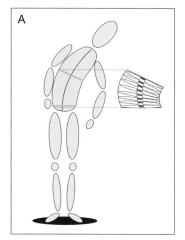

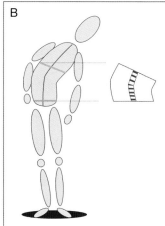

A: Deep stabiliser system providing segmental joint control of the spine. The action of strong superficial global muscles will not buckle the spine as they create force.

B: Without adequate deep stabiliser action, the long global muscles cause segmental buckling as they create force due to their long line of pull over multiple joints.

Ultimately this interplay between local and global muscles should lead to smooth efficient movement. To ensure a sound movement pattern, the *quality* of a movement should be emphasised in all aspects of training. In other words, pay as much attention to *how well* you perform the movement as you do to any other measure of a good training session. If you perform the movement accurately, you have a better chance of stimulating the correct pattern. Some athletes ignore this principle. For example, an endurance athlete's exceptional cardiovascular endurance may significantly outstrip their technique and their ability to cope with repetitive musculo-skeletal loading.

They nevertheless continue to prioritise their physiology over their biomechanics in training. Instead of addressing their weaknesses, they try to squeeze a tiny improvement out of a cardiovascular system which is already operating at maximum capacity. These athletes will commonly break down, or they peak early and then fail to meet their projected potential as they progress to higher levels of competition. Having familiarised yourself with this model of muscle function, it will now be applied to three primary stability zones: the Central Control Zone, the Lower or Pelvic Control Zone and the Upper or Scapular Control Zone.

The Central Control Zone: the Trunk

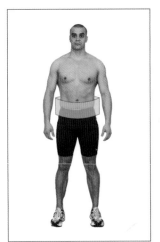

For pelvic stability and segmental stability in the spine, the local stabilisers **transversus abdominis** (TrA) and multifidus need to be functioning normally in partnership with the internal abdominal obliques, the diaphragm and pelvic floor. Between them, they represent the roof, floor and walls of your deep trunk stabilising system. In addition to their direct stabilising action via their musculo-skeletal attachments, these muscles coordinate their activity to create and control a balloon of pressure within the abdominal cavity. This pressure, known as *intra abdominal* pressure, contributes to the trunk stability mechanism in response to movement [42]. Breathing patterns, pelvic floor control and trunk stability are therefore intimately connected.

Wrapping around the trunk, TrA connects the front and back and upper and lower halves of the body. Through these connections, it plays a role in supporting the functional movement of the upper and lower limbs as well as stabilising the spine. With its extensive attachments, TrA is able to disperse force across a large surface area, decreasing load on isolated body structures. TrA has attachments to the cartilages of the lower six ribs, and reaches down to the upper surfaces of the pelvis. It spans around the trunk to connect into the **thoraco-lumbar fascia**, a thick connective tissue sheath that has attachments to the individual vertebral segments of the spine, as well as the pelvis and ribs.

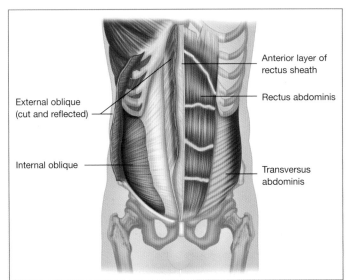

External oblique (cut and reflected)

Internal oblique

Anterior layer of rectus sheath

Rectus abdominis

Transversus abdominis

The muscles of the abdominal wall.

The thoraco-lumbar fascia helps to stabilise the trunk and pelvis when muscles connecting into it are tensioned [112]. Latissimus dorsi connects the upper limb into the thoraco-lumbar fascia, gluteus maximus connects the lower limb into the thoraco-lumbar fascia, the deep spinal stabiliser multifidus connects the spine into the thoraco-lumbar fascia along with TrA, and various other muscles including biceps femoris influence thoraco-lumbar fascia tension through attachments to ligaments which connect with it.

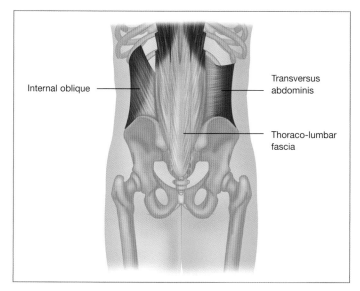

Transversus abdominis and internal obliques inserting into thoraco-lumbar fascia.

The upper and lower body are therefore anatomically integrated, with TrA and the thoraco-lumbar fascia providing a corset to connect them centrally. It can be appreciated then that TrA is involved in supporting powerful upper limb actions, as well as influencing leg movement by helping to stabilise the pelvis on the spine and creating a firm foundation for the strong leg muscles to pull from.

Transversus abdominis key points:

1. Local stabiliser.

2. Connects front and back, and upper and lower parts of the body.

3. Large surface area.

4. Connects into thoraco-lumbar fascia.

Personal Investigation

Face a wall, stretch your arms out towards it and place your hands on it at chest height. Lift one foot. Let your stomach relax completely, and perform a press-up against the wall. Note where in the body you are working most. Lifting gently from the top of your head, draw your body up against gravity so that your spine lengthens and you feel that you are picking up and placing your body onto your stance leg. You should feel your lower abdomen draw in as you lengthen your trunk.

Perform the single leg press-up again, being aware of keeping your lower back in the same neutral position throughout the movement. Notice that this requires some abdominal activity. When you performed the first press-up, you might have noticed that the main area of stress is in the shoulders and muscle of the upper body, even at this low load. If you performed the second one correctly, you might have noticed that the shoulder stress and load sensation on the upper body decreases slightly, balance is better and the total effort for the whole system is reduced. By reducing focal load and dispersing it over a larger area, transversus allows us to perceive a lower sensation of muscular effort to perform the movement.

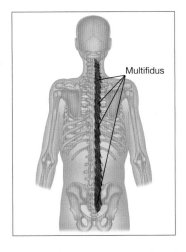

Multifidus

Multifidus muscles connect the individual segments of the spine in the cervical, thoracic and lumbar regions. Like TrA, multifidus reacts in anticipation of movement, providing close direct stability to the vertebral segments and contributing to tension in the thoraco-lumbar fascia in preparation for load. Like TrA, multifidus activity can be delayed or absent in response to pain [39]. Multifidus is also necessary for pelvic stability, so it should be assessed in athletes with groin or pelvic pain.

The muscular pairing of iliacus and **psoas major**, collectively known as iliopsoas, is usually listed as having a hip flexion action. However, psoas major, which has direct attachments to the segments of the spine, is now considered to have both local and global stabiliser roles. The posterior portions of the muscle act as local stabilisers, securing each segment for firm spinal alignment, while the anterior portions are thought to have a more global stabiliser role [31]. If you are an athlete in a contact sport, look back at the picture on page 37. If you are going to have to absorb the impact of a blow to your body, you will want all of those deep small muscles working to control the segments of your spine while your global muscles increase their bracing activity to control your overall trunk movement. The effectiveness of this mechanism is further increased by coactivation of the diaphragm and pelvic floor, so that your intra abdominal pressure is momentarily higher to withstand an impact. Athletes will often unconsciously pause their breath at the moment of impact to maintain this internal pressure as an automatic stabilising response, and then release it a split second after impact. The protection of your spine using these stabilising effects depends upon the timing and activation of the local spinal stabilisers.

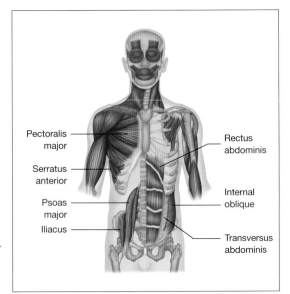

Pectoralis major
Serratus anterior
Psoas major
Iliacus
Rectus abdominis
Internal oblique
Transversus abdominis

Personal Investigation

Stand with your feet together and then step forward with one foot. Press your thumbs into the muscle on both sides of the spine. Keep your thumbs close to the spine. Rock your weight onto your front foot. You should feel the muscles under your thumbs tense. Rock back again and feel how they react to the movement. The muscle under your thumbs is multifidus. You should feel a response on both sides of your spine, although it will be a little more obvious on the opposite side to the stepping foot. Try the same exercise with the other foot forward and test whether both sides respond. Then try moving your thumbs a little higher or lower. If you have back pain, check the muscles in that area to see if they are working effectively. If you find that one area of multifidus is not responding as well, focus your awareness on that area. Find the area that isn't responding, and continue to transfer your weight forward and backward over your feet. Note how the other side feels, and work on gently trying to firm up the area which hasn't been responding.

Notes from the Clipboard

An elite female karate athlete presented for movement performance analysis. When asked what her training priorities were, she said that she needed more strength and power. To address this, she was lifting heavy weights in the gym, and in particular focusing on bench press. When asked how she'd like to fight however, she said that she wanted to be powerful and explosive, but quick, fluent and "light".

On assessment, it was obvious that the athlete's central stability was exceptionally poor, as was her pelvic coordination for driving quickly forward. She depended upon global muscles to provide stability, which made it hard for her to dissociate her movement. Her perception that she needed more upper body power was affecting how she was using her arms. Her movement was heavy and she was not meeting her potential for speed, despite the achievement of a European title as a junior.

The athlete was asked to perform the Wall Press as outlined on page 39. She primarily felt the load on her shoulders and arms, and even though she was capable of bench-pressing a substantial weight, felt that the Wall Press was an effort.

The athlete was then taught a simple postural cue, which established her central axis and activated her trunk stabilisers. Maintaining this position, she performed the Wall Press. She was surprised: her arms felt very little load. Instead she felt that the total body load was spread over her body so that nothing had to work too hard.

The thing to note here is that the athlete performed the majority of her strength work in the gym with her trunk supported fully, but did very little to integrate this strength into a total body pattern. When her arms were loaded without trunk support, she lacked the functional motor pattern to support the body efficiently. Stimulating a pattern which activated her central control mechanisms redistributed the load to achieve greater total efficiency.

After this experience, the athlete was asked to perform punch and kick movements as she had in her initial evaluation, but this time was given a specific cue. She was asked to fight with the imagery of a helium balloon lifting her spine against gravity. This stabilised and lengthened her central axis and activated TrA, released the muscles across her shoulders allowing them to drop into a more effective position, and decreased the tension levels in global muscles around her trunk and hips. The result was fluent, swift striking from both arms and legs and the disappearance of the heavy movements which had previously characterised her fighting style.

The important thing to remember about the local stabilisers is that they should activate automatically just before a movement occurs, and work for long periods at low effort levels. The problem in many exercise programmes is that these muscles are subjected to strengthening regimens. The primary problem with TrA and multifidus isn't weakness: it is that they aren't activating as part of a neuromuscular pattern, or do not have sufficient endurance to keep supporting movement. Priorities are therefore to switch on an inhibited muscle, and gradually increase its endurance within a total body pattern. The local stabilisers are a necessary foundation for safe, efficient technical movement, so they should not be neglected or overlooked.

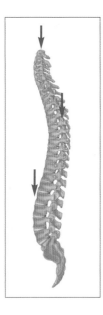

The Neutral Spine

TrA and multifidus activity is necessary to maintain and support a *neutral spinal position*. The spine is not a straight structure, but instead has a gentle inward curve in the cervical and lumbar regions. These curves allow the spine to share vertical load across many joints, and to decrease pressure on the discs which sit between each vertebra. The curves also allow for a certain amount of vertical shock absorption as we walk, run and jump, or if you are a rider, to absorb a horse's motion. If your spine was straight, the weight of your head would be transferred straight to the last disc in the spine, and this would break down quickly under the load. The neutral spinal position decreases the need for global muscle stabilising activity to maintain a postural position. Decreasing global stabilising strategies to maintain posture improves movement fluency and dissociation by reducing the stiffening effect over multiple joints. Good breathing patterns can be maintained and joint stresses are decreased.

The neutral spine: normal curves allow the spine to be mobile and share load evenly throughout the spine.

Athletes with poor local stabiliser activity in the trunk have difficulty controlling the neutral spine, and yet many sports depend upon this position for optimal technique, either in the sport itself or the training programme. Sporting examples of the sustained neutral spine are a freestyle swimmer, a weight lifter as they strongly drive up into a clean, a golfer in their address position, a gymnast in a handstand position, a dressage rider or a runner.

The spine does not have to be vertical to be neutral, and your hips can be at any angle as long as the shoulder to pelvis relationship is maintained and the spinal curves are normal.

Learning to control a neutral spinal position helps you to establish your central longitudinal axis (CLA), and as we discussed in Chapter 1, this axis is necessary for efficient rotational movement. It also prevents excessive joint compression, which occurs when your CLA collapses.

Neutral spine.

Extended spine.

Flexed spine.

If you consider the address position in golf, two common postural errors are seen. Some golfers flex their spine, making it appear rounded. The CLA is bowed outwards, and if the golfer then rotates, he will increase the stress on his lumbar discs. Other golfers collapse their CLA inward, making it appear as if they are sticking their bottom out. This position closes the joints in the spine, and rotation causes further compression of the joints. Both postures are collapses of the CLA in the sagittal plane. A neutral spinal position will disperse the load over multiple joints rather than focusing load on isolated structures.

Rotation will be strongest around a firm axis. This principle applies in sports which require rotation *within* the body, e.g. the golfer, the tennis player or the sprint kayak paddler, or for athletes who require rotation of the body in space, such as divers, gymnasts, hammer and discus throwers. Rotation around a firm CLA prevents the introduction of other planes of movement, maintaining technical movement and influencing consistency, accuracy, power and efficiency.

Transversus abdominis and multifidus normally activate regardless of the spinal position you need in your sport, whether this involves forward, backward, side bending or rotation movements. This makes sense: you need segmental spinal stability in all of these positions. Sports such as gymnastics require extreme spinal mobility, but transversus abdominis and multifidus must still support the joints throughout the full movement to make the movement optimally even and fluid. Although the overall position of the spine no longer looks like neutral, each joint is supported within its "neutral zone". This means that each joint has a range of motion which it is physiologically designed for. Moving beyond this zone increases stress on joint structures and injury risk. If TrA and multifidus are working effectively, they will support these joints in their neutral zone even in these dramatic positions.

Note the even curve of the spine, indicating that each segment is moving equally and no one part of the spine is under excessive stress.

A: Each spinal segment contributes evenly to the movement, giving the appearance of an even curve. Force is shared across many joints.

B: One spinal segment is moving more than the others, focusing forces in that area.

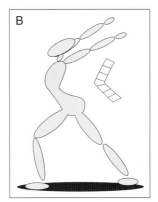

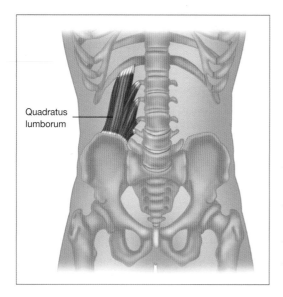

Quadratus lumborum

Stability of the CLA in the *coronal* plane has been found to correlate with lower limb injury risk [116]. In addition to the segmental support provided by TrA, multifidus and psoas, the ability to minimise displacement of the axis in the coronal plane is also dependent upon the action of **quadratus lumborum**.

This wide muscle runs across the waist from the iliac crest of the pelvis and the iliolumbar ligament (the ligament from the 5th lumbar vertebra to the ilium) to the lowest rib and transverse processes of upper four lumbar vertebrae (L1–L4) (pictured). Its action is to side bend the trunk, but also to withstand the trunk being pulled or pushed sideways in the opposite direction.

Stability of the CLA in the coronal plane is also dependent upon your pelvic control. If your pelvis tips from side to side due to weakness in the muscles around your hip, your spine will have to bend sideways also to keep you balanced, compromising your axis. Gluteus medius, a hip abductor, is considered to have the most significant role in this control, and weakness in hip abductor muscles has also been linked to lower limb injury risk [67]. The hip and pelvic muscles will be further discussed in the Lower Control Zone section of this chapter. Together, gluteus medius and the quadratus lumborum on the opposite side are considered to be a functional pair for coronal plane control.

At low levels, any sideways deviation in simple tests such as Single Leg Balance in Chapter 4 indicates a lack of CLA control in the coronal plane, while at higher levels, the jump with light push which also appears in Chapter 4 can expose coronal plane control issues more dynamically.

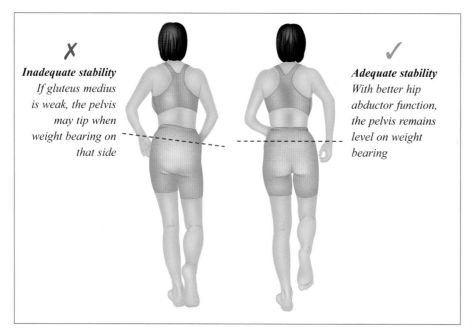

✗

Inadequate stability
If gluteus medius is weak, the pelvis may tip when weight bearing on that side

✓

Adequate stability
With better hip abductor function, the pelvis remains level on weight bearing

Hip abductor function.

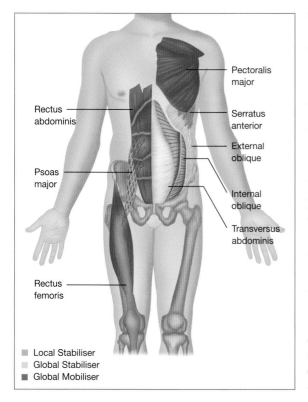

Pectoralis major

Rectus abdominis

Serratus anterior

External oblique

Psoas major

Internal oblique

Transversus abdominis

Rectus femoris

■ Local Stabiliser
▨ Global Stabiliser
■ Global Mobiliser

The Anterior Chain

There is a variety of possible neuromuscular strategies for stabilising the trunk. If we look at the front (anterior) surface of the body and consider the relationship between the abdominal muscles as part of a chain, TrA and internal obliques should work as local stabilisers, external obliques as a global stabiliser and rectus abdominis as a mobiliser. However, athletes often learn to use alternative patterns in order to compensate for poor local stabiliser activation. One of these patterns is the use of external obliques, rectus abdominis and superficial hip flexors as the main source of stability. This is not an effective method for stabilising the trunk, as these muscles do not offer segmental spinal control. They exert a compressive force over long lines of pull.

Ideally all of these anterior chain muscles should work in a coordinated fashion. A common poor pattern is the dominance of the red muscles, or red and yellow, without the muscles marked in green.

The external obliques decrease the mobility of the ribs by pulling them downwards towards the pelvis. Fixing the ribs in this way affects breathing patterns by preventing the lower part of the rib cage from expanding fully on inspiration. This will affect the potential for the large lower lobes of the lung to inflate fully, which in turn can influence the potential for oxygen and carbon dioxide exchange in this considerable area of the lungs.

The compressive action of external obliques on the ribs or the effect of rectus abdominis depressing the central rib cage can influence arm motion. To fully reach upwards with your arm, your trunk needs to lengthen and the space between your ribs should widen. If you are using compression to stabilise your trunk by activating external oblique-rectus abdominis, this lengthening action will be blocked. If you then need to reach for a high ball in basketball, or stretch for a longer stroke in freestyle swimming, you will have to make a compromise. You can either maintain your trunk stability pattern and not reach so far, or you can lose your trunk stability in order to allow your trunk to lengthen. Either way, optimal performance is lost.

Overuse of the superficial hip flexors is common in dysfunctional trunk stability patterns, and they often pair with the superficial back muscles (erector spinae) to compensate for poor local stabiliser activation and poor gluteal activation. The athlete with this pattern may stand with their pelvis tipped forward and an increased inward curve at the base of the spine. This combination of muscle actions produces a compressive or "buckling" force with a relatively limited attachment surface area. This makes the spine vulnerable in all planes.

Relative Flexibility and the Central Control Zone

As discussed in Chapter 1, relative flexibility is the tendency of one body part to move more readily than another. In the case of shoulder inflexibility, the spine tends to "give" into extension, collapsing the central longitudinal axis and allowing the spinal curve to deepen in order to get the arms overhead.

Personal Investigation

To investigate relative flexibility, stand with your side on to a mirror. Raise both arms so that they are straight above your head. Your hands should be directly vertically aligned with your feet. How easy was it to get your arms into this position? Did you need to increase your spinal curve to achieve the arm position? Did your pelvis shift forward so that your weight is supported on the front of your feet?

If so, bring your lower abdomen in towards your spine to help maintain its position, and try again. Can your arms go as high? If not, it is likely that your shoulders are not as flexible as you thought! You were "giving" in your lumbar spine. It is more "relatively flexible".

The same phenomenon can occur when the hip is relatively less flexible than the spine. When an athlete needs to bend at the hip, the spine bends first, collapsing the central longitudinal axis into flexion. There are different reasons for this, depending upon your body position. If you are trying to lift your knee or bring your thigh towards your trunk, poor hip mobility or hip flexion strength may cause you to bend your spine more readily.

This can be seen when athletes perform high knee lifts poorly in their warm-ups, allowing their chest to sink towards their knee instead of bringing the knee towards their chest. It can also be observed in rowers. If you are in a closed chain situation such as squatting, you may bend your spine instead of your hips due to poor gluteal action to control the hip angle, or poor body awareness.

When there is a compensatory pattern in the anterior chain, the thoracic spine (the spinal area from the point where your neck joins your trunk to the bottom of the rib cage) tends to be stiff and lacking in normal mobility. The nerve supply for TrA comes from the lower six thoracic vertebrae, and thoracic stiffness and transversus activation may be related. Applying the relative flexibility concept, stiffness in one area will tend to cause excessive mobility in another part so that the total amount of movement available to you remains roughly the same. When the thoracic spine is stiff, the cervical spine and lumbar spine will need greater motion to compensate, which can lead to instability in these areas. If you do not restore thoracic spine mobility, training TrA will only help in situations where you do not need good spinal movement.

Notes from the Clipboard

A professional surfer arrived at the clinic with lower back pain. He had been given exercises in the past for his poor trunk stability, but he was not improving. This young man's thoracic spine was extremely stiff, and as total spinal mobility is necessary for surfing, he had to move excessively somewhere else in the spine in order to perform. The excessive motion took place in his lumbar spine. The surfer's TrA function was inhibited, and his external obliques were trying to provide primary stability as well as rotational control and rotational torque. Some of his thoracic stiffness may have been due to this overactivity of the external  obliques. Muscle activation alone could not solve this athlete's problem. Without normal thoracic mobility, his lumbar spine would continue to move excessively despite local stabiliser training. To improve his situation, he needed to combine mobility training with his stability exercises. By restoring mobility in his thoracic spine, practising stabilising exercises which activated TrA to work as the local stabiliser and releasing the external obliques to work properly as a global stabiliser, the surfer was able to return to his sport without pain.

Main Messages

- Local and global muscles must work together to maintain smooth, efficient movement and normal breathing patterns.
- Breathing and trunk stability are interdependent.
- Local trunk stabilisers TrA and multifidus activate to provide a secure central longitudinal axis for efficient movement.
- Local stabiliser activity prevents spinal buckling under load.
- Trunk stability can influence the performance of your arms and legs.

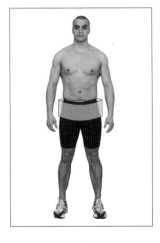

The Lower Control Zone: the Pelvis

The muscles of the trunk alone do not guarantee functional stability. Control of the trunk greatly depends upon the security of the foundation which carries and supports it. We therefore need to look a little further down the chain to that underappreciated group of muscles around the pelvis which primarily provide this support: the gluteals.

A large muscle with wide pelvic attachments, **gluteus maximus** (GMax) contributes to powerful hip extension for explosive activities like Olympic weight lifting, Nordic skiing, jumping and sprinting, as well as strong hip control as is needed for squatting, alpine skiing[40], uphill cycling[70] or a deep volley in tennis.

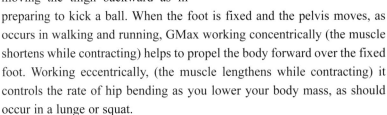

From a mechanical point of view, GMax performs key roles in controlling the relationship between thigh, pelvis and trunk. When the pelvis is

stabilised but the foot is not fixed, GMax acts as an extensor of the hip, moving the thigh backward as in preparing to kick a ball. When the foot is fixed and the pelvis moves, as occurs in walking and running, GMax working concentrically (the muscle shortens while contracting) helps to propel the body forward over the fixed foot. Working eccentrically, (the muscle lengthens while contracting) it controls the rate of hip bending as you lower your body mass, as should occur in a lunge or squat.

In partnership with gluteus medius and minimus, GMax controls the alignment of the knee with respect to the pelvis and the ankle, and therefore influences the amount of stress on the knee structures. For example, in a step-up, GMax should control thigh rotation and vertical alignment of the knee with the hip and ankle, while powerfully straightening the hip to press the body upwards. The hip, knee and ankle should remain in line so that the motion occurs in only one plane.

The lunge demonstrates eccentric action of GMax as the muscle is contracting as it lengthens to control the hip as it lowers.

GMax then contracts concentrically to straighten the hip.

If the gluteal group is weak or underactive, you will observe the knee moving inwards, and the pelvis tipping sideways. Under these conditions, the structures of the knee are put under abnormal strain due to poor alignment, and this can lead to pain at the front or inside of the knee. From a performance perspective it means that additional planes of movement are being introduced, which decreases the degree of force being applied in the most desirable direction.

Free movement at the hip and spine depends on healthy normal motion in the sacroiliac joints of the pelvis. These joints need a combination of muscles working in partnership to withstand the high forces that they must bear, and GMax plays a significant role in stabilising the sacroiliac joints by compressing the joint [49]. Like TrA, fibres of GMax attach into the thoraco-lumbar fascia. Via this thoraco-lumbar fascia, GMax forms a partnership with the latissimus dorsi on the opposite side to form the posterior oblique myofascial sling. Like modified rubber bands, myofascial slings store and release elastic energy, providing stability when they are under tension, and increasing movement efficiency when releasing. By forming a diagonal connection across the pelvis and lumbar spine, the posterior oblique sling increases sacroiliac joint compression to help support the body weight. In any movement that involves rotation of the upper body on the lower body, e.g. walking, running or kayaking, the sling stores and releases energy to make the movements more economical.

Weakness or underactivity in GMax will predispose the sacroiliac joints to injury and influence economy of movement by decreasing the effectiveness of the posterior oblique sling. If GMax is weak or underactive on one side, the body must compensate to protect itself from the high forces which impact on the sacroiliac joints. It may

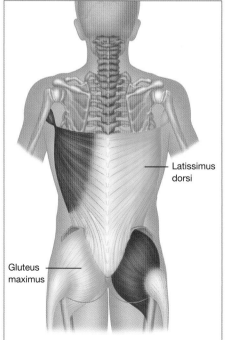

try to gain tension across the posterior oblique sling by increasing the activation of the opposing latissimus dorsi. If this happens, the trunk may tip to one side slightly, activation of the deep trunk stabilisers is affected, and it may appear that the shoulder is pulled down slightly on that side.

These effects are easily seen in weight-bearing movement such as a lunge, step up or knee raise. When you spot the shoulder moving slightly downwards, you should check the function of the gluteals on the opposite side. If the shoulder is pulled down by latissimus dorsi action in this way, shoulder biomechanics will change and an injury can appear. GMax function should be tested in athletes with shoulder injuries to make sure that it has not contributed to the development of the problem.

Latissimus dorsi and the opposite gluteus maximus work cooperatively to create the posterior oblique sling.

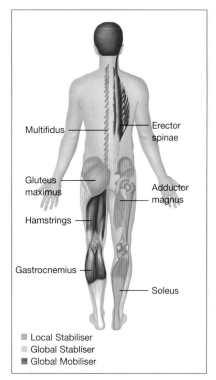

Multifidus

Erector spinae

Gluteus maximus

Adductor magnus

Hamstrings

Gastrocnemius

Soleus

■ Local Stabiliser
■ Global Stabliser
■ Global Mobiliser

These muscles should work in coordinated patterns. However, in dysfunctional patterns the muscles shown in red are often dominant, tight and overactive.

The Posterior Chain

If we look at the lumbar spine, pelvis and hip region from the back, GMax is the central link in a vertical chain comprising the superficial back muscles (erector spinae), gluteus maximus and hamstrings. These muscles should work in a coordinated partnership with the others in the chain, however GMax is weak and underactive in many athletes, causing the other links in the extensor chain to fire at high levels in the wrong sequence or timing. These muscles are not suited to this increased workload however: they complain bitterly by becoming chronically tight and susceptible to injury. Athletes who present with chronic hamstring "tears" or unusual levels of tightness in hamstrings and paraspinal muscles often exhibit poor GMax function on testing. Chronic groin strains can also be associated with poor GMax function. The largest of the inner thigh muscles, adductor magnus, has a role in extending the hip and supporting the thigh against the pelvis. Adductor magnus can increase its activity in an attempt to compensate for an underactive GMax, but this places abnormal strain on the muscle. Problems with GMax can start from seemingly unrelated injuries. A back or sacroiliac joint injury can switch off the muscle, but so can an ankle sprain [8] or a past knee injury. The original injury may have healed and been forgotten about, but it may have switched off GMax without it being noticed. Even though there is no remaining pain in the area, the athlete's technique may have altered over time for no apparent reason, and continues to resist improvement.

GMax Summary

Athlete presents with	What can it imply?	Likely finding
Tight/painful hamstrings or lumbar paraspinal muscles Insufficient forward or upward power production from the legs Pelvic position dropped when running	Faulty posterior chain muscle activation pattern	GMax weakness or delayed timing on same side
Tight/painful adductor magnus (inner thigh) Asymmetrical body orientation Better balance one side than the other	Faulty hip extension pattern: adductor magnus being over used to extend the hip	GMax function decreased on same side
Excessively tight latissimus dorsi (remembering that the dominant arm will often be slightly less flexible than the non-dominant one)	Faulty posterior oblique sling	GMax function decreased on opposite side

When acting as a stabiliser, the hip abductor **gluteus medius** (GMed) maintains a level pelvis when you bear more weight on one leg. This balances your trunk vertically with a minimum amount of postural muscle activity, which promotes good neuromuscular patterning in the trunk.

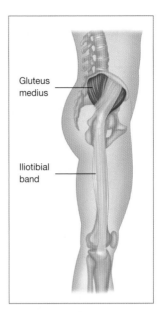

Gluteus medius

Iliotibial band

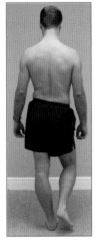 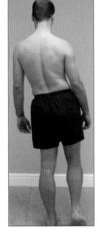

"Swagger gait"   *"Pendulum gait"*

If walking normally, the spine should respond to the force of striking the ground with your foot by rotating and counter rotating around a vertical axis, which keeps the trunk centred over the pelvis. The primary plane is rotation. You can easily see this action as you walk by noting that your opposite foot and arm move forward at the same time, indicating that your shoulders and pelvis are rotating in the opposite direction.

If the hip abductors are weak, coronal plane movement becomes more evident. This can expess itself in two ways. The pelvis may tip down on the opposite side to the stance leg, giving the appearance of a swagger on that side. This is known as a *Trendelenburg* gait. Alternatively, the individual will adopt a pendulum style of gait by shifting their whole trunk excessively over the weak hip. This is known as a *compensated Trendelenburg* gait. If adopting the pendulum style of walking to compensate for weak hip abductors, the trunk is only centred over the pelvis for a short moment in the gait cycle, and appears more like a side to side movement that markedly decreases efficiency and increases the activity of the trunk side flexors such as quadratus lumborum.

For athletes, the coronal plane movement that replaces efficient pelvic rotation around the CLA affects performance. It increases runners' foot contact time on the ground making each stride cost more energy, as their hip collapses slightly every time their foot strikes. In cyclists, it can be seen in excessive side to side trunk movement as they fail to keep a stable pelvis for the legs to push from. For footballers and basketballers it shows up as difficulty changing directions and controlling sideways momentum, and in skiers it will influence effective turning. GMed weakness is associated with many common sports injuries. GMed's fundamental pelvic stabilisation role in weight bearing influences the entire kinetic chain, and weakness can be associated with a variety of painful presentations including the knee, sacroiliac joints, and lower back. If working normally, GMed works in partnership with the GMinimus which lies deeper in the buttock, the adductor muscles of the inner thigh and tensor fascia latae (TFL), a superficial outer thigh muscle to keep your pelvis level as you stand on one leg. If GMed is weak then other muscles must increase their activity to compensate. TFL will become overactive if GMed is not functioning properly, and this causes tightness in the long fibrous band down the outside of the thigh, the iliotibial band (ITB).

Good hip abductor function maintains a level pelvis to support the trunk and the leg.

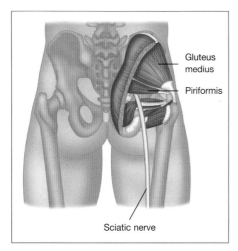

The small piriformis muscle is not well suited to compensating for the larger GMed muscle.

A tight ITB interferes with normal knee and pelvic mechanics, and can cause pain around the patella, sacroiliac joint problems, nerve compression around the head of fibula causing pain on the outside of the knee and even ankle pain due to altered biomechanics.

The other common responder to GMed weakness is piriformis, a deep buttock muscle which crosses the sacroiliac joint (SIJ). When overactive, piriformis interrupts normal pelvic and lower back mechanics and can cause sciatica and back pain.

An athlete may be able to balance on one leg, but have difficulty maintaining a level pelvis and vertical trunk while still looking relaxed. Many use excessive global muscular activity to compensate for loss of deep postural stabiliser function, and this can be observed in excessive ankle and foot activity, fixing of the ribs with the obliques, pinning down of the chest with rectus abdominis, pulling the shoulder blades back and deepening of forward pelvic tilt. Because of this, GMed can influence breathing, posture, shoulder mobility, balance, power production around the hip and multidirectional agility.

GMed Summary

Athlete presents with	What can it imply?	Likely finding
Swagger or pendulum gait	Faulty weight bearing strategy	Weak GMed
Tight quadratus lumborum (side trunk muscles)	Difficulty orientating the trunk vertically over the pelvis in gait, requiring overuse of side trunk muscles	Weak GMed opposite side
Tight piriformis	Faulty pelvic control in weight bearing requiring greater coronal plane control	Weak GMed same side
Tight ITB/lateral knee pain/knee cap pain	Faulty hip abduction or hip flexion strategy	Weak GMed, weak psoas same side

Main Messages

- The gluteal group must activate effectively to produce the short foot contact times necessary for fast running.

- The gluteal group is necessary for explosive lower body power.

- For the trunk to perform well, it needs to be set on a secure pelvic foundation provided by the gluteal group.

- Many common overuse injuries in the lower limb are associated with poor gluteal function.

The Upper Control Zone: the Shoulder Girdle

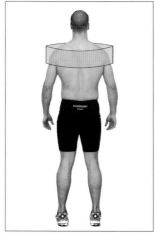

Whether you want power, fluency or precision from your arms, a stable shoulder girdle is essential to provide support and transfer of forces to and from the trunk. Compared to the pelvic girdle, the shoulder girdle is relatively delicate, but like the pelvic girdle, the shoulder girdle depends on its muscular attachments to provide a secure foundation for arm movement.

The scapula and the clavicle join at the acromioclavicular (AC) joint, making a roof just above the ball and socket joint of the shoulder. The clavicle then attaches to the sternum (breastbone) with ligaments, joining the shoulder girdle with the skeleton at the front. However, at the back of the shoulder girdle the scapula does not attach to the ribs in the same way. The scapula needs to be very mobile in response to arm movements, so fixing it to the skeleton with ligaments would reduce the movement possibilities in our arm. Instead of being fixed with ligaments, a coordinated muscular pattern around the scapula allows it to support the arm but still be very mobile.

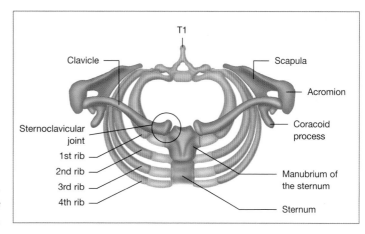

View of the shoulder girdle from above. Note that the only direct attachment to the skeleton is at the sternoclavicular joint.

Shooting requires static shoulder stability.

Some sports such as archery, dressage riding or shooting require a scapular position which is secure in a relatively static position. However, most sports need the scapula to be both *stable* and *mobile* simultaneously.

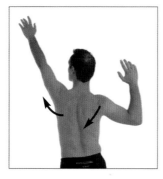

Dynamic scapular stability. To support the arm movements, the left scapula is rotating up and away from the spine, while the right scapula moves towards the spine.

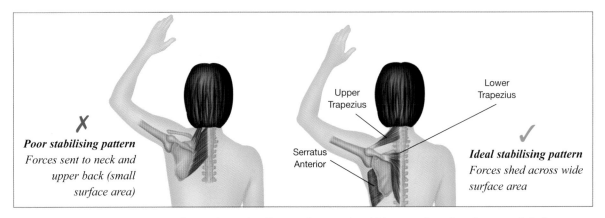

✗ Poor stabilising pattern
Forces sent to neck and upper back (small surface area)

Upper Trapezius

Lower Trapezius

Serratus Anterior

✓ Ideal stabilising pattern
Forces shed across wide surface area

Ideally, to produce or control optimum force, loading on the arm should be transferred to the central skeleton over the largest possible surface area. The muscles best designed for this function are lower trapezius and serratus anterior. These muscles work in partnership to secure the scapula onto the rib cage while dispersing forces across a wide surface area.

Personal Investigation

Can't feel your scapula? This isn't unusual! Their position means that we can't see them, so it is harder to notice the effects of using different scapular muscles.

1. Reach under one arm and around to the scapula on that side. Feel the edges of the bone and keep your fingers on whichever part of the scapula you can easily reach. Ideally, have your fingers around the bottom point of the scapula.

2. Lift that arm to shoulder height. Press your arm forward without moving your trunk. Did you detect your scapula gliding forward around your rib cage? This is called *protraction*.

3. Without bending your elbow, pull your shoulder back as far as it will come. Can you feel your scapula gliding back around your rib cage towards your spine? This is called *retraction*.

4. Try shrugging your shoulder. Your scapula will feel like it is being pulled upwards. This is called *elevation*. You can press it downwards also, which is called *depression*.

5. Put your feeling hand over as much of your scapula as you can reach. Lift your arm upwards in front of you. Can you feel your shoulder blade moving in response to your arm lift? This is called *upward rotation*. Becoming more aware of your scapulae and their natural movements can make it easier to activate the correct muscles around them.

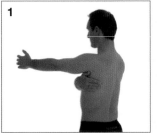
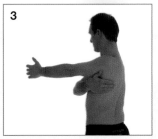
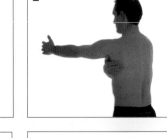
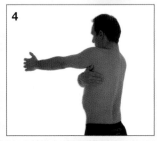

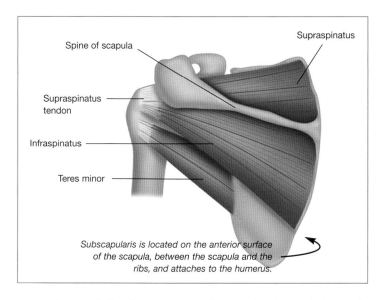

Spine of scapula

Supraspinatus

Supraspinatus tendon

Infraspinatus

Teres minor

Subscapularis is located on the anterior surface of the scapula, between the scapula and the ribs, and attaches to the humerus.

The Rotator Cuff

The collection of muscles known as the **rotator cuff** controls the motion of the head of humerus, or "ball" in the ball and socket joint of the shoulder. The "socket" part of the joint is part of the scapula, so as the scapula moves, so does the socket. The ball, or head of humerus, must be balanced in the socket as it moves. The rotator cuff muscles act to keep the ball of the shoulder balanced in the right position in the socket.

The rotator cuff group comprises supraspinatus, infraspinatus, teres minor and subscapularis. Each of these muscles has a unique primary action, but they also act together as a stabilising unit. When used for primary action, subscapularis acts as an internal rotator, infraspinatus and teres minor as external rotators, and supraspinatus as an arm abductor.

As stabilisers, these muscles exert a compressive force on the head of humerus to secure it in the socket as you move your arm. In effect they "suck" the head of your humerus into the socket, providing the fixed point for arm movement. If they did not perform this role, the more superficial movement muscles would pull the head of humerus across the socket as they contract. The fixed point, or movement axis will be lost, and the muscular pattern for force production and shoulder control will be altered. If the head of humerus is allowed to slide up or forward in the socket, it will press against bony and ligamentous structures in the shoulder, causing tissue trauma and eventually painful pathologies such as tendonitis and instability.

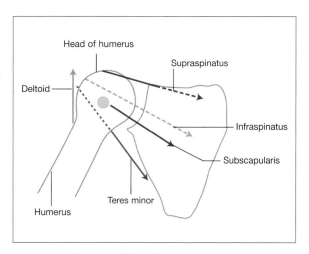

Head of humerus

Supraspinatus

Deltoid

Infraspinatus

Subscapularis

Teres minor

Humerus

Directions of rotator cuff muscle action.

Rotator cuff training alone will not ensure shoulder health. Scapular stability is necessary to ensure that the socket is controlled and well positioned for whichever forces it must deal with. Trunk and pelvic stability is necessary to provide a supportive foundation for the scapula. If your trunk stability is poor and you have a weak CLA it is likely that your scapula will be dragged into a poor position. Poor pelvic control can also alter scapular positioning, either directly due to excessive dependence upon latissimus dorsi, or indirectly by failing to provide a supportive platform for the trunk.

To protect the rotator cuff, make sure that your pelvic stability, trunk stability and scapular stability are secure in order to support good shoulder mechanics prior to performing resistance work for the upper body. The rotator cuff is addressed along with scapular stability in Chapters 5–8.

Poor Patterns for Managing Forces in the Upper Control Zone

Forces are supported by the neck in the weak elevated shoulder pattern.

Forces are supported by the stronger chest wall with this secure scapular position.

Elevation Pattern

Although the lower trapezius-serratus anterior pattern is ideal for supporting arm force, other patterns may dominate the shoulder girdle. The first of these is the use of the upper trapezius and levator scapulae muscles, which direct forces to the cervical and upper thoracic spine. These spinal structures provide a relatively small supporting surface area, and are not well suited to withstanding the heavy loads. Lifting weights while using this pattern can cause stress and even injury on the neck, upper back and shoulder.

The other outcome of sending forces to small regions in the neck and upper back is altered shoulder mechanics. The levator scapulae muscle which attaches to the mid cervical vertebrae, and rhomboideus minor which attaches to the upper thoracic vertebrae, pull the inner border of the scapula upwards. This tilts the scapula downwards.

Normal biomechanics of the scapula demand that as the arm is lifted, the scapula should rotate upwards, which moves the bony "roof" over the shoulder tendons covering the ball and socket joint of the shoulder out of the way. This avoids tendon compression that could eventually turn into tendonitis. Athletes with a downwardly rotated scapula therefore are at risk of developing an overuse injury of the shoulder. These athletes often appear to have very sloping shoulders.

If upper trapezius is over-pulling, you will look like your shoulders are pulled upwards, and you will feel tight and sore across the tops of your shoulders. This strategy increases stress on the neck.

Depression Pattern

The next possible pattern is overuse of the latissimus dorsi. From our discussion of the posterior oblique sling, we learned that you might increase your latissimus dorsi activity if the opposite GMax is weak. This can be observed when performing non-symmetrical activities such as standing on one leg or lunging. If the weight bearing side has an underactive GMax, the athlete will pull their opposite shoulder down slightly using latissimus dorsi. However, you may use latissimus dorsi as a primary strategy to provide some fixation for the scapula even without the influence of the pelvis, especially if you have been repeatedly told to pull your shoulders down. If this occurs, the scapula is pulled into depression and in some people downwards rotation, which alters shoulder biomechanics in overhead activities and increases risk of injury. **For this reason, it is better to ask young athletes to lengthen their neck or relax their shoulders rather than pull their shoulders down.**

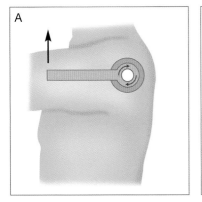
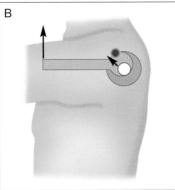

A: Head of humerus rotates around fixed point.

B: Fixed point is lost and head of humerus drifts forward and upward, pinching shoulder tendons.

Anterior Pattern

This pattern involves the overuse of the pectorals and anterior deltoid muscle to stabilise the shoulder girdle. This is exceptionally common in athletes, many of whom have been made to perform press-ups before their stability system was sufficiently developed, and who perform heavy pectoral strengthening resistance exercises. These athletes' shoulders are usually slightly rolled inwards giving the impression that there is a deeper groove than normal at the front where the arm joins the body. Pectoralis major is centrally secured to the sternum and clavicle and attached to the humerus, but as it does not actually attach to the scapula it is not an effective primary stabiliser of the shoulder girdle. Athletes with this pattern try to bypass the scapula by fixing their arm directly to the front of their chest wall, but as they are unable to secure the body of the scapula effectively against the ribs the biomechanics of the ball and socket joint of the shoulder are altered.

Athletes with the anterior pattern are prone to the head of their humerus being drawn forward in the socket. This is usually prevented through delicately coordinated cooperative muscle action. If the scapula is positioned and supported well, the rotator cuff's compressive effect on the head of humerus should keep it secure in the socket. If the head of humerus is allowed to glide forward, the axis for movement is lost and the shoulder becomes vulnerable. Athletes are prone to this pattern if they have allowed their shoulder joint to repetitively slide forward during chest stretching or strengthening exercises. In exercises such as Bench or Pec Deck Flyes and single arm chest stretches on the wall, athletes can be observed popping their shoulder joint forward as their arm moves backward. Instability and impingement of the shoulder tendons can result. To prevent this, ensure that as your arm moves backward, your shoulder stays secure and does not pop forward. Although this will feel as though you are not moving as far, you will be working more accurately in a position that will develop a stronger more robust shoulder.

Forward Scapular Tilt

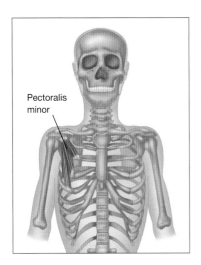

Pectoralis minor

The relatively small pectoralis minor has a small attachment to the scapula and connects this point to the upper ribs. If you find the midpoint of one of your clavicles and press your fingers into the muscle tissue below that point, you will find your pectoralis minor – it is often quite tender! If pectoralis minor is your primary strategy for stabilising your scapula, it will tend to tip your scapula forward, raising the bottom of it slightly off the ribs at the back. The scapula is therefore not secured to the rib cage effectively, so forces must be transferred and supported elsewhere on the skeleton, with the most likely areas being the neck, upper back or chest.

A Whole Body Approach

Personal Investigation

Sit in a slumped position looking straight ahead. Try to lift your arms as high as you can.

Now lift yourself against gravity so that you are in a relaxed upright posture. Try lifting your arms again. Do you notice a difference in your range of movement?

Your trunk position has influenced your arm movement.

Poor posture, poor trunk stability and poor scapular stability are directly related. A slumped spinal position and forward head posture alters shoulder biomechanics and makes overhead arm movements difficult. Athletes with general stability deficits will react to a force demand on their arms or a body balance challenge by drawing their shoulders upwards or forward. These athletes look tense, their movement fluency is usually poor and their trunk appears disengaged. Simply telling them to keep their shoulders down will not help. Improving their balance, trunk stability and pelvic stability will reduce their dependence on this strategy.

For explosive force production such as in a tennis serve, motion must move in a wave from the ground up, starting from the pelvis and trunk through the shoulder girdle and out into the arm and hand. If the athlete lacks control of their central trunk axis or cannot rotate the pelvis or trunk adequately around this axis, they will overuse their shoulder muscles to compensate for the lack of force production. If the athlete has poor pelvic or trunk stability, they are likely to use a strategy in their upper control zone that sends forces to the wrong areas.

Some athletes do have the correct pattern of activation, but do not have sufficient muscular endurance to sustain it for the duration necessary. As the stabilisers fatigue, other muscles are brought into play in order to maintain the position of the shoulders. Sports with relatively sustained postures like shooting and archery would be susceptible to this problem; however sports like kayak may provoke the same effect through sheer repetition of movement.

Similarly, the athlete's correct pattern may be available up to a certain level of load, but when this is exceeded, another muscular pattern emerges in order to cope. The increase in load may be actual weight to be lifted, or it may be the speed and complexity of movement involved. Progressing an athlete's training volume or intensity should therefore account for their overall movement pattern quality throughout the drill or exercise rather than simply achieving a number of repetitions at a given load. If this is not the case, improvements will eventually plateau, or the athlete will become injured.

Notes from the Clipboard

A 17-year-old female tennis player joined the national junior tennis academy. Although she achieved reasonable results, she was technically poor on serve and ground strokes. She had unstable shoulders which she said felt like they "pop out of place" and an unstable rib which caused her pain and stopped her from playing and training effectively.

On-court analysis showed that the player produced all her power shots with her shoulders raised and pulled forward in a "bracing" position. She demonstrated poor engagement of her trunk musculature, and poor trunk and pelvis rotation. Her pelvic stability was also poor.

There are several mechanisms to consider here. The player's global stability was poor, so in the absence of a secure foundation for power generation in her pelvis and trunk she adopted the "braced" shoulder posture, which uses muscle tension to provide a degree of stability for her arms. This does have unfortunate side effects, however. Playing with the shoulders raised tends to interrupt the trunk to shoulder girdle relationship, limiting the amount of power that can be generated from trunk rotation.

This position also compromises the axis of rotation in the ball and socket joint of the shoulder. With the head of humerus positioned forward in the shoulder socket, it was not possible for the player to achieve the shoulder rotation required to hit an effective serve safely. For an effective serve, the shoulder needs to move rapidly from lateral to medial rotation, but without a secure axis of rotation, the head of humerus will shift in the socket. This player cannot improve her serve action without putting herself at greater injury risk.

To improve the situation, the programme was as follows:

1. Improve central trunk and pelvic stability so that the player is equipped with a sound foundation for movement that alleviates the need for her to "brace" her shoulders.

2. Begin scapular stability training in a position where her balance is not challenged in order to allow her to experience correct activation patterning.

3. Once scapular control is improving, begin awareness training for the axis of rotation in the shoulder joint. This should be done simultaneously with activation of rotator cuff muscles.

4. Gradually increase the balance and stability challenges, ensuring that the player does not lapse into shoulder bracing positions.

5. Strengthen the entire system while simultaneously working on rotational action in the pelvis and trunk on court.

Main Messages

- Performance and health of the arms and upper trunk are dependent upon an athlete's total posture and stability.

- Total body movement should be considered in order to produce optimal force and protect the shoulder joints. Pelvic and trunk rotation should be checked and maintained for any sport which involves open chain force production from the arms, e.g. throwing, striking the ball with a bat or racquet, paddling, golf, tennis and volleyball.

- Forces should be dispersed across large surface areas of the trunk, not directed to the delicate structures of the neck.

- Moving your arm over your head requires your scapula to rotate upwards. If the movement you are going to perform involves taking your arms upwards, don't focus on keeping your scapulae squeezed back and down, as this is the opposite action. Instead, focus on maintaining a light tall posture, which naturally starts to open your chest and lengthen your neck to release unwanted muscle action and excessive tension.

- Pelvic and trunk stability is important to support an independent scapular position.

- The health of the rotator cuff is dependent upon scapular stability. Scapular stability should be established before undertaking resistance training for the arms if injury is to be avoided and optimal performance achieved.

Chapter Summary

- Muscles can be grouped according to their characteristics, but these groups have blurred edges and will continue to evolve as more research becomes available.

- The behaviour of our muscles and their relationships within patterns helps us to understand athletic movement. If the movement does not seem fluent, or if injuries occur, it is helpful to identify the patterns that might be the root of the problem.

- Poor patterns are usually the result of timing and coordination problems between muscle groups. Muscles that are habitually underactive need to be activated so that the pattern becomes efficient.

- Understanding the anatomy of stability gives us a foundation to start assessing movement to see how it is applied to body control. We will investigate this in Chapter 4.

Chapter 3: Key Stability Concepts for Efficient Movement

Posture
Breathing
Low Stress Abdominals
The Listening Foot
The Relaxed Face
Effortless Control
Compete in the Moment

The following concepts should be kept in mind throughout the entire training programme. Successful transference of the functional stability skills learned in the programme to your sporting movement depends upon these simple principles.

Posture

The foundation for efficient movement is posture, but not the rigid concept of posture that can be so difficult and uncomfortable to achieve. We often talk about good or bad posture, but it is more realistic to aim for what is an "ideal" posture for your individual body and the movements that you perform.

Ideal posture is a dynamic experience, whether you are in motion or in stillness. Nothing is locked or fixed, even when you are just standing quietly. You are simply and buoyantly supporting yourself against gravity, and allowing your body structures to move and interact in their least stressful, most effective relationships. An ideal dynamic posture should make movement easier, helping you to establish a central axis for balanced motion and allowing you to breathe freely.

The traditional view of posture is one of pure body alignment, as if our bodies were made of blocks stacked straight on top of one another. We are told "stand up straight, head up, shoulders back, stomach in" and so forth in order to achieve this alignment, but it costs high effort to bring all these body parts into line and sustain them in this "perfect" position. Increasing the effort increases the muscle tension, and it is hard to move freely when everything is holding tightly. Then we are told that we'll get used to it as we get stronger and more flexible!

The effect of effort can easily be seen in young athletes who are told to either sit up or stand up straight. They try to straighten up by increasing back muscle tension. Either they can't move freely or they fatigue quickly, so they collapse into their original posture. They become caught in a cycle of straightening and collapsing and fail to achieve the central axis that would permit a more relaxed and efficient movement.

Posture should not be rigid!

It is quite natural to fall back into old habits because postural muscles should actually work with *low effort* for long periods of time, not high effort as is often the case with the traditional approach to correction.

The good news is that the skeletal alignment model is appealingly simplistic but not entirely accurate. Posture isn't just about your skeleton: your nervous system powerfully influences your posture, making it possible to work more effectively with less effort. As gravity presses down upon our bodies, some parts can buckle forward and some buckle backwards. Trying to pull all these parts back into line is addressing the symptoms but not the cause of the problem. Perhaps instead we could get to the root of things directly by refusing to be compressed. How do we do this? Using neurological reflexes, we can stimulate your posture quickly and easily by learning to resist gravity. To do this we are going to use imagery.

Improving your posture is not about hard work, but about awareness of a new sensation. Stand in a relaxed, almost slumped posture. Imagine for a moment that a very large helium balloon on a string is attached to the back of the top of your head. Make it real for yourself by giving it a colour. Helium rises, so the role of the balloon is to gently lift the weight of your head up off your body. This releases the spine from the compression of gravity. Allow your body to decompress and lengthen without straining. Breathe freely now that the weight of your head has been lifted.

Now switch your balloon off. Feel how you collapse under the influence of gravity. Make a mental note of your shoulder position. Switch your balloon on again and you will find that your chest has opened and your shoulders have spread apart. This has happened even though you weren't thinking about pulling your shoulders back. Switch your balloon off again and put your hand on your lower belly. Switch on the balloon and you will find that your stomach moves inwards and possibly upwards. You have activated your trunk stabilisers without needing to think about it.

Compression causes buckling.   *Elongation restores alignment.*

You have achieved all of this by cleverly stimulating a reflex which was triggered by your head position. Most of us carry our heads slightly rotated backwards. "Ballooning" encourages you to gently rotate the head slightly forward, decompressing the back of the neck and encouraging the deep postural muscles to switch on.

Better posture should not be a strain. Allow your body to lighten up in order to decrease pressure on your joints and move freely. An ideal natural posture should be comfortable, repeatable and sustainable. Efficient posture is the foundation for movement: your effort should be directed towards your sporting activity, not just holding yourself up against gravity!

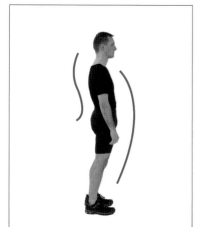 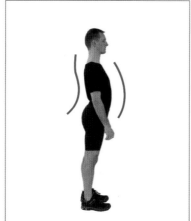 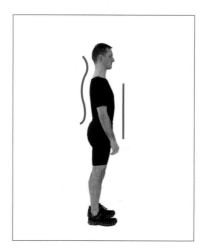

Buckling against gravity. *Over-strain.* *Ballooning for relaxed elongation.*

Athletes in such diverse sports as swimming, triathlon, karate, kayak, weight lifting, biathlon, football, athletics, tennis, golf and gymnastics are all applying the balloon principle, and they are finding that it unlocks their movement and provides a balanced, relaxed and dynamic foundation for their movement. It doesn't matter what position you are in: once you learn the feeling of low effort alignment triggered by your head position, you can apply it in any situation.

Notes from the Clipboard: Movement Dysfunction

A female long jumper presented to the clinic with a long history of severe shin pain. Although she had received substantial treatment including surgery, she was unable to run without increasing her pain.

This athlete's natural posture produced an inefficient running and walking style that led to overuse of the muscles on the front of her lower leg. In an effort to "run tall", she was throwing her shoulders back and raising her chin, which forced her hips backwards, arched her back and made it impossible for her to use her hip muscles effectively. This forced her to over use the small muscles of her lower leg as she tried to pull herself over her foot when transferring her weight, rather than pushing herself over her foot with the strong gluteal muscles of her hip.

By using the balloon cue, the athlete was able to lengthen the back of her neck, relax her shoulders and bring her hips under her trunk. This position felt strange at first, as she was accustomed to thinking that her slightly backward bent posture was in fact upright. Keeping the balloon cue in mind, she was asked to simply maintain the posture and roll onto her forefeet to initiate the movement. There was an immediate change in her movement pattern. Her stride length and forward propulsion increased, and she could feel the muscles on the back of her leg from her calf to her hip pushing her forward on each stride. The athlete's coach had identified a technical problem with her running style, but had been unable to change it. That style had eventually led to injury. Simple postural cueing enabled the athlete to access the muscles she needed to develop more efficient, less stressful movement.

Having trouble ballooning?

Occasionally it happens. You may be lifting the top half of your body, but disconnecting it from your bottom half. The curve in your spine appears to deepen, your ribs tip upwards at the front, and your pelvis tips downwards. This effectively shortens your body at the back, and lengthens it at the front. If you suspect you might be doing this, place your hands on your rib cage, fingers at the front and thumb at the back. When you perform the balloon postural cue, check that your fingers are not pointing upwards and your thumb downwards. If they are, relax the front of your rib cage back down so that your hand is level. Try tilting it again so that the fingers point upwards. Can you feel that your whole rib cage is rotating up at the front and down at the back? Relax the front back down until your hands are level again. Picture your rib cage sitting balanced and level on your spine.

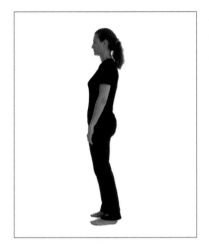  

You can also try this alternative image as an experiment.

Visualise your spine as a long sealed rubber tube, something like a bicycle inner tube. The tube runs from your tailbone all the way to your head. Now imagine filling that tube progressively with air from the bottom of the tube to the top. What happens? Most people feel their rib cage and pelvis come back into line as they inflate the inner tube, and as this occurs, the back of their necks release and the spine lengthen all the way to their tail bone. If this image works better for you than ballooning, use this one as you move.

Posture is Not Just About Your Body

Although muscle patterns and the way you react to gravity can affect posture, they are not the only factors to consider. Did you realise how much you are communicating with your posture? Imagine for a moment what these statements might look like in a person's posture: "I'm tired" (so don't ask too much of me), or "I'm not that confident right now" (so I'll make myself a little smaller so as not to attract attention) or "some day if I try hard I might be a winner" (but I haven't had any results yet and I don't want anyone to think I'm cocky).

Your thoughts, attitudes and mood can deeply influence your posture. Posture is one of the ways you can tell the world who you are. Decide what you want to say and "wear it".

Key Concept
Use light, effortless posture as the starting point for each exercise.

Breathing

Breathing is intimately related to both posture and stability. As discussed in Chapter 2, the diaphragm, TrA, the pelvic floor and multifidus all work together to provide primary stability for the trunk. Poor posture may change the breathing pattern by compressing the rib cage, and influence trunk stability by altering the activity of the diaphragm and TrA. Poor trunk stability may change the breathing pattern due to recruitment of global muscles that inhibit rib motion, and this abnormal muscle activity can distort posture. A poor breathing pattern can maintain these patterns and make them difficult to change. In order to improve posture, breathing or stability, all three must be addressed.

Although we all breathe, we don't necessarily do it in the same way, and some breathing patterns are more effective than others. A surprising number of athletes have poor breathing patterns, and when tested these athletes often demonstrate associated stability or balance problems, hyperventilation symptoms or performance differences between static and dynamic situations. Without an effective breathing pattern, stability training does not produce the best results.

When breathing normally, the lower ribs should expand in an outwards and upwards direction. However, if athletes have poor trunk stability, they may try to support themselves by using their external obliques as stabilisers. If this occurs, it is difficult for them to expand the lower ribs upward and outward. The athlete has to find another way to breathe, and the most likely strategy is to breathe in the upper chest instead. Physiological efficiency is compromised as the upper lobes of the lungs have a relatively small surface area for gas exchange compared to the lower lobes.

An athlete with this breathing pattern looks like their upper chest wall is moving up and down, instead of their lower ribs moving in and out. They look tense across the shoulders and tilt their head slightly back, which makes it difficult to efficiently activate the deep stabilisers of the abdomen. They may be repeatedly told by their coach to "pull their shoulders down", or simply to "relax", but unless their breathing pattern is retrained they can't respond to these instructions.

Do you know what your normal breathing pattern is? Fortunately it is not difficult to work out your own breathing pattern and learn how to breathe more effectively. Place one hand on your upper chest and the other over your lower ribs. Breathe normally and note which hand seems to move more. Now take a deeper breath. If your hands move apart or towards your head, you are using a "piston" breathing pattern. This means that your chest wall is moving up and down as you breathe instead of expanding outwards. It is likely that you are not inflating the largest part of your lungs efficiently.

 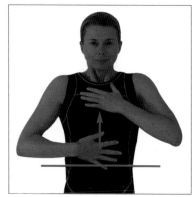 

Now place your hands around your waist, and gradually work them upwards until they cover your lower ribs. Place your fingers to the front and your thumbs to the back. The space between your fingers and your thumb will be wrapped around the side of your rib cage. Take a breath in. Your ribs should move out into the space between your fingers and thumb. If they didn't, it is likely that you felt your chest move upwards, or forward into your fingers. Breathe quietly, and notice whether your ribs move underneath your hands. You should see your fingers move slightly apart as you breathe in. Gradually increase the size of your inwards breath. You should start to feel your ribs move outwards and slightly upwards as you breathe in, and feel them move back down and in as you breathe out.

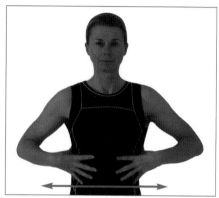

Now take a full breath in: make sure that the ribs move into that space between your fingers and thumb. Return to normal breathing. Now focus on your out-breath. The air should move freely out of your lungs without you needing to make any effort. The abdominals should only be used to breathe out under forced conditions, such as coughing, sneezing and extreme effort. Overusing them for normal breathing will affect their normal action. If you find that you are squeezing the air out with your abdominals, move one hand down over your belly button and focus on keeping these muscles relaxed throughout the breathing cycle.

This basic breathing exercise is useful to perform prior to starting your stability programme. It helps with your posture and makes it easier to activate the correct stabiliser muscles.

Breathing and Intra-abdominal Pressure

As mentioned in Chapter 2, the diaphragm, pelvic floor, TrA, internal obliques and multifidus create a container that controls pressure within the abdominal cavity. This intra abdominal pressure (IAP) has a stabilising effect on the spine[46], and a greater squeezing force of the superficial abdominals further raises the IAP to reinforce the spine in response to sudden load. Increasing the pressure in our abdominal cavity by breathing in or holding our breath is one of our natural strategies for increasing spine stability when producing forceful movements[35]. This can only be temporary however. Holding your breath can put the abdominal organs and muscles under immense pressure. Prolonged or repeated spikes in IAP have been linked to hernias and prolapses[20,18,27].

Athletes with poor local stabiliser function can often be observed performing relatively low load activities using breath holding and excessive superficial abdominal muscle activity to stabilise. Apart from the musculo-skeletal risks associated with a faulty deep local stabiliser system, this strategy increases the IAP repeatedly over long time periods, putting the athlete at possible risk of hernia.

Personal Investigation

Not sure about breathing in or breath holding? If you're sitting down, stand up. Did you breathe in or out?

Still not sure? Try lifting something nearby. Did you breathe in, out or hold your breath? Which one felt more comfortable?

Breathing is a natural part of movement. The habit of breath holding, however, can interrupt this natural response. Better awareness of your breathing pattern improved stability.

Key Concept

Breathe normally at all times during your exercises.

Low Stress Abdominals

There has been a great deal of confusion about how the abdominals should be trained to work in order to increase stability around the central control zone. Some athletes have been taught to simply pull their stomachs in, but this can lead to incorrect muscle patterning, a decrease in trunk mobility and problems with breathing. Some have been taught to "brace" their abdominals, and others have been taught a hollowing manoeuvre, all in the name of trunk stability.

In Chapter 2 you learned that transversus abdominis, a local stabiliser, is supposed to work at low levels over long periods in response to movement, and that it should normally activate automatically to do this. When you performed the balloon postural cue earlier in the chapter, you allowed your body to decompress. As you released your spine and allowed it lengthen, you had the sensation of your lower abdomen automatically drawing inwards and upwards gently. This did not require conscious muscular effort and concentration, so it will have had little effect on your breathing other than perhaps to make it a little easier. You should still feel that you can move freely and dynamically. This is the sensation that you are aiming for when training to move fluently at low effort.

This is an entirely different feeling from that which you would experience when you have to withstand a heavy blow from an opponent as you might in a combat or contact sport. The more superficial (global) abdominals must react to "brace" the spine for impact. An impact or unexpected load can cause a sudden forced bending or twisting movement of the spine. If your ribs are knocked sideways, for example, the spine is subjected to a rapid side bending stress, compressing the spinal structures on one side and overstretching them on the other. The powerful global muscles like external oblique abdominals and quadruatus lumborum help to maintain the alignment of your ribs relative to your pelvis.

Higher load core strengthening programmes therefore have a role to play in sports where the ability to "brace" your body is important.

Bracing helps to keep the trunk positioned over the pelvis despite coronal plane pressure.

Bracing generates a high level of global tension as a protective measure. It acts like a momentary suit of armour in the face of great force, but like a suit of armour it will restrict your dynamic movement if this is your only source of stability. Athletes in contact sports need to recognise the difference between training to brace and training for dynamic stability. Training to brace enables short bursts of high effort against strong resistance. Training to be dynamically stable fosters fluid, unrestricted movement with strength and control.

If your sport requires static control as in sports like archery, bracing yourself feels like it makes you stronger, but actually decreases your balance and makes breathing difficult. Bracing makes you rigid and decreases your stability by amplifying the small natural fluctuations in balance that occur in our bodies constantly. Aiming for "dynamic stillness" rather than a fixed static posture allows your body to absorb these fluctuations. Achieving a deeper level of stability releases excessive muscle tension and allows you to feel more grounded. Most sports require smooth movement and freedom of breathing. Bracing your trunk with high abdominal tension restricts both of these qualities. If you perform stability exercises with high levels of tension, the benefits are difficult to transfer back to your sport. When performing the exercises in this book, aim to build confident, controlled, fluid movement.

To be functionally stable, we use must therefore use combinations of abdominal muscle activity. With transversus abdominis providing a foundation, the other abdominal muscles act as layers of increasing support in response to the loading on your body. Remember though that with a greater proportion of superficial abdominal muscle activity to stabilise there will be a corresponding decrease in mobility. A balance is necessary.

This balance could be demonstrated in a well-coordinated golf swing or tennis ground stroke. In both of these situations, the local or deep stabilisers should provide a firm trunk axis, with the more superficial muscles taking on a powerful movement role as well as controlling the trunk through the movement. In both sports, the pelvis and shoulders must rotate with slightly different timing to optimise efficiency and power. The pelvis actually starts to rotate forward to initiate the swing-through before the shoulders have fully rotated backwards[9], which temporarily lengthens the trunk muscles. This sudden stretch stores elastic energy like a rubber band, increasing muscular efficiency when the upper body begins its swing through. If an athlete is using abdominal bracing as his primary stabilising strategy, he will lock his ribs and pelvis together and therefore find it difficult to separate the upper and lower body as is necessary for efficient technique.

The exercises in the next chapters will give you some cues to focus on to make sure that you are using an appropriate abdominal strategy. The main thing to remember is that if you are holding your breath or working hard to maintain your position, you are not using your most efficient pattern.

Notes from the Clipboard

A professional footballer presented with a history of chronic groin problems. He was a very powerful looking player, yet on simple low load testing he struggled for control, demonstrating lip biting, bracing and breath holding in order to perform the basic test movements. His was a familiar presentation, as many of the footballers and rugby players who have presented with persistent back and groin problems also demonstrated this behaviour. They all had excellent core strength and could withstand sudden bursts of force, but they lacked low load or "low threshold" stability. These athletes will often say that they know that they are fit, but yet they are always more out of breath than their team-mates. Adding simple Phase 1 and 2 activation exercises on a daily basis prior to training was sufficient to significantly improve symptoms and prevent recurrence to a surprising extent. These athletes are subject to body contacts of varying severity throughout a game, and it is possible that these sometimes painful knocks are sufficient to alter their muscle activity patterns. By supplementing the existing higher load programme with low load preparatory "switch-on" activities, hamstring, groin and back symptoms injury rates decreased throughout the player's whole team.

Key Concept

Aim for fluid strength and elastic movement rather than rigid resistance.

To develop deep local stabiliser effectiveness, breathe normally and use the lowest amount of muscle activity necessary to control the exercise perfectly. This can be difficult at first, because athletes are accustomed to experiencing muscle work rather than movement quality when performing trunk exercises. Remember that the deep local stabiliser muscles should give long duration support but allow for fluent dynamic action.

You are aiming to develop efficiency. If you use high effort for low level exercises, what are you going to use in a high level situation?

The Listening Foot

Balance, pelvic stability and posture are all heavily influenced by sensory information from the foot. The sole of your foot is sensitive for a good reason: it is constantly sending information into your central nervous system so that you can instantly and unconsciously adjust your body's alignment [98]. It also promotes a strong and stable pelvis in running, jumping or any other weight bearing exercise by triggering a connection called the *positive support reflex*, and this forms the foundation for closed kinetic chain exercise.

When the sole of the foot is stimulated by weight bearing it activates the extensors of the knee (quadriceps) and hip (gluteals) to withstand the load and prevent the joints from collapsing.

However, effective stimulation of the reflex is influenced by the joints of the lower leg adapting to the ground surface so that the sole of the foot can gather accurate information. The sole of the foot compares information across its surface in order to send instant information up into the central nervous system regarding where we should position our centre of gravity, and so is critical for dynamic balance. To access this critical sensory feedback, you need to have a mobile foot, ankle, and lower leg that will adapt to the surface you are moving on. This will allow the foot to maintain contact with the ground, even over uneven terrain.

In Chapter 1, we introduced the concept of functional rigidity. A functionally rigid foot and ankle complex will react to a balance or stability challenge by stiffening the muscles below the knee. This will sometimes show up as shortening or narrowing the foot, gripping the floor with the toes, wobbling from one side of the foot to the other or having part of the foot lift off the floor. If any of these reactions appears, the foot can no longer "listen" to the floor. It is no longer able to effectively compare information across its surface so its role in balance and stability is diminished.

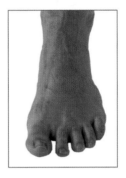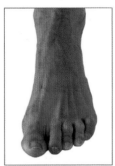

Excessive muscle activity around the foot and ankle usually indicates underactive gluteal muscles, so it will influence propulsive power. Because of its relationship with the gluteal group, the rigid foot is also associated with groin, pelvic, and lower back problems. Functional rigidity patterns in the feet and lower leg show up frequently in athletes, and are also associated with overuse injuries such as shin splints and Achilles tendonitis. The rigidity may have developed in response to poor stability elsewhere in the body, or it may be the result of a past ankle or knee surgery, where rotational mobility of the bones of the lower leg, the fibula and tibia has been lost.

The listening foot is one of the most important components of functional motor patterning. You will not achieve good transfer of gluteal activation and strength into your sport if the information coming up from your foot is poor. This connection via the positive support reflex helps to ground you, as is necessary in golf or judo, but it also fires up the muscular chain in your legs which allows for the short foot contact times necessary for running and jumping.

If you are not sure whether you have the functional rigidity pattern, take a look at your stance foot when standing on one leg. Are the tendons on the tops of your feet and front of your ankles markedly visible? Are your toes curling under, or lifting off the floor? Is your ankle making small adjustments while your foot maintains its broad floor contact as it should be, or is your whole foot rocking from side? If you close your eyes, does your foot narrow or tighten? If so, you may want to use the technique for developing a listening foot outlined below. Many athletes find that they have poor awareness and sensitivity in their feet and ankles, but are surprised to find that their balance and gluteal activation improves quickly when they improve their foot mobility and control.

Technique to Develop the Listening Foot

Sit on the front of a chair with both feet on the floor and no socks or shoes. Feel the surface of the floor under your feet, and with one foot at a time, explore shifting the pressure from one part of your sole to another.

Now place your hands around the top of your lower leg, just below the knee. Your knee will remain completely still. Move the pressure towards the outside of your foot, while still keeping it on the ground. You should find that your lower leg rotates with this movement. Move the pressure the other way and you should detect the rotation of your lower leg in the other direction.

Make this movement as smooth and slow as possible, aiming to eliminate any unnecessary tension until you can freely move the pressure from the outer to the inner portion of the sole of the foot. Repeat as often as you like throughout the day.

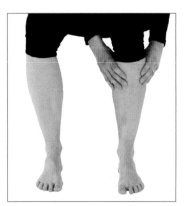 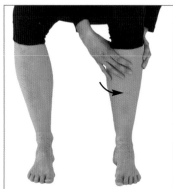 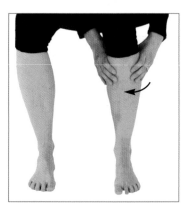

Key Concept

Aim for a supple, adaptable foot in all weight bearing exercises. Remember to check your foot to ensure that it is not rigid during the movements.

The Relaxed Face

Clenching the teeth, biting the bottom lip, sticking the tongue out of the side of the mouth, and folding the lips over the edges of the teeth are all behaviours that we use when we need a bit more control. We often think of them as indicators of concentration, but in fact they are telling us about our stability. These "fixing" behaviours appear when we are not using our balance and stability mechanisms effectively. If you are doing this as you perform a training exercise, you may manage that exercise a little better at the time but the benefit transference to your sport will be poor.

Immobilising the jaw affects the relationship between your head, neck and shoulders, so a short term apparent benefit of compensating for a weakness can come at a longer term cost.

 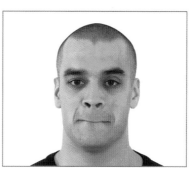 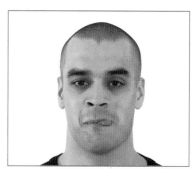

Initially, you may find that an exercise that was easy when you braced with your face is almost impossible when you keep it relaxed. Be positive: now you know what your real level is and can progressively improve. To prevent facial fixing you can whistle, count or repeat a word or phrase to yourself.

Notes from the Clipboard

An international-level sprinter presented with a long history of hamstring problems. She was asked to demonstrate some simple movements in her evaluation, including a lunge, which was a part of her normal strength programme.

The athlete performed the movements well, but used firm lip bracing throughout. When asked to repeat a simple phrase while performing the movement again, the athlete could barely keep her balance. Without facial fixing, she could barely stand on one leg, let alone perform some of the higher level drills.

Throughout virtually all of her non-track training, the athlete used facial fixing, but on the track needed to keep her face relaxed. The pattern that she trained off-track was not the one she needed to compete. It had just not been noticed until the injuries were impeding the athlete's performance.

This was one of the critical corrections needed to improve the athlete's neuromuscular pattern. She went on to run personal bests without injury.

Eye Fixing

Staring at a fixed point will help your balance as you perform standing exercises, but it will not improve your sporting performance if your sport requires that you have to move your head and eyes. Try to move your head and your eyes from time to time during standing movements to make sure that your body control is developing independently.

Key Concept

Aim for minimal tension in the face at all times.

Effortless Control

It is customary for athletes to perform exercises with maximal effort in training. They often display this effort visibly, even when performing exercises, which are not heavily loaded. Many look like they are trying hard as they train. They are then asked to look relaxed when competing. This is contradictory. For all of the exercises in this programme, the aim is to demonstrate effortless control. This does not mean that there is less commitment to the exercise. There should be total commitment to a perfect performance, but by aiming for an effortless looking movement, unnecessary muscle activity can be avoided leaving only the most efficient pattern.

Notes from the Clipboard

An elite sprinter was performing pulley pushes as outlined in Chapter 7. He was performing to the best of his ability and really trying hard, but he was finding the resistance quite a challenge. He felt that the weight was perhaps too great to enable a good performance.

He was asked a few simple questions. When he races, should a sprinter look like he's trying really hard, or should he look smooth and fluent? Who wins? The athlete who makes it look hard or the one who makes it look easy? This was an easy question to answer for the athlete.

This led naturally to the next question: "Why is it that in all your training you make it look like you are using high effort, but you want to compete looking relaxed?" This is a learned behaviour, and nothing to do with the actual demand of the exercise. It also trains a different motor pattern to the competition pattern, so it is a faulty training strategy.

This athlete had developed the look of effort when training to communicate to his coach and peers that he was giving 100%. Many athletes have a similar behaviour. He was asked to try the pulley push again, but this time to demonstrate a picture of effortless control and focused power. The athlete stepped up, performed the motion and nearly fell over with the unexpected increase in speed and ease with which he moved. He was shocked: the weight was exactly the same. The mind set had changed completely, and with it had come a better performance.

The same technique was used with a power lifter. The power lifter was using effort behaviours to communicate his strength to others in the gym. It looked and sounded impressive, and he believed that it was necessary in order to lift a heavy weight. A quiet observation was made that perhaps he might look more intimidating if he could lift a very heavy weight without apparent effort, rather than making it look like a strain. Adopting this attitude improved his technique and overcame a performance plateau, allowing him to lift greater weights. The athlete's effort behaviours had been holding him back.

Key Concept

Focus fully but make it look easy.

Compete in the Moment

Sometimes we forget to just move. Technique is incredibly important, but sometimes we have so much to think about that the movement starts to fragment into a sum of its pieces. We start to work against ourselves.

Train the skill components in drills and exercises. Let them embed the right patterns in your nervous system. Understand what they are all about. Be aware of these patterns as you move in training. Then integrate your brain and body by *remembering the feeling* of the peak moments that you produce.

When it's time to compete the brain and the body have to come together. This is not the time for your brain to be analysing every movement. It is the time to be in the moment. When the drills are over and it's time to really move, *feel it.*

Chapter 4: Functional Assessment

Basic Functional Assessment
Expanding the Assessment Parameters
Functional Mobility Testing and Mobility Training
Functional Assessment in the Elite Environment

How prepared is your body for the demands of training and competing? How well does it match the musculo-skeletal requirements of your sport? How well do you manage forces?

By assessing simple movements, it is possible to create a profile of your basic control. By identifying the mobility and stability demands of your sport, increasingly specific tests can be added to guide you towards the type of exercise you should be incorporating into your programme.

The components of a basic functional assessment are:

- Balance/central axis control.
- Functional mobility: mobility specific to the training and competitive demands of the sport.
- Function of the lower control zone: pelvic stability.
- Function of the central control zone: trunk stability.
- Function of the upper control zone: scapular stability.

The sequence of tests below covers the basic foundations which athletes in any sport should be able to perform well. These are low load movements designed to expose fundamental motor control deficits. An athlete should be able to perform these simple movements without difficulty. Surprisingly, many elite athletes struggle with this level of testing. Most athletes are skilled at compensating and can hide movement dysfunctions easily in fast or complex movements, so basic control issues may have been missed. By using simple tests, it is easier to detect control problems.

Testing for movement quality and control is difficult to quantify absolutely objectively. Rating the degree of dysfunction from minor control problems to major instability is subjective and based on experience with this type of testing. For this reason, the degree of dysfunction has been eliminated from the scoring procedure. Each test has a list of possible errors. You only need to decide whether the error is present. Total up the number of errors to score the movement. The aim is to achieve a score of 0. The higher the score, the more stability dysfunction has been identified. The result should give you an impression of overall functional control.

If you have limited time, you can simplify the testing further. If the movement is performed with none of the errors, it passes. If any errors appear, it fails. Think of the tests as a series of checks that will give you an insight into your movement control.

Once you can perform these foundation movements effectively, additional movements can be added to assess control at higher load and skill levels. The functional checks outlined below can be used to supplement the structural and physiological testing provided by sports medicine and sports science personnel as a part of athlete profiling. As a coach or athlete, these checks will highlight areas which need to be worked on as part of training.

Should any of the tests cause pain, seek the advice of a qualified medical professional.

○ Scoring

For all of the tests excepting balance, perform the movement three times and score the third one. If the pattern is inconsistent, watch a further three movements and score the most frequently occurring problems.

You are aiming for a score of zero. A result of greater than zero indicates that problems should be addressed. A score of 2 or greater indicates a high priority issue.

The total score for the selected tests can be kept, and the scores can be compared when the athlete is reassessed at a later date. In this way they can be monitored for changes in their physical profile.

○ Automatic Points

Foot Fixing

As mentioned in Chapter 3, an indicator of possible stability problems is the use of excessive tension around the foot and ankle. When weight bearing normally, the foot should relax into the floor with small adjustments occurring in the ankle to account for balance fluctuations. You should not see the foot itself shortening, narrowing or lifting any part of its sole from the floor. These signs indicate that the foot itself is becoming rigid in response to fluctuations in balance. This is a poor balance strategy, which is often associated with decreased pelvic stability and hip control on the same side.

Note what the foot looks like prior to the test movement and compare it to its behaviour during the movement. If any of the foot rigidity signs appear and are sustained throughout the test, an automatic 1 point is added.

Facial Fixing

As mentioned in Chapter 3, lip biting, clenching of the teeth, pressing the lips together very firmly or poking your tongue out are all facial fixing behaviours which can enhance central stability. Even if you think it is only happening because you are concentrating, it is more likely that it is helping you to maintain control. These tiny movements can subtly influence your trunk stability, and make test movements look very good when in fact they are not completely sound. On clinical testing of a simple test movement like a lunge, some athletes have changed from a low score indicating reasonable control to a maximal score indicating very poor control simply by eliminating their facial fixing.

The test movements are very simple and should be performed without effort. If any of the facial fixing behaviours appear during a test, it will mask potential problems, so the test must be repeated without the fixing behaviour. To eliminate facial fixing, repeat a simple word or phrase during the test movement. This keeps the face mobile and relaxed without adding complexity to the task. Whistling can have the same effect. This is preferable to the more commonly used technique of placing the tongue on the roof of the mouth behind the top teeth, as some athletes will press their tongue firmly enough up into their palate that they are able to increase their trunk tone for increased stability. If the facial fixing cannot be eliminated, an automatic point is added to the test score.

If you eliminate the facial fixing, be aware that you may shift your need to "fix" instead of stabilise to somewhere else in the body. You may increase foot fixing, or even stiffen your elbows or hands to increase limb tension in an attempt to stabilise. Most subtly, you can even "fix" with your eyes: people using this strategy adopt a staring quality to their gaze. If you are observing your own movements in a mirror you are unlikely to be fixing your gaze; however if you are observing someone else, ask them to look at you as they perform the movement as this stops them from adopting the glassy eyed stare of visual fixing.

All of these strategies can mask an athlete's true level of control on testing. If you do not account for them, you may be missing possible control problems, which may occur when normal breathing and dynamic movement in more complex situations is required. Lack of attention to detail during testing can lead to failure to identify problem areas, and this in turn can misdirect conditioning and injury prevention programmes.

What to do next

If your scores are coming in higher than 1 on basic assessment movements, you will need to address the problems. For each exercise a short list of relevant initial exercises is provided to get you started on your way to improving.

Basic Functional Assessment

Section 1. Static Balance

Although it is rarely the nature of sport to stand still, the static balance test looks at some fundamental foundations for movement control. Performance in this test examines:

- The sensory communication between your foot and your central nervous system.
- Control of the CLA over each leg.
- The ability of the body to make small adjustments without rigidity so that you can easily move your limbs without affecting your trunk position or balance.

Test 1: Eyes Open

Stand on one leg with both arms above your head. Maintain a 'soft' knee.

Move one arm down to your side and back up. Move the other arm down and back up.

Move both arms out in front of you. Take one arm out to the side and back to the front.
Repeat with the other arm.

Lift your arms to a horizontal position and bend your elbows. Keeping your pelvis facing forward, turn your upper body to the left and to the right.

Move your free leg out in front of you as far as you can.

Take it back behind you as far as you can.

Take it out to the side as far as you can. Take it across your body to the front. Take it across your body to the back.

Observation notes

- Does your trunk tend to tip to one side more consistently than the other? This is a loss of the central axis into the coronal plane.

- Has your foot become rigid in response to this challenge or is it relaxed and adapting well to your movement to help you to balance?

Scoring

For both of the balance tests, score only for the worst error that you see. For example, if you wobble, but then touch the floor for support, you will score three points.

Relaxed accurate performance	0
Wobbles but does not touch the floor	1
Violent wobbling or shifting of stance foot to regain balance	2
Needs to touch the floor at any time	3
Facial fixing	add 1 point
Rigid foot	add 1 point

Total:

What should I do to improve my performance?
A training athlete should not test poorly on eyes open balance testing. If your balance is poor at this stage of testing, focus on pelvic stability work and establishing a listening foot.

Key exercises
- Basic Balance, Eyes Open and Eyes Closed (Chapter 5).
- Progressions for Balance Training (Chapter 6).
- Listening Foot (Chapter 3).
- Bridge, Clam, Standing Knee Press (Chapter 5) and Progressions for pelvic stability.

⬤ Test 2: Eyes Closed

The body has three main balance systems: vision, somatosensory, and vestibular. The *somatosensory system* provides feedback from the skin, joints, tendons and muscles to tell your nervous system where you are in space. The *vestibular system* is the delicate balance organ of the inner ear, and it responds to changes in your head position and movements of the head. These three systems work together to maintain your balance. If you close your eyes, you eliminate one of the three systems, and this exposes how well the other systems are working.

Some athletes are overdependent upon their vision to stay balanced, which makes them vulnerable to injury if their eyes are moving or engaged in another task. Their body orientation may change quickly as would happen on takeoff as a pole-vaulter. They may be quickly scanning their environment as they run, or catching a ball on the move as in basketball or netball. They may be a skier who encounters poor conditions like "flat light", but needs to be making split second adjustments to the surface under their feet. Vision is not enough if you are running over uneven ground: you need your somatosensory system to be very responsive in order to make quick, fine adjustments for balance and the safety of your ankles and knees. You may have to move in poor or patchy light as a dancer may have to on stage, so your eyes cannot give you consistent feedback. You need the other balance systems working well to cope with these situations.

Testing with your eyes closed can tell us a little about how well your balance system really works, and how much you depend upon your eyes. Testing poorly on this can indicate an overdependence on vision for balance, and inadequate somatosensory feedback from the body. The reflex which links hip and knee muscle activity to sensory feedback from the sole of the foot is involved in this, so problems with feedback can also compromise pelvic and leg stability.

Repeat the same sequence as above.

⬤ Scoring

Relaxed accurate performance	0
Wobbles but does not touch the floor	1
Violent wobbling or shifting of stance foot to regain balance	2
Needs to touch the floor at any time	3
Facial fixing	add 1 point
Rigid foot	add 1 point
Total:	

What should I do to improve my performance?

- Basic Balance, Eyes Open and Closed (Chapter 5).
- Progressions for Balance Training (Chapter 6).
- Listening Foot (Chapter 3).
- Bridge, Clam, Standing Knee Press (Chapter 5) and Progressions for pelvic stability.
- Lunges with Eyes Closed (Chapter 6).

Section 2. Functional Mobility

Functional mobility differs from flexibility in that it represents relationships between body parts rather than muscle length alone. Investigating functional mobility highlights the effect of one body part's movement on another in the movement chain so that the relationship is easily seen. This relates both to the concept of relative flexibility and also to body awareness.

As we investigated in the previous chapters, the ability to move one body part independently from another is called *dissociation*. Dissociation problems can be caused by poor stabilising patterns, which do not allow you to be both fully mobile and stable at the same time. If an athlete can only maintain stability by limiting limb or trunk motion, they are in fact functionally rigid, rather than dynamically stable. They may appear to have true physical restrictions in mobility, but these limitations may in fact be due to excessive activity in global muscles responding to inadequate postural or motor control. They may be "fixing" instead of being stable. The movements below are simple but each one represents an important movement element. It is helpful to video the movement if you are new to evaluating movement in this way. You are looking for the ability to move only one body part, unless otherwise stated and symmetry of the movement from right to left.

Test 1: Double Arm Raise: Shoulder-Trunk Relationship

The relationship between shoulder and trunk movement can be influenced by poor shoulder mobility and poor trunk control. In this test you are assessing:

- Trunk stability in the sagittal plane.
- Active shoulder mobility.
- The effect of shoulder movement on trunk posture and control.

The movement is performed in a standing position, and the best place to view is from the side. If you are rating someone else, instruct them to raise his or her arms straight above their heads. Do not give any further instructions regarding the quality of the movement: you want to see what their natural response will be.

1. Forward rotation of the pelvis. This will pull the lumbar spine out of neutral into extension causing the central axis to collapse in the sagittal plane. This may be due to inadequate shoulder mobility, underactive transversus abdominis or poor awareness of lumbar spine position.

2. The pelvis slides forward, shifting the body weight towards the front of the feet and once again pulling the lumbar spine out of neutral. The central axis has collapsed in the sagittal plane. The same factors as above may contribute with the possible addition of a stiff thoracic spine limiting shoulder motion.

3. The shoulder mobility is limited to less than 180 degrees. This is not necessarily a problem for all sports, but any sport which requires a controlled trunk position with overhead arm activity or incorporates overhead arm activity in cross training will need to address this. This includes activities such as a gymnastics handstand, swimming freestyle, a football throw in, jumping to intercept a ball in basketball, performing a shoulder press in the gym, blocking a ball in volleyball, stretching to catch an overhead ball in baseball and many other situations.

Observation notes

The ideal response would be to see the arms move through a 180-degree arc, with the pelvis maintaining its position. The central axis is maintained in the sagittal plane. There are several possible movement dysfunctions, which may interrupt an ideal shoulder-trunk relationship.

Scoring

Pelvis level	0
Pelvis rotated forward-spinal curve deepened	1
Pelvis-weight shifted forward	1
Shoulders less than 180 degrees	1
Total:	

Further testing:

If you find that the performance is poor, investigate the Double Arm Shoulder Press to confirm your findings.

What should I do to improve my performance?

- Floor Presses (Chapter 5).
- Greyhound (Chapter 5).
- Wall Press (Chapter 5).

Test 2: Seated Hamstring Test: Hamstring-Trunk Relationship in Sitting

Hamstring tightness is often blamed for lower back pain, and in many sports is thought to impact on performance. However, it is not only hamstring length but the proprioceptive awareness of lumbar position and the stability to control it which also play a part. This test was originally developed for sprint kayak and martial arts but has become a useful marker for any sport as it demonstrates available hamstring length against a neutral spinal position as well as proprioceptive problems in the lumbar spine. Performance in this test examines:

- Active hamstring length.
- Trunk proprioception and control.
- The relationship between hamstring lengthening and lumbo-pelvic control.

Sit with your foot on the front of a Swiss Ball. Sit up onto your seat bones so that your spine is in neutral. Maintain this spinal position and push the ball out away from you until you feel the limit imposed by your hamstrings.

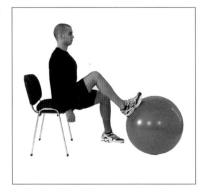 

Observation notes

An ideal performance will show an athlete who can maintain a neutral spine with their leg straight and hip at 90 degrees. The problems associated with this movement will be:

1. Your pelvis slips into backward pelvic rotation before the hamstrings reach a tension point. This indicates poor proprioception and stability around the spine.

2. You cannot straighten your knee. This indicates hamstring length restriction.

3. You slip into backward pelvic rotation once the hamstrings are under tension. This indicates greater relative flexibility in the spine than in the hamstrings.

4. You tip your pelvis sideways to relieve the pressure on your hamstrings.

Scoring

Spinal position is lost at any time	Y =1	N=0
Knee fully straightens	Y=0	N=1

Total:

What should I do to improve my performance?

- Straight Up Hamstring Mobility (Chapter 5).
- Standing Leg Swing (Chapter 5).
- Tail Up (Chapter 8).
- Any trunk stability exercise in an unsupported neutral spine position, e.g. Wall Press and Ball Bouncing (Chapter 5) or at a more advanced level, Over the Top (Chapter 6).

Test 3: Total Body Rotation

This movement looks at the total available rotation from the foot to the top of the spine. There are few sports that require only one body part to rotate. Usually rotation occurs as a result of many parts contributing to the total motion. One of the best examples of total body rotation is the golf swing. In the more comprehensive functional mobility assessment section, tests to examine each component are available. Performance in this test examines:

• Total joint rotation availability from foot to head.
• Correct foot pressure changes in response to rotation.

Stand with feet hip-width apart. Turn and look behind you, noting a spot that you can comfortably see. Do not strain yourself. The test seeks to determine what movement is naturally available to you. Turn back around the other way, noting a spot that you can comfortably see.

 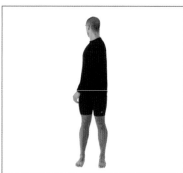 

Once you have noted how much motion is available, turn your attention to your feet. Note the pressure changes in your feet as you turn. It should follow the same pattern: as you turn to the left, the left foot pressure moves towards the outer part of the foot, and the right foot pressure moves to the inner part of the foot. In other words, the pressure moves in the direction of the turn.

Observation notes

1. Note whether the feet alter their pressure in the correct pattern.
2. Note whether rotation is markedly restricted in one direction.

Scoring

If you are standing at the top of the circle and can turn all the way around, you score 0. If you have poor rotation and only make it into the first third of the movement, you score 2. If your feet do not alter their pressure in the correct direction, add 1.

What should I do to improve my performance?
• Total Body Rotation (Chapter 5).
• Pelvic Rotation Over a Fixed Foot (Chapter 5).
• Listening Foot (Chapter 3).

Section 3. The Lower and Central Control Zones: Pelvic and Trunk Stability Relationship

⬤ Test 1: Static Lunge

The Static Lunge is the least complex of the lunge group of exercises and is therefore suitable as a baseline assessment. It is alternatively known as the Split Squat, but considering it as a Static Lunge establishes it as the start point for a clear path of progression.

- Pelvic stability.
- Eccentric GMax activation.
- Loaded functional hip mobility.
- Control of the leg from the hip to the foot.
- Central axis control for the trunk.
- Basic balance.

Stand with one foot in front of the other, hip-width apart. Raise your back heel. Put your arms straight out to the side. Keeping a vertical trunk, take your body straight to the floor.

Note: your body weight should not be moving forward. Your back knee should move straight to the floor.

Observation notes

1. The knee moves inwards. If this is the case, it is unlikely that GMax and GMed are functioning correctly.

2. Pelvis tips sideways. This demonstrates loss of control in the coronal plane for the pelvis, and indicates a GMed dysfunction.

3. Hips move backwards. This may be visible as the lumbar spine deepening its curve when observing from the side, and indicates that GMax is either not functioning well eccentrically (as it lengthens), or functions poorly in outer range (when it islongest). Instead of the hip moving downwards, you move it backwards where it is easier to access the back extensors and hamstrings to help you.

4. Trunk tips sideways. This demonstrates a loss of the central axis control.

5. One arm drops lower. This may indicate a dependence on latissimus dorsi on that side.

Scoring

Knee moves inwards	1
Pelvis tips sideways	1
Hips move backwards (lumbar curve deepens)	1
Trunk tips sideways	1
One arm drops lower than the other	1
Lip biting or facial fixing	1
Rigid front foot	1
Total:	

Each lunge variation examines a slightly different combination of elements. It is useful to look at each of them for this reason. However, if the static lunge is performed poorly and you are short of time, the following variations can be skipped until the static lunge improves sufficiently to be tested at a higher level.

Athlete performing a static lunge poorly. The pelvis has tipped downwards on the left, and the knee has moved inwards. Note that the left hand is lower than the right with the elbow bent. This athlete is trying to use her left latissimus dorsi to compensate for poor right gluteal activation.

Test 2: Eyes Closed Lunge

To recap on the information provided in the balance testing section, in many sports, your eyes are moving, either to track a ball movement or the position of an opponent, or due to your own movement through space. Some athletes are over-dependent on their eyes for balance, and are weaker in their other two primary balance systems, the somatosensory (information coming from the receptors in your skin, muscles and joints) and vestibular (your inner ear). This means that they may test well when they are allowed to look at a fixed point, but this result does not reflect what their control might be like if their eyes must move.

It is useful to test both the Eyes Open and Eyes Closed Lunge. The Eyes Open version indicates whether the pelvic stabiliser muscles are capable of controlling the movement. The Eyes Closed version looks at the relationship between sensory feedback and pelvic control. The procedure is exactly as above only with the eyes closed.

Scoring

Knee moves inwards	1
Pelvis tips sideways	1
Hips move backwards (lumbar curve deepens)	1
Trunk tips sideways	1
One arm drops lower than the other	1
Lip biting or facial fixing	1
Rigid front foot	1

Total:

What should I do to improve my performance?

- Bridge, Hip Pops, Hip Swivels (Chapter 5).
- Clam, Standing Knee Press (Chapter 5).
- Supported Lunge (Chapter 6).
- Lunge Progressions (Chapter 6).

● Test 3: Dynamic Lunge

Performance in this test examines:

- Higher level trunk stability and proprioception.
- Ability of the athlete to push effectively from the leg instead of throwing their shoulders back to generate momentum.

Start standing straight with feet together and arms straight above your head. Step forward into a lunge while maintaining an upright trunk, and push back to the start position again. When moving back to the start position, check that the motion is initiated from the foot, not from driving the shoulders back to generate momentum.

● Scoring

Knee moves inwards	1
Pelvis tips sideways	1
Hips move backwards-lumbar curve deepens	1
Trunk tips sideways	1
Trunk collapses forward	1
Moving shoulders back initiates return to start position	1
Lip biting or facial fixing	1
Rigid front foot	1
Total:	

This test can also be performed with eyes closed, for the same reasons as mentioned for the Static Lunge.

What should I do to improve my performance?

- Bridge, Hip Pops, Hip Swivels (Chapter 5).
- Clam, Standing Knee Press (Chapter 5).
- Wall Press (Chapter 5).
- Supported Lunge with arms up above head (Chapter 6).

Test 4: Standing Knee Lift

Performance in this test examines:

- The ability to easily position the CLA over each stance leg.
- Symmetry.
- Lateral pelvic stability.
- The foot-hip connection.
- Hip flexion pattern.

Stand with feet together and arms out to side at shoulder height. Lift one knee to hip height. Replace the foot and swap sides.

Note: It is most useful to alternate sides on each repetition. This exposes any issues and makes them easier to see.

Observation notes

1. Hip hitching. This is a fault in the hip flexion pattern. Instead of the femur moving straight upwards in the sagittal plane with clean hip flexion, the pelvis tilts in the coronal plane, allowing you to stabilise your trunk by using the trunk side flexor, quadratus lumborum. This is not a pattern that you would want to see in anyone who needs to move quickly or efficiently in a forward direction as the movement has been diverted into the coronal plane.

2. Stance hip moves out to the side. The pelvis should remain straight and level throughout this movement; however if GMed is weak, it will not keep a firm control over the femur to pelvis relationship. If the weak muscle cannot pull into its shortest range and maintain this position, it will allow the pelvis to drop on the lifting side, or permit the hips to drift sideways. An athlete showing this response may find that driving sideways off this leg, landing on it or jumping off it is slower or less powerful than the other side.

3. One arm moves lower. This indicates possible use of latissimus dorsi to compensate for decreased trunk or pelvic stability.

4. Trunk tips sideways. This loss of the central axis is usually a compensatory response to loss of pelvic position, but can also indicate that the body is not well balanced over the stance side.

5. Leg does not lift straight. Weakness in iliopsoas may cause you to recruit other muscles to flex the hip.

○ Scoring

Hip hitches up on the lifting side-trunk shortens on that side	1
Stance hip moves out to side	1
One arm moves lower	1
Trunk tips sideways	1
Leg does not lift straight	1
Facial fixing	1
Foot fixing	1
Total:	

What should I do to improve my performance?

- Clam, Standing Knee Press (Chapter 5).

- Bridge, Hip Pops, Hip Swivels (Chapter 5).

- Supported Lunge (Chapter 6).

- Lunge Progressions (Chapter 6) particularly with your arms stretched upwards to improve the CLA and minimise the effect of latissimus dorsi overuse.

Test 5: Seated Knee Lift on Ball

The seated knee lift on the ball is quite a sensitive test, which examines trunk stability and vertical alignment of the trunk on the pelvis. It will highlight any asymmetry in weight bearing between the left and right sides of the pelvis as well as control of the CLA. Performance in this test examines:

- Trunk stability.
- Vertical alignment of the trunk on the pelvis and control of the CLA.
- Symmetry of weight bearing through left and right sides of the pelvis.

Sit on a Swiss Ball with hips and knees at approximately 90 degrees and your feet together flat on the floor. Position your arms so that they are parallel to the floor. Maintaining an upright trunk, lift one knee so that your foot comes off the floor.

Scoring

Hip hitches up on the lifting side-trunk shortens on that side	1
Pelvis moves out to side	1
One arm moves lower	1
Trunk tips sideways	1
Leg does not lift straight	1
Facial fixing	1
Foot fixing	1
Total:	

What should I do to improve my performance?

- Seated Knee Lift on a Chair (Chapter 5).
- Bridge, Hip Pops, Hip Swivels (Chapter 5).
- Clam, Standing Knee Press (Chapter 5).
- Ball Bouncing (Chapter 5).

Section 4: The Upper Control Zone: Scapular Stability

Test 1: Scapula-Shoulder Relationship: Diamonds

This simple test looks at active shoulder external rotation mobility with respect to scapular control. Tennis players, volleyballers, swimmers and handball players should all be able to perform the movement well. Performance in this test examines:

- Scapular control against the rotating arm.
- External rotation mobility and control of the shoulders.

Lie on your stomach with your forehead resting on the floor. Place your arms in a diamond shape on the floor so that your fingertips touch. Draw your scapulae slightly towards your toes. Lift the forearms and hands off the floor and hold them there for the count of 5.

Observation notes

1. Scapulae moving towards the ears instead of maintaining a consistent position, which indicates a shoulder dissociation error or a scapular stability error.

2. If the arms raise less than 10 cm from the floor it indicates insufficient shoulder mobility, which may be due to stiffness or poor patterning of the movement.

3. One or both shoulders sink towards the floor as the arm lifts.

Scoring

Shoulders move towards ears	1
Hands lift less than 10cm	1
Shoulder sinks towards floor	1
Total:	

What should I do to improve my performance?

- Diamond exercises (Chapter 5).
- Superman exercise (Chapter 5).
- Wall Press exercise (Chapter 5).
- Doorway Stretches (Chapter 9).

Test 2: Scapula-Trunk Control Relationship: Wall Press

The Wall Press is a low load movement, which looks at coordination of the shoulder girdle to the trunk. It does not require strength but does require coordination. Performance in this test examines:

- Scapular stability.
- Sagittal trunk stability.
- Coordination of upper body to lower body.

Stand with your hands on a wall at shoulder height in front of you. Your arms should be straight. Stand tall, and then bend your elbows to perform the press up movement, keeping your body alignment consistent. Press out again.

Observation notes

1. The head rotates backwards. This puts your head into backward rotation on your neck, which switches off your local trunk stabilisers.

2. The shoulders hitch up towards the ears, or wing off your rib cage. This indicates poor scapular stability.

3. The pelvis drifts forward relative to the trunk. This means that the trunk stabilisers have switched off.

4. The stomach protrudes. You are not using TrA to control your trunk.

5. Bend forward with your upper body and leave your hips behind. You have found a way to avoid using your abdominals and load your upper body.

Scoring

Head rotates backwards	1
Shoulders move up, or scapula wings off rib cage	1
Pelvis drifts forward	1
Stomach protrudes	1
Upper body bends forward	1

Total:

What should I do to improve my performance?

- Wall Press (Chapter 5).
- Greyhound (Chapter 5).
- Ball Bouncing (Chapter 5).

Section 5: Basic Global Control

This exercise requires coordination of all three control zones. Performance in this test examines:

- Scapular stability.
- Pelvic stability.
- Trunk control.
- The coordination of all three zones.

Superman

Start on hands and knees. Hands should be positioned under shoulders, knees under hips. Press out with one heel and stretch out with the opposite fingertips so that you have a straight line from fingers to heel. Your chest and pelvis should be parallel to the floor.

Observation notes

1. Head drops, or rotates up and back. This is a poor head control response to loading of the shoulder girdle and trunk.

2. Scapula on the supporting side lifts off ribs. This indicates poor activation of stabiliser muscles.

3. Chest drops on unsupported side. This indicates an upper zone weakness, which could implicate both scapula and rotator cuff stability on the supporting side.

4. Pelvis rotates upwards on the unsupported side. This is usually an indicator of poor inner range GMax activation, poor hip mobility, or a poor hip extension movement pattern.

5. Pelvis rotates downwards on the unsupported side. This indicates weakness in GMed on the supporting side.

6. The spine moves from neutral into a deeper curve. This indicates a proprioceptive deficit in the trunk as the spine moves out of its neutral position into extension in response to a hip extension stimulus. The TrA will switch off in this circumstance.

Scoring

Head rotates backwards	1
Shoulders move up, or scapula wings off rib cage	1
Chest drops on unsupported side	1
Pelvis rotates upwards or downwards on unsupported side	1
Stomach protrudes-spinal curve deepens	1

Total:

What should I do to improve my performance?

- Bridge, Hip Pops, Hip Swivels (Chapter 5).
- Clam, Standing Knee Press (Chapter 5).
- Supported Lunge (Chapter 6).
- Wall Press (Chapter 5).

Once you have completed the basic functional assessment, you should have an impression of your overall foundations for movement. You may have performed well in some sections but not in others. You may have highlighted a difference between one side and the other. Note your findings, and see if they relate to injuries or technique issues that you may have. The programmes outlined in Chapters 5–8 provide exercises to address problem areas which you may have identified.

Expanding the Assessment Parameters

Having used this set of basic tests to establish your overall motor control profile, you can then extend the testing according to your capabilities and the demands of your sport.

In order to progress the testing procedure, additional elements can be added. These may include:

- More comprehensive sports relevant mobility testing.
- Dynamic force management: jumping and landing.
- Momentum control: forward and lateral.
- Control in multiple planes.
- Control of external forces: predicted and unpredicted.
- Increased dynamic demand.
- Increased cognitive demand (body control is maintained when the mind is distracted).
- Increased speed.
- Increased load.
- Increased skill.

The testing difficulty level is limitless, and can become increasingly sports relevant. It is important to expose limitations and assess coping strategies, so depending upon your capabilities or those of the athletes you work with, you can progress as far as is necessary using the methods listed above.

For example, after testing the static and dynamic lunge with a tennis player, you may add rotation to it. If the player performs this well under controlled circumstances, they might be asked to perform a deep dynamic lunge to catch a thrown low ball. This would look at automatic postural control responses, pelvic and trunk stability, functional strength through available range, balance and recovery. By increasing the dynamic demand as well as adding a cognitive task, additional systems are examined for their effect on the soundness of the basic movement. Despite the added coordination requirement, the trunk, pelvis, and leg control should still be controlled and efficient during the lunge.

Similarly, a basketballer may have good trunk control in slow, focused movements, but has to cope with a variety of dynamic demands when playing. You may therefore test his jump landings by pushing him from the side as he jumps to see whether his trunk control is sufficient to counteract an external force. You want to see how far he lands from his takeoff point, how far his central axis is pushed off line under resistance conditions, and how he positions his legs on landing. The basic tests are applicable to all sports. The list below provides options to gain further insight, assuming that you have already tested the basic movements. If you are not sure which additional tests will be relevant to your sport, use the list below as a guideline. The list is by no means comprehensive: there are many additional tests which can reflect the demands of your sport.

Features of the sport	Examples	Jumping and landing	Hop and stop-hop and return	Rotational jumps	Lunge progressions	Lumbo-pelvic mobility	Leg swing	Press-up	Double arm floor-press	Supine hip flexion	Thoracic rotation	Shoulder internal rotation	Step-up	Seated forward tilt	Mini squat	Active pelvic rotation
Multidirectional/move off either leg equally/ jumping	Football, tennis, handball, skiing	*	*	*	*		*						*		*	
Symmetry of body alignment	Equestrian, sprint and distance running, jump sports					*	*						*			
Control of pelvic motion in a seated position	Equestrian, rowing, kayak					*										
Hip bending mobility and control	Rowing, cycling									*						
Even pressure and power through both legs	Cycling, running sports				*								*			
Arm motion	Volleyball, tennis, golf, waterpolo, swimming							*	*		*	*				
Control of spinal angle/ coordination of trunk angle with hip bending	Show jumping, skiing, golf, kayak, rowing, throwing sports													*	*	
Kicking sports							*			*						*

Scoring, as for the foundation tests, can be as simple as a Pass/Fail rating. However, if you wish to numerically score, a system has been provided.

Functional Mobility Testing and Mobility Training

The mobility tests listed in the basic functional assessment can be augmented with additional movements which are relevant to your sport. Checking mobility is as important as checking any other aspect pertaining to stability. Insufficient mobility or a distorted pattern for achieving mobility is often associated with poor stability. If you don't have sufficient mobility in the right planes, somewhere else will "give" instead.

Many of the exercises listed below can be used as exercises as well as assessment. They comprise movement elements which train awareness and control as well as mobility. If you or an athlete you are working with fails a movement, it is advisable to practice it in order to improve. There are as many tests for mobility as there are sporting movements, and it is impossible to account for all of them in one resource. The exercises listed below can be used to augment the more familiar procedure of muscle length testing for sports where very specific flexibility is required.

Test 1: The Ball Follow

This is a useful movement to gain an impression of total body movement. It is not necessary to score it.

Two people hold a Swiss Ball up between them using one hand. They should start with their hands directly opposite each other with fingertips pointing upwards. One person leads the movement in any direction, trying to push the other into large changes in position. The first  thing to look for is good transference of body weight during a movement. Some athletes are surprisingly static, preferring to reach awkwardly to the side instead of shifting their weight for a smoother performance.

The athletes should be able to keep their trunk relatively upright by bending in their hips, knees and ankles. If they do not bend sufficiently in the legs, it will look as though they are leaning forward, collapsing their trunk and causing them to lose contact with the ball. Upper zone control is also exposed with this movement. The athletes should be able to keep their shoulders quite relaxed. They should not draw their shoulders upwards, and their scapulae should not lift off their rib cage.

Scoring

Score one point for each of the following:

- Movement is not smooth and fluent.
- Shoulders are tense or hunched.
- Hips not bending.
- Weight is not shifting from side to side with the movement.

Test 2: Mini Squat: Hip-Trunk Relationship

This is a small movement, which exposes hip-trunk timing and movement proportion. It is not a squat motion: the objective is to keep the trunk in an upright neutral position while bending the hips and knees. It is a quick test for athletes in any weight bearing sport to examine active hip to trunk coordination in the sagittal plane. Imagine a tennis player receiving a serve. She may be leaning forward as she prepares, but at the moment just prior to the impact of her forehand, she will straighten her trunk and soften her hips and knees in equal proportion. This test reflects such a movement.

The movement is simple. Stand with feet hip-width apart. Keeping body upright, bend at the hips and knees so that your centre of gravity moves straight downwards.

There are several possible movement dysfunctions, which may interrupt a hip-trunk relationship.

1. The hips do not bend in proportion to the knee. The hip has relatively little bend, and the trunk may look like it is slightly tipping backwards. Poor eccentric GMax performance is associated with this pattern.

2. The pelvis immediately moves backwards. This enables an athlete to avoid controlling their hip with eccentric GMax contraction.

3. The athlete excessively curves their lumbar spine. This is often associated with faulty squat training.

4. The knees fall inwards and the arches of the feet flatten.

 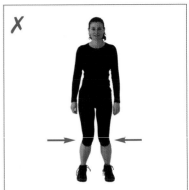

Scoring

Trunk tips forward	1
Trunk appears to tip backward	1
Lumbar spine curve deepens	1
Knees fall inwards	1

How can I improve?

- Improve hip awareness with Hip Pops (Chapter 5).
- Improve hip to trunk alignment as well as knee control with supported lunge and supported single leg squat.

Test 3: Double Arm Floor Press: Shoulder-Scapula-Trunk Relationship in Supine

This enables you to look at the relationship between the shoulder, the scapula and the trunk. The test was initially introduced when looking at swimmers but has become a standard test for any athlete requiring good shoulder mobility.

Start by lying on your back with your knees bent and feet on the floor. Keeping a straight elbow and the hand facing inwards, move your arm over your head, keeping the movement in line with the shoulder joint. Your spine should lengthen along the floor, with your arm moving smoothly to the floor overhead.

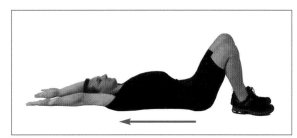

There are several possible movement dysfunctions, which commonly appear with this movement.

1. The lumbar spine lifts off the floor. If the shoulder has lost mobility or latissimus dorsi is tight, the athlete will allow their lumbar spine to deepen its curve in order for the hand to reach the ground.

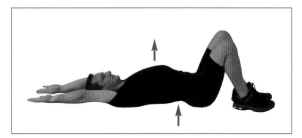

2. The elbow bends, or the arm moves outside the line of the shoulder. Both of these indicate insufficient mobility at the shoulder.

3. The scapula becomes clearly visible more than 3cm beyond the line of the chest wall. This indicates insufficient shoulder mobility, and possibly stiffness of the thoracic spine.

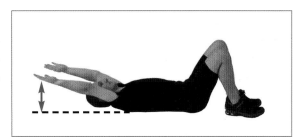

4. The arm does not reach the floor.

Scoring

The lumbar spine lifts off the floor	1
The scapula becomes visible outside the line of the chest wall	1
The arm does not reach the floor when elbow is straight and arm is in line with trunk	1

How can I improve?

If the primary problem is shoulder mobility:

- Latissimus dorsi stretches (Chapter 9).
- Greyhound (Chapter 5).

If your finding correlates with testing results that show overuse of latissimus dorsi in the lunge and the standing knee raise, you will also need to address pelvic stability.

Test 4: Hip Flexion-Pelvis Relationship in Supine: Supine Hip Flexion

This assessment was introduced into the functional mobility collection when evaluating rowers, cyclists and skiers, but it is relevant to many sports. It is used to determine whether backward pelvic rotation in response to hip bending is due to primary stiffness in the hip, or is a hip-pelvis coordination and control problem.

Lie on your back with one leg straight and the other hip bent to 90 degrees. Place your handson your raised knee. Keeping the straight leg pressed to the floor, pull your other knee slowly towards your chest. You should manage an additional 30 degrees before you feel your pelvis start to move.

The issue here will be primary hip stiffness. This will cause the pelvis to rotate backwards rather than the hip freely flexing. You will see the other leg lifting slightly off the floor when this occurs as hip flexor tension pulls its femur up when the pelvis rotates.

If this test appears normal but the athlete rotates the pelvis in response to *active* hip flexion, the seated knee lift and standing knee lift should be examined to introduce other contributing factors such as the athlete's trunk stability and hip flexor strength.

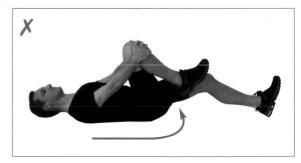

 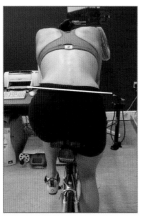

Athlete with poor left hip mobility. When her right hip is flexed as her right knee moves up, her pelvis remains level and her spine is not stressed. When her left knee moves up, the pelvis tips sideways to compensate for the left hip stiffness. The spine is forced to rotate.

Scoring

Pass/fail. To pass, the additional 30 degrees of hip bending will not cause any pelvic tilting. If you are numerically scoring, a fail will incur 1 point.

How can I improve?

- Hip Ranger (Chapter 8).

Test 5: Seated Lumbo-pelvic Mobility

It is easy to see why these tests are relevant to the seated sports such as rowing, paddling and equestrian events; however they also give additional insight into the symmetry of weight bearing in any athlete.

The tests can be practiced as exercises if a problem is found.

Test 5.1: Forward and Backward Tilting of the Pelvis

Athletes who use their back extensors and hip flexors to stabilise the pelvis on the trunk have difficulty with this movement, partly due to the physical restriction of tight muscles and partly due to poor awareness. Because of this they may have difficulty achieving and maintaining a neutral spinal position.

Sit on a Swiss Ball with feet flat on the floor. With minimal ball movement, collapse your spine so that you feel yourself roll off the back of your sitting bones, causing the lower spine to form an outward curve. If your sitting bones were arrows, they would be pointing forward. Then lift your body upwards and roll up and over your seat bones, causing the spine to form an inward curve. Your sitting bones will be pointing backwards. Finally settle your weight straight through your seat bones, which will give a neutral position. Your sitting bones will be pointing straight downwards.

Scoring

Scoring is a simple pass/fail.

To pass, the spine and pelvis should move into a lengthened outward curve as pictured above, and then into a shortened inward curve. The head should stay in a constant position. In a failed test, the spine shape changes very little, but the ball moves significantly forward and backward. The head can be seen to move backwards and then forward.

It is possible to perform this test on an ordinary chair but it is simply easier to detect problems with a ball.

If you are numerically scoring, a fail will incur 1 point.

Test 5.2: Side Tilt of the Pelvis

Athletes who stabilise by shortening one side of the trunk with latissimus dorsi and quadratus lumborum will have difficulty with this movement. You will have noted this when you tested the Static Lunge and the Standing Knee Lift.

Pelvic Side Tilting can expose weight bearing asymmetries and central axis control problems. It is often uneven in athletes with groin problems or chronic back and hamstring pain. It should also be checked when evaluating chronic shoulder problems, as an inability to perform lateral pelvic tilt changes the trunk's ability to lengthen, and this in turn can affect shoulder mechanics.

Sit on a Swiss Ball with both feet on the floor. Press one side of your pelvis down into the ball so that the pelvis tilts sideways. The hip and shoulder on that side will seem to move away from each other as your side lengthens and your spine curves gently. Your head should stay in the same position.

Usually one side moves well, and the other does not. On the side of poor lumbo-pelvic movement, the head will seem to move sideways. This is because this side of the trunk has not released and lengthened, so it tips instead.

Scoring

Scoring is again a simple pass/fail. To pass, the movement is symmetrical, with head staying in the centre as the pelvis tilts. If you are numerically scoring, a fail will incur 1 point.

How can I improve?

If you cannot press your pelvis down on one side, lift your arm up on that side and rest your hand on your shoulder blade. Your elbow will be pointing upwards. Stretch your elbow up as you press your pelvis downon that side.

Test 5.3: Rotation of the Pelvis: Knee Creepers

As your foot moves forward in walking or running, the pelvis advances on that side also, while the opposite shoulder moves forward to create a spiral or rotation in the spine. This continuous symmetrical rotation and counter rotation is a fundamental component for efficient locomotion. Athletes are usually unaware that they rotate far more on one side than the other.

The ability to smoothly rotate the pelvis is also necessary to kick a football, strike a golf ball, hit a strong tennis forehand and advance one hip in a dressage saddle. Lack of rotation causes an increase in coronal plane movement and this is rarely desirable from a technical perspective in any sport.

Sit on a chair or Swiss Ball with your arms crossed over your chest. You will keep your chest facing forward throughout the movement.

Make sure that you start with your knees level. Slide one knee forward and the other one back and note how far you move. Start again with knees level. Repeat the movement with the other side.

Problems that you might see are:

1. A difference in the amount of rotation between the two sides.
2. An inability to keep the chest facing forward.
3. A tendency to hitch the hip upwards instead of sliding it backwards.

Scoring

Pass/fail. For a pass, the movement is symmetrical between left and right with none of the compensations listed above. If you are numerically scoring, a fail will incur 1 point.

Test 6: Seated Forward Trunk Tilt

Sports such as golf and kayak require a forward tilt of the trunk and pelvis on the hips. A simple forward tilt maintaining a neutral spine minimises pressure on the structures of the back, and creates a good axis for rotation. However, few athletes can manage the movement with a neutral spine.

This test is best done with a partner, who can observe you while you perform the test.

Sit on a chair with both feet on the floor and knees at 90 degrees. Place your hands behind your head and sit directly onto your sitting bones so that your spine is upright.

Tilt your whole trunk forward, bending only at the hips. Count to 10 and return to the start position.

Observation notes

The shape of the spine should not change at any time during the movement. If there are problems with this movement, you will see one of two things:

1. The spine collapses, and the trunk bends. The spine looks like an outward curve.

2. The lumbar spine deepens its natural inward curve, causing the spinal muscles running down either side of the spine to over work.

Scoring

Pass/fail. If either of the two problems occurs, add 1 point.

How can I improve?

- You need to develop a more secure CLA, and learn how to bend at the hips instead of in your spine.

- Ball Bouncing (Chapter 5).

- Greyhound and Progressions (Chapter 5).

- Seated Knee Lift (Chapter 5).

- Wall Squat (Chapter 5).

Test 7: Thoracic Mobility: Seated

Stiffness in the midback area is a common problem. It may be caused by postural problems, sustained positions like driving or sitting at a computer, or may indicate overuse of secondary stabilisers to compensate for poor primary stability.

To investigate thoracic mobility, sit on a firm Swiss Ball with feet hip-width apart and your weight straight through your sitting bones. Cross your arms over your chest so that the backs of your hands are placed on the sides of your face. Keeping your weight evenly distributed through both sides of your pelvis, turn your trunk and head as one unit.

Note: Your starting posture will make a difference to this movement. If you sit upright too rigidly, supporting your weight in front of your sitting bones, the joints of your spine are more compressed and the muscles are under tension. This will decrease your available movement. The balloon position is sufficient as a starting posture.

Indicators of a poor test would be:

1. Visible asymmetry in available motion.
2. Shifting the weight off one side of the pelvis as you rotate.

3. Trying to shift the arms across to make it appear as though you are moving further.

Scoring of correct pattern

The measurement marker is the point at which the arms cross over the chest. The more restricted the movement is, the higher you will score.

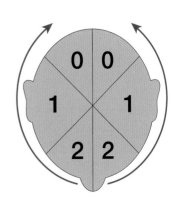

How can I improve?

- Your movement can be restricted due to overuse of your obliques abdominal muscles to stabilise, and also due to joint and muscle stiffness.

- To rebalance your trunk stability strategy, you need to learn how to activate TrA without over recruiting the obliques.

- Chapter 5 exercises such as Greyhound, Ball Bouncing, Superman and Wall Press can be progressed into OTT exercises in Chapter 6.

- Exercises to address rotational mobility include: Thigh Slides (Chapter 5); Total Body Rotation (Chapter 5); Revolving Lunge (Chapter 6); Hip and Spine Twist (Chapter 6); Cork Screw: Chest Opening Spinal Twist (Chapter 8).

Test 8: Active Pelvic Rotation

Kicking sports require an ability to sustain a firm trunk position over the supporting leg while rapid lower body rotation occurs. Testing of footballers has shown that this is not always present. Poor stability and restrictions in hip internal rotation of the supporting leg can cause a collapse into spinal side bending or back bending. Groin and back problems can be associated with a poor performance of this movement.

Stand upright with arms out to the side and lift one knee until it is approximately level with your hip. Move the knee across your body, keeping the chest facing forward. Your knee should move easily past your supporting leg.

Scoring

Trunk-shoulders tip backwards	1
Trunk-shoulders collapse forward	1
Knee does not move past supporting leg	1

How can I improve?

* This test requires good rotational mobility of the pelvis on the stance leg and the pelvis on the trunk, but also demands a secure, vertical trunk.

* To improve the CLA and therefore the trunk control, start with Chapter 5 exercises such as Greyhound, Ball Bouncing, Superman and Wall Press, which can be progressed into OTT exercises (Chapter 6).

* To improve the pelvic action on the trunk, use Cork Screw: Chest Opening Spinal Twist (Chapter 8).

* To improve rotation of the pelvis on the stance leg, use Total Body Rotation; Pelvic Rotation Over the Fixed Foot (Chapter 5).

Test 9: Standing Leg Swing

This movement checks for a fluid sagittal leg motion pattern on the foundation of a secure central axis and controlled pelvis. All runners should be checked for this balance and symmetry.

Stand on one leg, and swing the other leg fully back and forth, allowing your arms to move normally. Your trunk should stay vertical and your leg should swing in a straight line. Your pelvis should remain in a constant position, so your spine should not move.

Observational notes

Your powerful leg muscles need a stable attachment to pull from to achieve their most efficient performance. The muscles involved in this test are attached to the pelvis. If you observe your lumbar spine deepening its curve when you move your leg back and flattening its curve as you move the leg forward, you are not maintaining the pelvis in a stable position for your legs to pull from most effectively.

Scoring

Trunk tilts sideways	1
Pelvis rocks forward or backwards	1
Balance is poor on one side	1
Any "fixing" behaviour	1 for each behaviour observed
Jerky, non-fluent movement	1

How do I improve?

- Greyhound, Superman and Wall Press to secure your CLA, and Basic Balance (Chapter 5).
- Hip Pops to learn how to straighten your hips without bending your spine (Chapter 5).
- Quad stretches and hip flexor stretches to improve muscle length (Chapter 9).

Test 10: Windscreen Wiper: Active Shoulder Internal Rotation

Rotation of the ball in the socket of the shoulder joint is fundamental for overhead sports [29]. The Diamond test investigated active external rotation and its relationship to scapular control. This test examines control of internal rotation.

Lie down on your back with your elbow bent to 90 degrees, your upper arm level with your shoulder and the back of your forearm and hand as close to the floor as you can without pushing. Relax everything before you start. If you feel that your shoulder lifted closer to your ear when you positioned your arm, shift

it back down so that it is level with your other side. Place your other hand over the front of your shoulder. This hand will monitor the movement of the "ball" in the socket of your shoulder joint.

Keeping your elbow secure on the floor, lift your forearm so that your arm rotates and your hand now points to the ceiling. Imagine this position as 12 o'clock on a watch face. This completes phase 1 of the test. Keep moving in the same direction until you cannot continue without shifting your shoulder position. This completes phase 2 of the test.

Observational notes

1. You should be able to perform this movement without feeling your shoulder pushing upwards or rolling forward into your hand. If you detect the "ball" pushing into your hand, it means that it is losing its position in the socket by sliding forward. If this happens repeatedly as it can when throwing a ball, swimming, spiking a volleyball or serving in tennis, it stresses the structures at the front of the shoulder. Painful shoulder instability can occur as a result.

2. The shoulder mobility required for different sports varies widely. However, you should be able to reach 10 o'clock with your forearm.

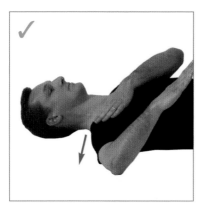 

Scoring

Phase 1: A Pass or 0 score means that the "ball" of the shoulder stays in a consistent position throughout the first phase of the movement. Any movement of the "ball" constitutes a Fail, or 1 point.

Phase 2: To gain a Pass or 0 score, you reach 10 o'clock without the "ball" pushing into your hand. A Fail, or 1 point, demonstrates insufficient mobility.

How do I improve?

- Establish scapular stability and learn how to separate ball-in-socket movement from scapular movement with Diamonds (Chapter 5).
- Mobilise the shoulder with Chicken Wings (Chapter 8).
- Practice Windscreen Wiper as described above.

Jumping

We often assume that athletes can jump and land effectively; however even in sports where this is a necessary component, movement dysfunctions can be commonly found. Sports such as volleyball and basketball are obvious candidates for testing landings, but it would equally apply to footballers, handballers and skiers.

Jumping

A common dysfunction is overuse of the upper body and spine on take off. To look at this, first perform a natural jump and feel how high you have moved off the ground.

Next, put your hands on your head and try the jump again. There should not be a dramatic difference in height.

You should not feel your shoulders drive back either – this would indicate that you are not maintaining a neutral spinal position in the air. Your trunk should look like it is driving upwards, not backwards.

Your knees should not draw together on take off. Your hips, knees and ankles should remain parallel as you dip slightly before take off and launch yourself upwards.

Athlete demonstrating poor knee control on takeoff.

Scoring

To rate a jump take off, scoring would be:

Marked drop in jump height with hands on head	1
Shoulders driving backwards	1
Knees drawing together	1

On the pass/fail system, appearance of any of the above issues will rate the test as a Fail.

Test 2: Single Leg Jumps

Greater hip and knee control is necessary to generate a good jump off one leg. The pelvis must remain level, and the knee aligned with the ankle and hip. Marked loss of power is often associated with poor pelvic control.

Scoring

Loss of pelvic alignment on preparation for takeoff	1
Knee moves inwards or outwards.	1

Landings

Landings are a common source of injury for athletes. Poor landing technique has been positively linked with anterior cruciate injuries [52], and high loading on knee structures [22]. Female athletes in particular have been shown to have inadequate sagittal joint control, higher ground force reactions and poor lower limb alignment [12,73,38]. However, poor landing strategies can be observed in male athletes also.

A good landing should absorb force through the hips, knees and ankles; the muscles on opposite sides of the joints work in partnership to allow the extensor group to first lengthen and then shorten again quickly to absorb and control joint bending. However, this does not necessarily come naturally to some athletes. Instead of "springs" in their joints, the muscles supporting the joints fail to change length in a coordinated fashion, so they land with their joints locked, causing a jarring sensation. Landing with a relatively straight knee absorbs less energy, and can therefore be associated with higher ground force reactions and greater knee stress [17].

The other landing problem is the issue of landing heavily. The heavy lander does not maintain a level of tension in the muscles during the landing. These athletes usually exhibit too much motion in the joints, giving an appearance of them "folding". Without this level of tension; elastic energy storage in the muscle-tendon unit is diminished and a quick takeoff in any direction is virtually impossible.

Finally, landing should occur with the legs in normal alignment. If landing on both feet, legs should be parallel, and if landing on one foot, the alignment rules that we investigated in the lunge apply. To do this, you need good sagittal control in your hips and knees so that the force of landing is absorbed vertically. Without this control, the force seeps out of the sagittal plane, and the knees move towards each other on impact. This is an extremely common landing pattern in female athletes and in children.

Scoring

To rate a jump take off, scoring would be:

Hips, knees and ankles not absorbing impact	1
Loss of balance on landing	1
Loud-heavy landing	1
Knees move together	1
Total:	

Single Leg Landings

To progress this investigation of landings, take off into a jump off two feet, but land on one. You are looking for the same issues as you did in the basic lunge in terms of pelvic and lower limb control; however now the speed of muscle activation has increased.

Scoring

Knee moves inwards	1
Pelvis tips sideways	1
Hips move backwards (lumbar curve deepens)	1
Trunk tips sideways	1
Trunk collapses forward	1
Wobbling	1
Lip biting or facial fixing	1
Rigid front foot	1

Depending upon the dynamic demands of the sport, this theme can be extended.

Examples of this would be landing with the eyes closed to observe the athlete's anticipatory preparation for landing, or jumping sideways and landing on the outside leg with balance.

How do I improve?

Phase 1:

- Clam (Chapter 5).

- Standing Knee Press (Chapter 5).

- Basic Bridge (Chapter 5).

Phase 2:

- Supported Lunge (Chapter 6).

- Supported Single Leg Squat (Chapter 6).

- Static Lunge and Progressions (Chapter 6).

- Space Invaders (Chapter 6).

- Sway (Chapter 6).

Higher Level Trunk Control Testing for Jumps and Landings

Trunk control and activation of preparatory or feed forward neuromuscular responses when landing from a jump are critical for athletes who can be contacted while in the air. This anticipatory action is extremely fast to restore and maintain joint stability [68] and minimise risk of injury. Footballers, netballers, and basketballers would fall into this category.

Step 1 is to evaluate a jump with a light sideways push to the pelvis and ribs while in the air. You want to see that the trunk remains straight and the landing is not far from the takeoff spot.

Step 2 will add light resistance only to the ribs, which is a higher demand on the trunk to stabilise itself in the coronal plane.

Step 3. Compromising vision's contribution to landing control can change the motor pattern [102]. Engage the eyes by throwing and catching a ball during the movement and see if this influences landing control.

Step 4 will repeat the movement but land on one leg. *For safety, this should always be the opposite leg to the side being pushed.*

Scoring

Trunk moves off centre in the air	1
Landing is rigid or heavy if compared to a basic jump	1
Knee alignment is lost	1
Total	

How do I improve jumps and landings?

You need to be willing to bend your hips and knees freely to generate and absorb force. To do this, you need an active GMax and GMed to control the hip joint and knee alignment.

- Phase 1 activation exercises include Basic Bridge, Hip Pops and Wall Squats.
- Phase 2 exercises include Supported Lunge, Supported Single Leg Squat, Static Lunge and Progressions.

These can be progressed into jumping and landing tasks, starting very simply with no distraction and aiming for quiet landings with "springs in ankles, knees and hips". Basic jumps can be further challenged by:

1 Adding a visual distraction such as catching and throwing during jumping.

2 Jumping and turning the body in the air to land with feet at 90 degrees to the start position. This can be progressed to a 180-degree turn (see also Rotational Control; page 127).

3 Jumping in different directions.

4 Adding a mild push while in the air, aiming to land securely.

Higher Level Pelvic Control Testing

Test 1: Lunges

Lunge testing can be progressed almost indefinitely to meet the demands of your sport. This is a sequence used for an international level badminton squad.

Start in the lunge position as previously outlined. With arms crossed in front of you, keep your head facing forward and turn your shoulders in the direction of the front leg. All movement markers are the same as for the static lunge. Turning the shoulders should not cause the knee to collapse inwards.

1 Add rotation to the lunge. In order to be truly systematic, you would test a static lunge with added rotation before a dynamic lunge.

2 Perform the same movement, but allow the head to turn with the shoulders. The knee should still be facing straight ahead.

3 Perform the rotation movement in conjunction with the dynamic lunge. Start with arms crossed in front of you. As you step forward, turn your shoulders, keeping your head facing straight ahead.

4 Perform the same movement, but allowing the head to turn.

5 Perform multidirectional lunges with sound form and no trunk rotation. Include side steps, angled steps, forward and backward steps.

6 Perform multidirectional lunges returning to stand on one foot.

Interestingly, the badminton players performed this poorly and thought that it was an unreasonable level of testing. The former Olympic Gold medallist who now coached in the national programme performed it perfectly.

⬤ Test 2: Step-up

The step-up offers a different method for examining force management between the foot and the hip. If you have to propel yourself forward or upward, or produce maximum force from alternate legs or a single leg, this test is a very useful one.

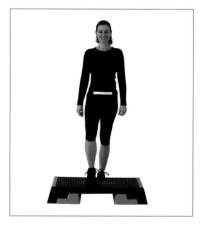

Stand with one foot on a standard step. Make sure the foot is fully on the step. Check that your pelvis is level before performing the movement.

Raise your body onto the step and stay balanced on the supporting leg. Slowly reverse the movement to and return to the start position. You are only watching the working leg.

Observation notes

1. The pelvis should remain level throughout the entire movement.

2. The hip should not move out to the side.

3. The knee should maintain its alignment with the hip and ankle.

If you see the pelvis tip down on one side, the hip move outwards or the knee move inwards, the muscular force you are producing is being lost sideways and is not being used effectively to propel you. The force you produce should be contained between your foot and your hip, like a cushion of air pressure between two plates. If this pressure is maintained, you can absorb shock effectively, and the force you produce can be controlled and focused in the most effective direction.

Scoring

Pass if none of the markers listed above are observed. Fail if any of them are observed. If you are numerically scoring, 1 point for each marker can be given.

How do I improve?

Phase 1:

- Clam (Chapter 5).
- Standing Knee Press (Chapter 5).
- Basic Bridge (Chapter 5).

Phase 2:

- Supported Lunge (Chapter 6).
- Supported Single Leg Squat (Chapter 6).
- Static Lunge and Progressions (Chapter 6).
- Space Invaders (Chapter 6).
- Sway (Chapter 6).

Momentum Control

Lateral Control

The Standing Knee Raise was a static method for testing stability of the pelvis when weight bearing on a single leg. This lateral hip-trunk control relationship can be tested more dynamically. Any sport which requires lateral hip control is a candidate for this type of testing, so it is as relevant to downhill skiing as it is to multidirectional sports.

Test 1: Hop and Stop

From a normal standing position, take a large sideways leap with your right leg, bring your left leg across it and take another large side leap to balance on your right leg.

Observation notes

1. If timing and coordination are a problem, you won't organise your trunk in space so that it will land balanced and upright on the outside leg. This will look like your trunk is tipping sideways on landing.

2. The pelvis will not be level on landing if GMed and the other hip abductor muscles are weak or their response is poorly timed. It will be higher on the landing leg side, lower on the non weight bearing side.

3. If GMed and the other hip abductor muscles lose control of the pelvis-femur relationship, your knee will move inwards.

Athlete failing to control her trunk momentum.

Scoring

Pass/fail.

For Numeric Scoring

Trunk tips sideways	1
Pelvis tilting sideways	1
Knee moving inwards	1

Test 2: Hop and Stop

This time, you will land on your outside leg and immediately push off it in the opposite direction.

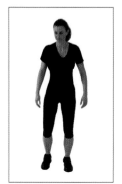    

The main problems are the same as for the Hop and Stop test, but are usually easier to see. If there is a tendency for the hip to collapse and the pelvis to tilt sideways due to a GMed weakness, you will usually see the trunk move past the hip on landing, instead of arranging itself in the air in preparation for landing. With this pattern, you will use trunk momentum to try and assist you with jumping back when you should be using GMed strongly. This is not a powerful strategy, and puts more stress on the inner knee.

Scoring

Pass/fail.

For Numeric Scoring

Trunk tips sideways	1
Pelvis collapses	1
Knee falls inwards	1

Don't be concerned about the leg that you finish on. It is the leg that controls momentum and pushes you back to the start point that you will be scoring.

These tests also relate to cutting manoeuvres, where inadequate planning and postural adjustment have been found to increase rotational and sideways stress on the knee structures [6]. More complex dynamic tasks introducing unanticipated changes of direction can be designed to investigate these patterns at a higher level.

How do I improve?

Phase 1:

- Clam (Chapter 5).
- Standing Knee Press (Chapter 5).
- Basic Bridge (Chapter 5).
- Wall Press (Chapter 5).

Phase 2:

- Supported Lunge (Chapter 6).
- Supported Single Leg Squat (Chapter 6).
- Static Lunge and Progressions (Chapter 6).
- Space Invaders (Chapter 6).
- Sway (Chapter 6).
- OTT (Chapter 6).

Test 3: Rotational Control

Over-rotation on landing from a turning jump can greatly increase the risk of knee injury. If your sport is multidirectional and involves jumping, this simple test highlights a major control problem.

Hips and knees bend to drop centre of gravity.

Stand with feet hip-width apart. Soften your knees and hips, then jump to land facing in the opposite direction. Ask someone to watch your knees: they should not continue to rotate or fall inwards. This is a basic pass or fail movement. If you land with good knee alignment, you pass the test.

Increased level of testing for court sports such as handball, netball or basketball
If you are working with a partner, have them challenge your anticipatory responses by getting you to catch a ball thrown to you just as you are landing.

Test 4: Forward Control

This is a difficult movement to score objectively; however it is interesting to see differences in strategy between athletes. Problems are usually obvious. Slow changes of direction and a toppling forward of the trunk indicate momentum control problems.

Ask someone to observe your movement. You will run as fast as you can in a forward direction, and react to a clap or noise to brake and reverse your direction to run backwards for a few steps.

Performance points to note:

1 Height of pelvis from the ground.

2 Number of steps needed to brake.

3 Head and pelvis relationship.

A higher pelvis and forward head posture is not so effective for braking.

Your centre of gravity is located at around the level of your pelvis. Athletes with good agility will respond to a change of direction stimulus by bending at the hips and knees to drop their centre of gravity, or pelvis. To use the movement direction concept outlined in Chapter 1, these athletes counteract forward motion by introducing another movement direction, the downwards direction. To change direction or to control momentum, drop your pelvis quickly to initiate the change.

Agile athletes may additionally angle their trunk slightly backwards to initiate and prepare for the brake, and they shift their weight off their toes back onto their mid foot to make effective counter movement possible. The combination of these factors makes it possible for these athletes to use a minimal number of steps to achieve a brake.

Athletes who manage forward momentum poorly collapse their trunks forward and try to stop their motion by increasing the step rate of their feet rather than using the braking mechanism of dropping their centre of gravity. Their heads drop forward but they do not effectively drop their pelvis.

The movement of the head with respect to the pelvis can be obvious in these cases. Athletes who manage this movement poorly will have a higher pelvis position and a low forward head position. This makes it difficult to produce an effective counter movement. Athletes with this strategy need a greater number of steps to achieve a brake.

How do I improve?

When you need to check forward momentum, focus on dropping your hips.

To combine braking and turning, sprint forward, brake on command and turn 180 degrees to run forward in the opposite direction. Look for the same ease of movement on left and right turns. Check this: some athletes will avoid one side by pushing off the same foot regardless of which way they are turning.

CHAPTER 4: FUNCTIONAL ASSESSMENT

Notes from the Clipboard

During routine screening of professional footballers, one of the players was found to have decreased control of his right leg and pelvis, and greater foot rigidity on that side. His right static and dynamic lunge were not well controlled, nor was his standing knee raise. On the brake and turn test, he turned and pushed off well to the right, but performed poorly to the left. On further questioning, the player admitted that he would do anything to avoid pushing off his right leg when he turned. He would literally run around the ball so that he could move off his left leg. His right leg was not painful, but he did not have confidence in it.

A quick practice on Single Leg Wall Press, cueing the player to lift himself up and place his trunk over his right leg, some lunge training with corrections and external resistance with hand pressure, and a small amount of listening foot exercise increased the pelvic stability responses in the right side. The player became aware of his gluteal group, and as he repeated the movements, his control began to improve. When tested again on brake and turn, he had improved. The player was relieved: this problem had bothered him, but he had not known what to do about it. Assessing simple movements made it possible to identify a performance problem and correct an asymmetry.

Scapula-Trunk Relationship Control

The Wall Press is the basic movement for foundation testing; however it is a very low load exercise. If an athlete can perform it well, it is necessary to increase the load to control a larger proportion of body weight.

Step 1

With thighs on a Swiss Ball, position yourself so that you look straight at the floor with your head, neck, and spine in a straight line. Perform a press-up by bending your elbows and make sure that you do not push the ball backwards. You are looking for the same issues that you did in the Wall Press.

Scoring

Head rotates backwards-drops down.	1
Shoulders move up towards ears, or scapula wings off rib cage.	1
Lumbar spine curve deepens.	1
Stomach protrudes.	1

129

Step 2

Surprisingly few athletes can be tested to the level of a full press-up. Most show scapular control problems at much lower loads. However, a well-coordinated athlete with ideal functional motor patterns should be able to perform a full press-up correctly.

Start in a plank position with arms and trunk straight, and hands positioned under shoulders. Lower yourself to the floor and press back up to this position. All the same observation points apply, with the addition of hip flexion. The hips should remain straight, but athletes who do not have adequate trunk control can commonly be observed using a combination of hip flexor and back extensor activity to control the trunk-pelvis relationship.

Scoring

Head rotates backwards-drops down	1
Shoulders move up towards ears, or scapula wings off rib cage	1
Lumbar spine curve deepens	1
Stomach protrudes	1
Hips flex-bottom sticks up	1

Functional Assessment in the Elite Environment

A great deal of money is currently invested in athlete screening, or profiling as it is now more commonly known, but the return from this investment is variable depending upon the integration of the multidisciplinary team and the administrative structure of the sport. In order to justify the cost of profiling, a clear action pathway should be established. First it is important to establish the expectations of a profiling procedure. Why do we do it?

Most commonly, profiling is seen as an injury prevention measure, and as such is usually performed by sports medicine personnel. It is normally expected that if no issues are identified, the athlete should be able to cope with normal training and competition demands without breaking down, and able to make technical improvements where necessary. When including functional tests in the profiling procedure, it could also be expected that profiling may give us an insight into an athlete's movement efficiency, and any technical difficulties which may be persistent. To achieve this, the professionals involved in profiling must have sufficient knowledge of the sport's mechanics and a good relationship with the coach.

The barriers to gaining insight into functional reasons for injury or technical barriers are:

1 Insufficiently sports relevant tests.

2 Insufficient technical knowledge in the tester.

3 Insufficient communication between coach and tester.

4 Insufficient time allowed for testing.

From a technical movement perspective, there are many possible tests to examine whether an athlete can create and control forces to a level which meets the demands of their sport. The questions you may want to ask when selecting tests will include:

- What are the main mechanisms of injury? Are they traumatic or biomechanical-overuse?
- What physical issues might contribute to these injury mechanisms?
- What are the most common technical problems?
- What are the main components of the sport? Examples may be jumping or landing, control of unexpected forces, symmetry of weight bearing, or control of more than one plane of movement.
- How does the athlete generate and control force?

If issues are identified, appropriate action should be taken. This will fall into two categories:

1 The athlete has fixable biomechanical or motor control issues which can be addressed to prevent injury and enhance performance.

2 The athlete has unchangeable physical issues which require modification in technique, equipment or training methodology.

Although it seems logical that action will be taken, it is not necessarily the case. The sporting organisation may take one of a variety of pathways in response to testing information. The passive pathway does not respond at the time to collected information. If enough data is collected over time, it may lead to the recognition of trends within the sport which may be acted upon, but often the information is merely stored as part of the monitoring process.

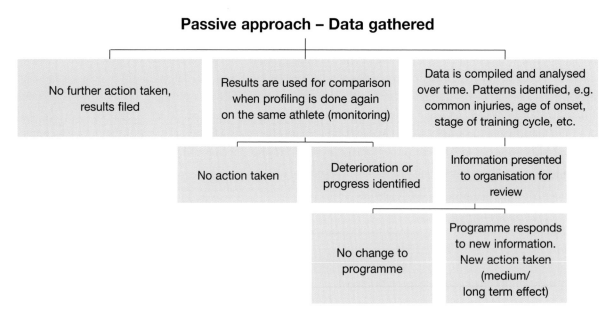

The active approach to profiling findings is to implement a direct intervention. However, this may be unidisciplinary or multidisciplinary.

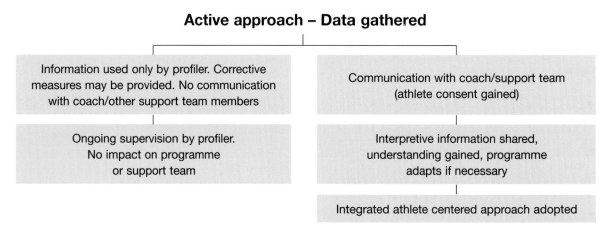

Sporting organisations are either *reactive* or *responsive* to profiling data. The *reactive* organisation suffers from non-integration of coaching, sports medicine, and sports science personnel. Athlete screenings are conducted by sports medicine personnel, but these findings do not impact upon the training programme unless the athlete becomes injured. Communication between professions in this system is often impaired and athletes can become stressed by differences of opinion between the disciplines. In the reactive system, supplementary exercise is presented as injury prevention and as such is usually provided by sports medicine personnel. It tends to be perceived by the athlete as being separate and additional to his or her training programme. Compliance with injury prevention work is poor in this circumstance.

In a *responsive* sporting organisation, athlete screenings are followed immediately by meetings between professional personnel to discuss the impact on the training programme and the best route forward to ensure optimal training progress with the least risk of injury. A commitment within the multidisciplinary team to respect the opinions and expertise of others is necessary in order for this to work, as differences in opinion will naturally arise. Supplementary movement control work is presented as having the dual purpose of injury prevention and movement optimisation. It may be initiated by sports medicine personnel but its principles will be carried throughout the training programme by all personnel. Because they are a part of normal training procedure, athlete compliance is maintained.

Profiling and the Athlete

If you are trying to implement a stability programme for your sport, functional profiling can help to stimulate athlete interest. If poorly presented, athletes often perceive functional stability work as irrelevant and uninteresting. If the exercises selected for them are quite general and without a clear benefit, motivation will not improve. Using simple functional tests can help them to identify their own movement habits. This helps them to understand the purpose of the exercises, and provides a way of gauging improvement.

The perceived relevance of functional athlete profiling can be increased by including a self-assessment section. Questions for the athlete to think about can include:

1 What does a good athlete in your sport look/move like?

2 How is this different to your movement?

3 Why do you think that is?

4 Which technical aspects do you find difficult to improve?

5 Which technical aspects would you like to perform better?

6 Which technical aspects does your coach think are most important for you to improve?

7 Are there any training or competition movements that you are less confident about?

8 Are there any training or competition movements which feel risky to you from an injury point of view?

9 What are your strengths as an athlete?

Surprisingly, some athletes have difficulty answering questions like these, but this self-reflective process can help them to develop an internal feedback system, rather than exclusively depending upon external feedback.

The feedback from this type of questioning can be combined with functional assessment findings to help athletes to engage with the process, especially when test findings can be related to technique. It may be that an equestrian athlete finds that vertical trunk orientation is not as good over one leg on balance testing, and that this relates to more difficulty on one rein than the other. A handball player drives much better off one foot than the other and on testing finds that he has more pelvic control on that side. A swimmer may find that his scapular stability is not symmetrical and that the weaker side is the same as the one which does not "hold the water" as well. A footballer who consistently lands poorly from contesting a high ball may find deficits in his trunk stability, or that he absorbs shock poorly in his hips and knees due to inadequate pelvic control.

Engaging athletes by illustrating relevance to their sport can help the athlete and coach to establish common goals, and provide a meaningful language for discussion between strength and conditioning professionals, coach and athlete. If the tests highlight a weakness, some components of the athlete's programme will need to be modified to make sure they are corrected. It is therefore important that everyone involved understands the concept.

If you are a sports science, sports medicine or coaching professional, you may decide to analyse the role of profiling for your sport. Questions to reflect on may include:

- Is profiling having an impact on your programme right now? If not, why not?
- How often is it performed in your system?
- Does the content of the procedure reflect the demands of your sport?
- Is relevant data communicated, and if so to whom?
- Is data compiled for longitudinal analysis?
- How integrated and cooperative is your team?
- How does your system respond – is it active or passive? Responsive or reactive?

Case Example

The client: An international netball team. Netball is a fast, multidirectional sport involving jumping, catching, attack and defence, and traumatic injuries of the knee and ankle are common.

The problem: A high injury rate and poor training compliance.

The professional team: The coach, strength and conditioning trainer, physiologist, and physiotherapist.

The players: Women of age ranging from 18–32, with varying training ages and international competition experience.

The programme: With the introduction of a new strength and conditioning coach, the training had taken a much greater emphasis on weight lifting in addition to agility training and cardiovascular work. Injuries were occurring more frequently, and conflict had arisen between strength and conditioning and sports medicine. Player stress was rising. Player compliance with training was diminishing.

Intervention

Functional sports specific profiling was undertaken. Basic functional assessments were performed followed by progressively more task specific movements relating to jumps and landings, change of direction strategies, balance and ball control. All professional personnel attended, so that each could understand the implications of the findings to their specific disciplines. Fundamental stability, balance, and control issues were identified.

At a meeting following this, the findings were discussed. The coach now had insight into the physical reasons for some of the technical problems she had been working on, the strength and conditioning coach understood why his exercise selection was sound for the future but too advanced for the current level of control, and the physiologist understood that the periodised programme that she had designed would need to be modified.

With framework to establish common goals and a commitment to respecting the opinions of other professionals, the conflict was eliminated and an integrated plan made.

The players were given a five week supervised remedial programme to work on movement control, stability, balance, and mobility. Their awareness of good quality movement in training and playing contexts was systematically increased, ready for integration back into their normal training programme. The strength and conditioning programme was adjusted to reflect the current level of the players rather than their assumed level.

Maintenance exercises were integrated into coaching warm-ups and drills, and good movement principles emphasised in all aspects of training.

Result: A dramatically reduced injury rate, good training compliance, and improved technical performance.

Chapter 5: Building Fluent Movement
Phase 1: Activation and Awareness

The Central Control Zone
The Lower Control Zone
The Upper Control Zone
Activating Stability Relationships
Functional Mobility

Developing fluent, controlled movement is like building a well-constructed house. You need to start with secure foundations. There are no short cuts if you want a structure that will perform well over time. For this reason, the programme in this book is systematic and progressive. Instead of presenting a general collection of exercises, it provides a pathway to follow, methodically developing abilities which lead to progressively higher levels of control.

The programme aims to help you to move well. As discussed in Chapter 1, functional stability depends on multiple factors, and the programme therefore contains exercises which complement each other as they address different aspects of your movement. As discussed in Chapter 2, the stability and movement of the upper, central and lower control zones are often closely linked. Because of this, the relationships between the control zones are developed from the early stages of the programme and progressed together, rather than presenting separate upper, central and lower body programmes.

The programme has been divided into four phases:

1 *Activation and Awareness.* This is the most important phase but it is often mistakenly skipped over in favour of bigger more exciting movements. It makes the links between your brain and the muscles you are trying to activate, using simple movements.

2 *Integration.* This phase progresses your new neuromuscular connections by teaching you to control your trunk against movement of your limbs.

3 *Global Coordination.* This phase develops Phase 2 skills into whole body movements and introduces multidirectional movement.

4 *Dynamic Control and Stability Conditioning.* Optimising your movement ultimately requires more than one aspect of control. This phase improves your neuromuscular responses to dynamic control challenges, when speed and coordination of your response is most important. It also introduces higher load demands, requiring greater strength to maintain central axis control.

Do not bypass Phase 1. If you are serious about exploring new neuromuscular pathways, you need to activate your system first and familiarise yourself with some new movement habits. If you skip Phase 1 when these muscles are not a part of your normal functional motor patterning, the higher level exercises will simply teach you to compensate in new ways.

Starting at Phase 1 does not mean that you are weak. Competitors at the highest level usually have to start at this point because their methods for compensating are so well established. Their existing pathways between brain and muscle have been reinforced by thousands of repetitions. Trying to establish a new pattern is not always easy, so simple focused movements are used to create new connections.

When you are able to progress to Phases 2, 3 and 4 exercises, a small selection of Phase 1 exercises in the warm-up ensures that you do not slip back into old patterns as the skill or load of the exercise increases. Phase 1 exercises focus your awareness on the body parts to be worked, allow you to release unnecessary tension which may inhibit the stabilisers, and wake up the communication between the balance, stability and sensory systems. These exercises give you the opportunity to attend to the finer aspects of your movement, pick up control problems or asymmetries before they turn into injuries and pre-activate patterns to prepare for sporting activity.

Your programme will eventually contain elements from each phase. You may find that your trunk stability allows you to progress to Phase 2 quite quickly, but that your balance needs more time at Phase 1 level. You may be able to perform Phase 4 mobility tasks, but find Phase 3 stability exercises more relevant to your sport. You may also find that some exercises are particularly effective for you, and you can retain these throughout your programme. All of this is appropriate, as long as you have started at Phase 1 and worked your way forward.

When performing the exercises, aim for a perfect movement each time. As you fatigue, you start to use unwanted muscles, and when this happens, it is time to rest or change exercises. The aim is to establish a new pattern, so persisting with an exercise with a poor pattern is not productive. It is better to perform two sets of five repetitions well than to perform ten repetitions if the last four are poor.

Be open to finding out something new about your movement. Awareness itself can lead to new physical possibilities. Many athletes have quite poor awareness in specific parts of their bodies but have experienced improvements by making new sensory connections. When performing the exercises in this programme, many athletes have mentioned that they have been given such exercises in the past but have not felt them working before. For these athletes, an increase in awareness and a greater attention to the quality of small movements have made the difference. It is not the exercise itself but the quality with which you do it that matters most.

Good stability work does not need to be complex. Complexity can be added for variety once the skills have been consolidated, but unless it is necessary for the sport, simplicity is a good policy.

The following exercise outlines are therefore very specific. Don't just look at the pictures and think that you'll be doing the exercise correctly. *Read the instructions carefully*. If you follow the instructions, you will benefit from the exercises. If you just copy the pictures, you are likely to miss the key point that triggers the correct response. Be patient. These initial small movements are an opportunity to find something new in your body.

You might think "I can't feel anything!" but this is usually because you are accustomed to your more accessible muscles creating lots of obvious sensory feedback. The muscles we want to train are more subtle, so listen carefully for them. The most important thing to remember is that although you should be focused, the movements should look effortless. This means that there should be no facial grimacing, lip biting or tension. Breathe naturally. The aim is *efficient* movement, so make it look smooth and easy.

A Note on Equipment

Most of the equipment used in this programme is straightforward if used correctly, but Swiss Balls, sometimes known as Fitness or Stability Balls, require a little background knowledge. These guidelines will help you to gain the full effect of the exercises which use the Swiss Ball.

If the ball is inflated correctly, it will be firm but not hard. You should be able to sit on it with your hips and knees each forming 90-degree angles. Your hips should never be below your knees. Nor should you feel that you are perching on the front of the ball because it is too big.

Do not use a ball that is too big for you and then underinflate it to make it smaller. You should have a sense that you and the ball are pushing against each other. When you push into it, it should push back. Working with a squashy ball will tend to switch off the deep stabilisers.

Size recommendations can only be general due to differences in people's body proportions and also the materials that the ball is made of. Poor quality balls tend to stretch due to the thinness of the material used, so a ball that fits you today can be too big next week. However, with a good quality ball, the average person up to 5'7" will find a 55cm ball suitable and up to 6'2", a 65cm ball will be suitable. If you are over 6'3", a 75cm ball will be preferable.

Phase 1: Activation and Awareness

Phase 1 incorporates simple activation exercises for the stabiliser muscles in each control zone. It also includes basic balance exercises and a selection of mobility exercises which complement the activation exercises. The exercises are low load and low complexity, so you have the opportunity to increase your awareness in different body parts. Use Phase 1 to establish your central longitudinal axis.

The actual number of repetitions and sets is relatively small, but each system is involved in more than one exercise. A variety of stimuli can enhance motor learning and transferability more than a single exercise. The Phase 1 programme will be performed for two weeks in this form. It may be performed for longer, but after two weeks you would be expected to add Phase 2 elements. Phase 1 elements will continue to appear for preactivation, or as part of warm-up or cool-down. Progressions for Phase 1 exercises have been provided so that you can continue to progress as you improve.

The Central Control Zone

Gaining control of the Central Longitudinal Axis (CLA) will be one of the most important elements to achieve early in the programme. In order to do this, Phase 1 Central Control Zone exercises will start to develop awareness of the CLA while activating some of the key muscles which control it.

Of these muscles, the most frequently discussed is transversus abdominis (TrA). It is a muscle which causes great confusion regarding how it should feel and whether it is working. As discussed in Chapter 2, TrA is a support muscle that responds automatically to the stimulus to move [43]. For this reason, we will be using simple movements initially to trigger a TrA response, rather than trying to consciously activate the muscle without a movement stimulus.

TrA works at low levels for long periods in order to support our movements. We are generally not attuned to perceiving low levels of activation from our muscles. This is especially the case with TrA because it is not one of our movement producing muscles, so our brains do not recognise its activity as readily as they do for our more familiar movement muscles. We know how it feels to activate a bicep: we can see it, make it perform a movement and feel it contracting more and more as we increase the load on it. There is a strong clear pathway between our brains and our biceps through regular repetitive useage, so it is easy to recognise.

TrA will not give us that same type of feeling. We can't see it contracting and if it is functioning normally, we don't notice when it is working. This can be frustrating when we are trying to exercise it, so we try to create a stronger, "louder" feeling around the area of the muscle to help us to "hear" it. This stronger feeling is actually other abdominal muscles working, which makes us feel strong in the trunk while we perform the exercise but doesn't make us move any better when we stand up. When you start to master these early exercises, you will notice a subtle sensation which is most easily felt deep in the lower abdomen just above your pubic bones. It won't feel like a muscle contracting in the sense that you are accustomed to. It is more like a sense of something securing your position.

You are aiming for a sense of effortless control around your trunk and pelvic area. You should feel that it is easy to maintain your trunk position and move your arms and legs. That fools a lot of people into thinking that they are not doing anything, but remember that the objective is to move effortlessly, not to strengthen an individual muscle. The exercises below encourage TrA to activate, making you aware of the trunk control it gives you.

The exercises in the first three phases of the programme focus on working your abdominal wall in a neutral position in order to secure your CLA. You may be accustomed to working your abdominals in curling actions, so this will be a different sensation. The initial exercises are easy awareness movements.

Ball Bouncing

This exercise teaches you to support your spine without buckling against vertical forces. This ability reinforces the CLA. Bouncing slightly amplifies the effect of gravity on your body, which stimulates a stabilising action in the small muscles located close to your spine.

Sit on a ball with your feet and knees hip-width apart. Find your sitting bones with your hands. Slump your body and feel yourself roll off the back of your sitting bones. Straighten up and feel yourself roll over the front of your sitting bones. Now find the position where you are sitting straight down on your sitting bones. This is the pelvic position for all your seated work.

Stretch both arms above your head, feeling the stomach draw inwards in response to the arm raising movement. Initiate a bounce by squeezing your glutes on and off, making sure that you land each time

directly on your sitting bones. If you do this, you will achieve the correct trunk response. If you land either with your pelvis tipped slightly forward or backward, you will use back extensors or hip flexors to stabilise.

Perform 6 x 30 seconds sets prior to other exercises to pre-activate the trunk stabilisers.

Where should I feel it?
* You should have a general sense of the lower abdominals working at a low, consistent level, and a secure spine.

What would a poor performance look like?
* Landing in a slumped position or landing in too much back arch.

The Greyhound

The Greyhound allows you to develop a secure CLA with low effort and increase your awareness of your abdominal stabilisers. This is a great exercise when performed well, but it is usually performed with too much effort. There are two things to consider. Firstly, you will be lying fully supported by the floor. Secondly, you will only be moving your limbs at a low load level. The combination of these two factors means that you should not be using high abdominal effort. The question to ask yourself is, "how little effort can I use to perform these movements perfectly?" Most abdominal training is done to produce high force. TrA training aims to produce efficiency and economy of movement. This means the least effort for the best result.

If you have spent your athletic career performing high force abdominal exercises for rectus abdominis and obliques, you may have difficulty with this exercise at first. Don't reject it for that reason: this means that the Greyhound is something you need to do! It teaches you how to effortlessly maintain a neutral spinal position to support arm and leg motion without the need for superficial muscles to act as stabilisers. For this reason, it can alleviate feelings of stiffness and restriction in the hips and shoulders. Many people will be able to move from Greyhound 1 to Greyhound 3 within several minutes. Greyhound 1 and 2 teach the basic pattern so that the Greyhound 3 exercise will be correct, but you do not need to spend much time on them. View them as a short warm-up.

Greyhound 1.0

Lie on the floor with your knees bent and feet flat on the floor. Start by releasing any unnecessary activity in the abdominals. To do this, rest one hand on your ribs and the other on your lower abdomen below your navel. Note your normal breathing pattern for a few breaths. Now try to gently inflate your abdomen, then let the air seep out again. Try not to squeeze your air out with your abdominals – it is a poor habit when there is no respiratory demand on you. Once you have done this, return to your normal breathing pattern.

Keep the hand centrally on your lower abdomen just above your pubic bones and raise the other one to the ceiling. Slowly take it over your head focusing on allowing your spine and ribs to lengthen along the floor. Feel the abdomen drop from under your hands. Just like a greyhound, your abdominals have sunk towards the spine between your ribs and your legs. Maintain this dropped abdominal position, and with the least amount of effort possible, lift your arm back up to the ceiling.

Note for therapists: Instead of trying to consciously activate TrA, we are inhibiting the muscular strategy we don't want (rectus abdominis and external obliques) in order to stimulate the body to find an alternative automatic stablilising response to movement. The best results occur when people focus on releasing the spine, instead of focusing on the stomach area.

 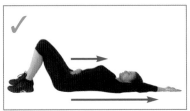 

What would a poor performance look like?

- Arching your back off the floor because you have not allowed your back muscles to release.

- Pressing the lower back down into the floor instead of lengthening it along the floor.

- Trying to tense or tighten the abdominals muscles instead of allowing them to drop down towards the spine. Once you can feel the abdominals sinking and the sensation of the spine relaxing and lengthening along the floor, move straight to Greyhound 2.

Greyhound 2.0

Repeat the above action but this time take both arms over the head, remembering to lengthen the body along the floor. Using the least possible amount of abdominal activity, bring the arms back up again.

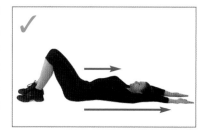 

Where should I feel it?

- You should only feel a vague sensation very low in your abdomen. If your spine is relaxed on the floor and you are moving your arms without effort and without bracing your abdominals, you are doing a great job. If you make your abdominals feel like they are working hard, you are training yourself to use more effort than is necessary. This is the opposite of training efficiency. Keep aiming for smooth movement without effort.

- If Greyhound 2 is easily controlled without tension, move to Greyhound 3.

Greyhound 3.0 (A): Increasing Skill

Start with both arms up to the ceiling and both knees bent with feet on the floor. Perform a Greyhound 2 exercise to establish the correct action. Now combine this arm action with sliding one heel out along the floor, once again focusing on lengthening the body along the

floor. Press your heel as far from your fingertips as you can to feel a deep stretching and narrowing around your midsection. Maintain this feeling of narrowness, and with as little effort as you can, smoothly bring your arms and legs back to the start position. Make sure you maintain an even pressure under both sides of your pelvis.

Reps	10 reps alternating sides
Sets	3

○ Greyhound 3.0 (B): Increased Load

Start in the bent knee position as for the above exercises. You will not move your feet this time. Hold a 2kg weight in your hands. With the philosophy of using as little muscle activity as possible, you will take the weight over your head, making sure that you focus on lengthening the spine along the floor. Maintaining the sunken feeling in the lower abdomen, pull the weight back up.

  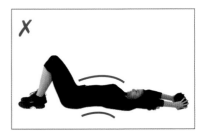

Reps	10 per side
Sets	3

From this point, progress from stage to stage as you master each exercise.

○ Greyhound 3.1: Increased Skill

One set comprises three different movements. 1. Perform the Greyhound 3.0A exercise and come back to the start. 2. Then move only the arm on the sliding leg side, lengthening this side of the body. Bring your arm and leg back in. 3. Now from the start position, move only the opposite arm to the sliding leg side.

The three movement combinations = 1 set	
Sets	10

Greyhound 3.2: Supine Running

To increase the skill without load, and build coordination and endurance to this pattern, we will now progress to alternating arms and legs.

Start with your right arm straight over your head and your right leg straight. Your left knee will be bent and your left arm will be by your side, with your elbow bent. Settle your breathing and reverse your arm and leg position, maintaining the length of your spine along the floor and a level pelvis.

Reps	10 reps alternating sides
Sets	3

Greyhound 4.0: Increased Load

Perform the *Greyhound 3.1* exercises as previously outlined but instead of sliding your foot out, move it out so that it is 10cm from the floor at full extension.

Greyhound 5.0

Start in the knees bent position and support one knee with your hand. Maintain the long, relaxed spine and using as little effort as possible, raise the other foot. Put your foot back down.

Greyhound 5.1

Start in the knees bent position and support one knee with your hand. Maintain the long, relaxed spine, and using as little effort as possible raise the other foot. Now straighten this leg all the way out, releasing at the hip and maintaining your spinal position with as little effort as possible. Bring the leg back and replace it on the floor.

Greyhound 5.2

Athletes often start at Greyhound 5.2, but very few can initially manage this level of loading with the correct abdominal pattern. If you can't manage it well, do not spend time performing multiple repetitions of a poor pattern. Select a more appropriate level for the majority of your set, and spend a little time in the middle of your set working on this new more difficult level. Sometimes athletes are taught to do this with their hands under the pelvis to prevent their backs from lifting. This enables you to perform the movement but does not teach a correct pattern, so it is not recommended for the aims of this book. Start with your knees bent and your feet close to your body. Place one hand on your abdominals and reach the other arm towards the ceiling. Lift one foot off the floor until your knee points to the ceiling. Now try to lift the other foot without your abdominals popping up into your hand. Once you can do this, try it with both arms towards the ceiling.

What would a poor pattern feel like?
- Your lower back tenses and lifts from the floor.
- Your abdominals pop up into your hand.
- Your hips feel locked in position.

Greyhound 5.3

Start with your arms to the ceiling and your hips and knees at 90 degrees as shown in Greyhound 5.2. Maintaining your hip and knee position, lengthen both arms over your head, allowing the spine to relax into the floor.

Greyhound 5.4

Perform Greyhound 5.3, adding the straightening of one leg out along the floor as the arms move over the head. Your fingertips and heel should be stretching away from each other and an inch or so from the floor before you bring the arms and leg back in with effortless control of your pelvis and spine.

Trunk Control Against Hip Flexion: Seated Knee Lift

Many athletes experience the sensation of tightness in their hip flexors. Usually we tend to think of stretching a tight muscle, but what if stretching doesn't seem to help?

If your trunk stability is poor, you may use your hip flexors to improve control. Constant activity of the hip flexors in a stabilising role can cause the perception of tightness in the hip, but unless you improve your stability, the hip flexors will continue to work in this way, making stretching ineffective. It also means that the hip flexors may not contract effectively through a full range. Your hip flexion action may actually be quite weak, especially if your trunk is not sufficiently stable to support a strong hip flexion action (the trunk does not provide an adequate fixed point for muscles to pull from). Even international-level competitors have had to start with this most basic of exercises to establish a normal relationship between the trunk and hip flexors.

Sit on the front of a chair with both feet on the floor hip-width apart. Make sure you are sitting directly on your sitting bones. Lift both arms out to the side until they are level with your shoulders. This will help you to monitor your trunk position. Before moving, take a deep breath and check your rib movement. Keeping your weight evenly pressing through both of your sitting bones, lift one knee and hold it in this position for 5 seconds. Your arms should not have moved, and you should see no visible abdominal activity occurring. If you have kept your position correctly, your lower abdominals should be working to support your hip flexors. Check that you can still breathe by expanding your lower ribs. Your lower leg should hang straight to the floor without turning. If it doesn't, straighten it so that your foot will place itself precisely on the floor once you lower your knee.

What would a poor performance look like?

- Your ribs draw downwards and inwards because you are overusing your oblique abdominals.
- Your trunk shifts sideways due to poor stability.
- Your trunk shortens on the lifting side due to poor stability.
- You collapse your trunk forward due to poor stability.

Reps	10 per side
Sets	2

Progression

- Sit on a wobble cushion, and eventually a Swiss Ball to perform this movement. The challenge is far greater, as you must keep your weight evenly distributed over the left and right sides of your pelvis. The distance between your armpit and your hip must remain the same on both sides during the movement so that only hip flexion is occurring.

The Lower Control Zone

GMax Activation

Coordination around the hip and pelvic area and the responsiveness of the gluteal group are intimately connected. Although many athletes practice strengthening exercises for this group, the key to improving their function is actually practicing small good quality movements which unlock the pelvis from the spine and the hips from the pelvis. These movements are often new to the athlete and the increase in awareness that comes with them develops a relationship between movement and muscle. Very simple movements are needed at first.

Basic Bridge

The bridge is a simple movement which can help an athlete to restore mobility between the spine and the pelvis, unlock tight back muscles and discover the relationship between the *hip straightening movement* and GMax.

Stage 1

Start by lying on your back with your knees bent and your feet flat on the floor. Keep your feet hip-width apart and bring them towards your body. Placing your feet further from the body will bias the hamstrings, and we want to minimise this effect.

Relax your abdominals and start to tip your pelvis back towards you by pressing down through your feet.

Once you are in this position, you need to check which muscles you are using to stay up there. Feel across your lower back. If your spine feels like a deep valley between two large hard ridges of muscle running down either side of it, it is likely that you are using a little too much back extensor and not quite enough GMax. If you feel any discomfort in your lower back, it is also likely that you are using too much back extensor.

To rectify this, put your hands on your pelvis with the thumbs up and the fingers down. Drop your hips slightly and tip your pelvis a little more back towards you. Recheck your back – is the valley a little less deep? It is normal and desirable to have some back activity, but it should feel like gentle hills as you run your hand over them, not the Himalayas.

CHAPTER 5: BUILDING FLUENT MOVEMENT: PHASE 1

Notice that if you have tilted your pelvis a little, you may find that your quadriceps feel stretched. This is an extra benefit in this position.

Once you are accustomed to feeling the difference between using your glutes and using your back, turn your attention to your hamstrings and adductor (inner thigh) muscles. Feel the muscles with your hands: are they firm or soft?

If you suspect that your adductor muscles are working too hard, maintain your bridge and move one knee outwards, maintaining your trunk position and a level pelvis. Move the knee back in and repeat with the other side. The adductors must release to allow you to move your knee.

You will sustain the position for the count of 10 and then return to the floor by slowly uncurling, placing one vertebra after the other on the floor. Try not to use your abdominals to help, as this will decrease GMax's role.

What would a poor performance look like?
- Pushing hips and back straight up instead of rolling the pelvis into position.
- Using too much abdominal muscle to create a pelvic tilt.
- Hanging on with back muscles and hamstrings.
- Hanging on with adductors.

Where should I feel it?
- You should feel your buttock muscles working.

Reps	10
Sets	2

Progression

- While holding the position, move one arm out to the side, ensuring that you keep your pelvis level. Bring it back up and switch to the other arm.

Observation notes

Some people will worry that the spine is not in a perfectly neutral position here. However, the aim of this exercise is not neutral spine control. The aim is to put the pelvis in a position which favours GMax and disadvantages the back extensors. As discussed in Chapter 2 the primary posterior chain dysfunction involves too much hamstring and back extensor and not enough GMax. The aim here is basic re-patterning, and it is a little like balancing the treble and bass on your stereo system. We are not trying to switch one thing off and another thing on. Instead we are trying to increase activity in one area and decrease it in the other until we have a balance. The neutral position against gravity is usually too difficult when early re-patterning is occurring. The pelvic tilt gives us a means to actively change the conditions for each muscle and once the pattern starts to recalibrate, a more neutral position can be aimed for. The control of a neutral spine is being addressed with other exercises in the programme and once a balance has been achieved between the gluteals, back and hamstrings, they can be worked on in a neutral position.

The pelvic tilt also teaches you to dissociate (independently move) your pelvis from your spine, gently mobilising your lower back. Many GMax deficient athletes are dependent upon fixing their pelvic position with their back muscles to maintain stability, making it even more difficult to activate GMax and producing a feeling of stiffness. Improving this dissociative ability can help greatly with activation.

Although you have been instructed not to use your abdominals in this exercise, this does not mean that no abdominals are working! The muscles that you have direct control of at this time are more likely to be rectus abdominis and obliques. If you try to relax these muscles, the deeper TrA can activate more effectively. Clinical experience has shown that actively trying to relax the superficial abdominals also tends to encourage the GMax work more effectively in this exercise, as it becomes the primary movement producing muscle.

Stage 2: Hip Pops

The ability to straighten the hip without over-bending the spine is a critical movement for many sports. Without it, the contribution of GMax to the total power of the movement will be markedly reduced. Remember that GMax is a big, broad muscle, and it is hard

to compensate for the loss of its contribution. Hip pops address awareness of the hip extension movement and inner range activation of GMax.

Perform the bridge as above, and place one finger on the crease of the hip and another directly opposite at the back of the hip. The two fingers should be pointing towards each other through the hip joint. This is your awareness focus. Move the top finger towards the bottom finger by softening the hip into a slight bend. Be aware of this movement. Now move the bottom finger towards the top finger, squeezing GMax and causing the hip to straighten. Be aware that the hip has moved but the spine has not bent. Count to 3. Repeat without coming back to the floor.

Reps	10
Sets	2

Progression
- Once you have the idea of the hip movement, perform it with both arms to the ceiling as shown above.

Stage 3: Hip Swivels

As discussed in Chapter 1, pelvic rotation is a critical movement for normal efficient walking and running. This exercise teaches GMax activation in combination with pelvis and hip rotation. Start in the Basic Bridge position. Put your hands under your buttocks. Keeping one

side up, let the other side drop down into your hand. This will look like your pelvis has rotated down on that side. Press it back up by squeezing the GMax on that side. Repeat with the other side.

Reps	10 per side
Sets	2

Progression
- Once you have the idea of the hip movement, perform it with both arms to the ceiling as shown above.

○ Wall Squat

The wall squat takes this basic GMax activation and applies it to a vertical position. Having achieved an inner range contraction of GMax, we want to link an awareness of hip bending with a neutral spine position while working GMax into a greater range of hip bending. This exercise is not intended to mimic a barbell squat in the weights room. Its postural position is vertical as opposed to tilted. Its priority is awareness and control of the neutral spine, control and smooth motion of the hip, and eccentric/concentric GMax activity.

○ Stage 1

Stand with a Swiss Ball behind your back at waist level. Walk your feet forward to a comfortable point and allow the ball to accept your weight. Straighten up so that your shoulders are

directly above your hips. Place your hands under your sitting bones. You will sit directly down into your hands, squeezing your glutes as you go. Pause when your knees are at 90 degrees and experiment with relaxing your glutes to make your quadriceps take more of the load and then switching the glutes back on to feel the load shared between the two muscle groups. Press your body straight back up again.

The three main errors for this exercise:

1. You may not bend your hips as much as your knees, so your shoulders end up behind your hips. To correct this you can place your hands into the crease at the front of the hip to remind your body to release this movement and allow a vertical alignment.
2. You may forget to keep your knees in line, so you need to focus more on your GMax to control your thighs.
3. You may sneak your pelvis under the ball for extra support and sensory feedback. In this case, with your hands under those sitting bones, focus on the bones going

straight down to the floor instead of back towards the wall behind you. If you feel that your weight is being supported more on one side than the other, lift this heel and perform the squat. Reducing the support on this side shifts more weight onto the other leg.

Where should I feel it?

- You should feel your thighs and buttocks. You will notice your thighs more.
- Once you can perform 10 of these with good form, you can progress to stage 1+.

Stage 1.1: Increasing Trunk and Hip Control

Start as for stage 1, but this time take your arms above your head in a streamlined position. Repeat the squat but make sure that your sitting bones do not sneak backward, increasing your lumbar curve. It is much more challenging to keep the spine neutral in this position.

Stage 1.2: Trunk Control Against Moving Arms

Start with a Swiss Ball and a light weight in your hands. As you move down into your squat, take the ball above your head. Focus on keeping a consistent trunk position, because it is easy to collapse into back extension with this exercise.

Increasing Coordination

Place your right hand on your left thigh. As you squat down, take the arm up and across your body, finishing above your right shoulder. Your knees and hips should remain pointing forward throughout the motion. This exercise can also be performed with a light weight or medicine ball.

Reps	10
Sets	2

GMed Activation

Gaining awareness and some basic endurance in GMed is helpful before trying to activate it in weight bearing.

Clam

Lie on your side with your top arm on the floor in front of you. Draw your knees and hips up, then push your top thigh forward along the line of your bottom thigh. Your top knee will overlap your bottom knee by about 5cm. Notice that this pulls your trunk and pelvis into slight forward rotation.

Drawing your lower abdomen in towards your spine, lift the top knee by pivoting between your feet and your hip joint. Keep your pelvis forward: it is easy to let it roll slightly backward to access stronger more easily activated muscles. Count to 10. If you have performed the movement correctly, your top knee will land with the same amount of overlap that you started with.

Reps	10
Sets	2

Where should I feel it?
- As you lie there feel for a bone in the side of your top hip. You will feel the work just behind this bone, and you may feel it on the moving leg side or the supporting side.

What would a poor performance look like?
- Rolling the top hip back as you lift your leg.
- Lifting the top foot.

Once you have a basic GMed foundation, it is time to apply it to weight bearing.

● Standing Knee Press

Stand next to a wall with feet together. Lift one knee and place it on the wall. First you need to focus on your stance leg. Place your hand over the bone at the side of the hip. Draw your body up over your hip. You should feel the hip bone under your hand move further underneath you. This is where it must stay throughout the exercise.

Straighten both arms up into a streamlined position. Press out with the knee into the wall, keeping the pelvis facing forward. Count to 10.

Where should I feel it?

- Feel for a muscle working hard in the depression just behind the hip bone on the stance side.

Reps	5 each side

The Upper Control Zone

Awareness Around the Scapula

If you need to improve your upper control zone, better awareness around your scapula can help you to feel the muscles in that area. We are not generally very aware of our scapula: we often don't relate well to body parts that we can't see or put our hands on easily. If you are not experienced at activating scapular stabilisers, try this awareness exercise first.

Lie down on your side with your knees bent and your arms out in front of you with the palms together. You are aiming to move with the least possible amount of muscle tension. Slowly and smoothly slide your upper hand out over your lower hand as far as you can. Notice how your scapula has moved over your rib cage, sliding forward and around in response to your hand movement.

Once you have reached your limit, pause, make sure that everything is relaxed, and begin to move your hand back to the start position again without letting your elbow bend. Your scapula will move back around your rib cage again, sliding towards your spine. Repeat the movement up to ten times slowly and then relax.

The Diamond

As well as being a good quick test, the diamond works well as a simple exercise to activate lower trapezius and teach scapula-shoulder dissociation.

Lie on your stomach with your forehead resting on the floor. Place your arms in a diamond shape on the floor above your head so that your fingertips touch. Draw your scapulae slightly down towards your toes. Lift the forearms and hands off the floor and hold them there for the count of 5.

Where should I feel it?
- You will feel muscles working in your mid back area.

What would a poor performance look like?
- Tightening up the neck muscles. Your upper trapezius and neck muscles should be completely relaxed throughout this exercise. If they are not, ask someone to tap you on either side of your spine at the level of the bottom of your scapula. Aim to bring your scapulae towards the tapping finger before you lift your arms.
- The other error is to collapse the front of your shoulders towards the floor as you lift your hands. To avoid this, just before you lift, be aware of the shape created between your arms and chest and the floor. Maintain that shape as you lift. If you collapse one shoulder, it will move closer to the floor, distorting the shape. If this happens, focus on maintaining the ball-and-socket joint in a consistent place throughout the movement.

Reps	10
Sets	2

Windscreen Wiper: Active Shoulder Internal Rotation

As well as being useful as a test, the Windscreen Wiper teaches you to control internal rotation of your shoulder joint while maintaining a stable scapula.

Lie down on your back with your elbow bent to 90 degrees, your upper arm level with your shoulder and the back of your forearm and hand as close to the floor as you can without pushing. Relax everything before you start. If you feel that your shoulder lifted closer to your ear when you positioned your arm, shift it back down so that it is level with your other side. Place your other hand over the front of your shoulder. This hand will monitor the movement of the "ball" in the socket of your shoulder joint.

Keeping your elbow secure on the floor, lift your forearm so that your arm rotates and your hand now points to the ceiling. Imagine this position as 12 o'clock on a watch face. This completes phase 1 of the test. Keep moving in the same direction until you cannot continue without shifting your shoulder position. This completes phase 2 of the test.

Where should I feel it?

* You are aiming for a smooth effortless movement, so it is not a question of where you should feel it, but where you shouldn't. There should be no sensation of tightness in your neck and no overstrain in your pectoral (chest) muscles.

* You should be able to perform this movement without feeling your shoulder pushing upwards or rolling forward into your hand. If you detect the "ball" pushing into your hand, it means that it is losing its position in the socket by sliding forward.

Reps	20
Sets	2

The Sphinx

This basic movement acquaints you with your serratus anterior and gives you an appreciation of a scapular motion.

Start on your stomach propped up on your elbows. Make sure that the elbows are in line with the shoulders and wrists and that the arms are parallel to each other. You can start by sagging between your shoulders and then press your arms into the floor to lift your upper body into a strong position with your neck in line with your spine. Hold for a count of 5.

You are aiming for your back to look smooth, with the scapulae pressed firmly onto the rib cage.

Where should I feel it?
- This should not be hard work. You should feel general muscle activity around the back of your shoulders.

Common error
- Dropping the head, or tipping it backward. Keep a long, neutral neck.

Reps	10

Activating Stability Relationships

Stage 1. Wall Press: Developing the CLA and Shoulder-Trunk Integration

A Wall Press is a good basic level test but is also a foundation movement for coordination of the shoulder girdle with the trunk. It looks deceptively simple due to its low load but few athletes perform it well. A former European Junior Champion in triathlon attempted this in the clinic and could manage 5 repetitions before her TrA fatigued.

Place a Swiss Ball on a wall at chest height. Your arms should be straight and your body upright. Switch your balloon on to stimulate your abdominals to draw inwards and your shoulders to relax. Keeping this entire set up consistent, bend your elbows so that your body moves towards the ball. You should be looking into the ball if you have kept your head position. At the point where you are closest to the ball and about to press out again, you should especially focus on maintaining your lower abdominal position, as it is tempting to let it relax and sag outwards.

Main points
- Long back of neck.
- Relaxed shoulders so that you can press from your upper control zone.
- Lower abdominals maintain a gentle inwards feeling.

What would a poor performance look like?
- Head tips back.
- Shoulders draw upwards.
- Back sags forward when the abdominals switch off.

Where should I feel it?
- You are aiming for a strong secure feeling in your trunk and shoulders. Focus on feeling how your lower abdominals work to prevent your spine from sagging forward.

Note for therapists
The best places to cue are at the base of the skull with a light upward pressure to prevent the head rotating backward, and with fingertips just below the navel to provide sensory feedback for abdominals.

Reps	10

If 10 repetitions are easy, progress to Stage 2.

Stage 2. The Single Leg Wall Press: Shoulder, Trunk and Hip Integration and Rotational Trunk Control

Start in the set up position as above but lift one leg. Draw your body up over your hip so that your GMed is triggered and your spine is aligned vertically over your stance foot.

Perform the press, making sure that your shoulders and pelvis stay parallel to the wall and that you do not lose your abdominal activation.

Reps	10 each side

Stage 1: Superman

This is another common and useful exercise when performed well but it is of little use if it isn't performed accurately. It coordinates the pelvis, trunk and upper body and increases awareness in all three zones while activating muscles at low threshold.

Start on hands and knees with your head and neck in straight alignment with your spine. Hands should be positioned under shoulders, knees under hips. Draw your lower belly upwards, and press your chest slightly away from the floor until

your upper back is flat. Press straight out with one heel keeping your pelvis level, making sure that your supporting hip does not sag out to the side. Stretch out with the opposite fingertips so that you have a straight line from fingers to heel. Your chest and pelvis should be parallel to the floor. Focus on this position feeling strong and secure as you really stretch your fingertips from your heel. Hold the position for the count of 5 and come back to the start position before switching sides.

Check points

- Head and neck in line with body, not dropped down or rotated upwards. These head positions will switch off TrA and distort the scapular stability pattern.

- Chest pressed away from the floor to keep it level. This prevents the scapula winging, or your chest rotating around your shoulder.

- Heel, not toe, pressing out so that a strong straight line from the trunk through the hip is achieved.

- Feel that TrA is tucked up towards the spine.

- Pelvis level, not rotated or sagging out through one hip (as shown in Chapter 4, Superman).

> Once you can perform 10 repetitions each side, move on to Stage 2.

Variation 1: Start in your basic superman position with opposite arm and leg outstretched. Move your arm out to the side, then under your body, and straight out in front again. Your trunk should remain still throughout the movement.

Variation 2: Increase speed of dynamic control. Perform the Superman as described above; however this time snap your arm and leg out into position and then hold for a moment to ensure that you have hit the target position. Bring your arm and knee back under your body. Keeping your back neutral, repeat this quick, accurate movement.

Stage 2: Hovering Superman

Take up the Superman position, and then lift your knees from the ground. Maintain your balance and press one heel out behind you until your leg is level with your back. Lift your opposite arm and maintain your position for a count of 5.

Add Variations 1 and 2 as outlined for the basic Superman position.

Basic Balance

Simple static balance. The purpose of the basic balance exercise is to connect the foot to the hip, decrease unnecessary muscle activation so that your limbs can move freely and increase low effort stabiliser activity. When the eyes are closed, basic balance exercises can help to integrate the vestibular and sensory-motor balance systems. This is important when you cannot depend on using your eyes as your primary balance system. If you need your eyes to judge an opponents movement, track a ball or cope with variable lighting conditions, this type of training will help. If you have to move over uneven surfaces, decreasing dependence upon your eyes and increasing the responsiveness of your sensory motor-systems will help to avoid injury.

Stand upright in your balloon posture. Lift one leg and move both arms directly above your head. Relax any gripping action around your ankle, and soften the foot so that it can "listen" to the floor accurately. Lift your body up over your hip to ensure that you are activating GMed.

Move one arm down to your side and back up.	Take both arms out in front and move one to the side and back.	Bend the stance knee and turn your trunk one way and then the other.	With arms outstretched, bend your upper body to one side so that one arm points upwards and the other one downwards.

Move the other leg forward as far as you can, back as far as you can, to the side and across your body diagonally.

Once you can do this, practice the same routine with your *eyes closed.* This can be progressed onto a balance board for increased challenge.

Star Hold: Global Stability Connecting the Hip, Trunk and Shoulder

Lie on your side with your feet together and your body in a straight line. Press up onto one hand, creating a straight body line. Reach the other hand to the ceiling. Make sure your hips are straight.

Count to 10 and perform 10 repetitions on each side.

If this is easy, start in the basic star hold position and hold the top leg up.

Where should I feel it?
* You may feel your shoulder muscles, or the sides of your trunk and hip.

What would a poor performance look like?
* Allowing the hips to bend and move backward.

Functional Mobility

The following exercises combine stability and mobility in the same exercise. This helps to teach you good movement habits and encourages the body to support itself effectively while releasing tight muscles.

● Straight Up Hamstring Mobility

Sit on a chair with one foot on the front of a Swiss Ball. Sit up onto your sitting bones. Push the ball away with your foot until you feel a stretch in the back of your thigh/knee/calf, maintaining your trunk position. Move the ball in and out 4 times and on the last one hold for a count of 10.

What would a poor performance look like?
• Letting the back sag as the foot moves away from you.

● Wind-up Stretch

This stretch increases mobility between the leg and the trunk.

Take up the same position as above, pushing the ball out until you feel a stretch in the back of your leg. Staying up on your sitting bones, put your hands on your head and turn your trunk one way, and then the other – one way should feel tighter and the other should feel looser. Slowly rotate your chest from left to right 4–6 times.

● Floor Presses

This simple technique combines trunk control with shoulder mobility.

a) Lie on your back with your knees bent. Take one arm over your head, palm facing upwards. Keep your elbow straight and your arm close to your head. The other arm stays by your side, palm facing downwards. Prevent the back from arching by lengthening the spine and press both hands into the floor for the count of 5. Swap arm positions and repeat.

What would a poor performance look like?
- Arching the back off the floor. Allow it to relax and lengthen.
- Bending the elbow. This will decrease your shoulder mobility.

b) Lie on your back with your shoulders and elbows at 90 degrees resting on the floor. Your back must remain relaxed on the floor. Press down into the floor with both elbows and wrists for the count of 5.

Standing Leg Swing

This movement develops a fluid, straight leg motion pattern on the foundation of a stable trunk and pelvis and a secure CLA.

Stand on one leg and bring your hip bone under you to activate GMed. Stay tall and swing the other leg fully back and forth, allowing your arms to move normally. Your trunk should stay vertical and your leg should swing in a straight line. Your pelvis should remain in a constant position throughout the movement.

What would a poor performance look like?
- The pelvis tips forward (and backward) instead of staying level as the leg moves.
- The trunk tips sideways to stay balanced.

Scapular Awareness

Many years ago while on an inspiring Feldenkrais workshop, I was introduced to the concept of using low effort, self-exploration movements to improve awareness and efficiency. This next exercise improves awareness around the scapula and can be used prior to performing scapular stabilisation exercises to improve their effectiveness. In sports such as golf, tennis and swimming, the movement releases tension around the shoulder and neck and improves scapular mobility.

Lie on your side with both arms stretched out in front of you. Place the palm of your top hand on your bottom hand. Relax. As slowly and smoothly as possible, slide your top hand forward over your bottom hand. Don't rush: you need time to feel what is going on. Notice your scapula sliding forward over your ribs. Once you have reached as far as you can, pause, relax, and slowly begin to slide your hand back towards you without bending your elbow. Notice your scapula sliding back towards your spine.

Repeat this movement again, but even more slowly. This time notice whether you are using muscles that you do not need. Notice your neck muscles and the muscles at the front of your shoulder: these are often overactive. If you notice tension anywhere, pause, relax, and then in your own time continue on with your movement. You are aiming for effortless sliding of your scapula. Repeat as many times as you like, but at least perform six or seven full movements.

Restoring Rotation

Rotation occurs throughout the body and is essential for normal movement. The body needs to rotate in a spiral from the feet to the top of the neck, and the spine needs to counter rotate to decrease spinal stress and increase movement efficiency.

Thigh Slides

This is an easy "feel good" mobiliser of the midback. Sit comfortably upright with your hands on your thighs. Making sure that your head stays facing forward, slide one hand forward and the other hand back towards you, allowing your shoulders to turn fully into the movement.

Knee Creepers

Small movements make big differences. You may have used this technique as a test in Chapter 4, but it can be used as an easy pelvic mobility exercise to encourage symmetrical pelvic rotation as is needed for walking and running.

Sit comfortably upright with your hands on your knees. Keeping your weight even on both sitting bones, slide one knee forward and the other one back. This motion causes a rotation of your pelvis and lumbar spine. Smoothly and easily reverse directions so that your pelvis and lumbar spine rotate the other way.

Pelvic Rotation With Weight Transference Over the Fixed Foot

The combination of pelvic rotation and weight transference is necessary for tennis players, golfers, footballers, and baseballers but some people have a mobility awareness block around this area of their body.

Stand up with your arms relaxed. You are going to turn your body to the left, allowing your right heel to lift so that your foot can pivot to allow your pelvis to freely rotate over your left foot. Letting your arms swing freely, turn to the right, lifting your left heel to allow your pelvis to rotate. Increase your awareness by noting which way your weight is moving when you rotate.

If one side feels a little restricted, hold the rotational position and smoothly shift the pressure inwards and outwards under the sole of the foot on this side as you did in the previous exercise. You should feel the restriction ease after a few repetitions. The following exercises were inspired by the movement philosophy of Moshe Feldenkrais. They should be performed slowly to allow you time to notice your own movement.

Total Body Rotation

This movement restores mobility to a stiff midback, as well as increasing the mobility deep in the hip. It integrates the rotation from the foot to the top of the neck. If you used the total body rotation test in Chapter 3, this technique addresses any restrictions you may have found.

Stand with your feet hip-width apart. Turn and look behind you, noting a spot that you can comfortably see. Do not strain yourself. Turn back around the other way, noting a spot that you can comfortably see.

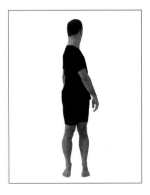 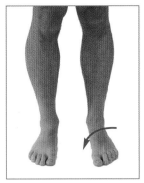 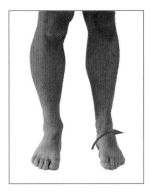 

Once you have noted how much motion is available, turn your attention to your feet. Note the pressure changes in your feet as you turn. It should follow the same pattern: as you turn to the left, the left foot pressure moves towards the outer part of the foot, and the right foot pressure moves to the inner part of the foot. In other words, the pressure moves in the direction of the turn.

Decide which direction is more restricted. Turn in this direction and stop when you have reached your comfortable limit. You should have your weight on the outside of that foot. Keeping your body in the same position, focus on smoothly shifting the pressure under your foot from the outside to the inside surface. If you place your hand up around the top of your thigh, you will notice that the foot motion is causing your thigh to rotate. You may notice as you continue that you feel the movement deep in your hip.

Once you have completed ten smooth pressure shifts with your foot, keep your weight on the outside of the foot and turn in the opposite direction. This will feel strange because it is not your normal method for moving. Perform several turns with the weight maintained on the outside of your foot and then come back to standing normally on both feet. Retest your movement by turning in the direction of the original restriction, allowing your feet to move normally. You should find that you move much further.

You can repeat the movement but try shifting the pressure under the other foot. Instead of performing pressure shifts with the left foot when you are turning left, try doing pressure shifts on the right foot, as you turn left.

Counter Body Rotation Around the CLA

Counter body rotation, as discussed in Chapter 1, is the basis for efficient gait, whether it is walking or running. Restrictions in pelvic rotation decrease your ability to shock absorb and they increase stress on lower body structures. Good pelvic rotation engages small muscles around the spine to increase stability in your lower back. This movement aims to increase awareness and mobility in your spine.

Lie on your side with your hips and knees bent to 90 degrees. Pause before beginning the movement. Slowly slide your top knee forward over your bottom knee. As you slowly try to draw it back again, focus on maintaining a long, relaxed spine. The most common error is tightening the lower back muscles as you slide the knee back. Focus on keeping the lower back the same length throughout the movement. If you do this, your CLA is being maintained and the correct muscles will be working. Repeat this movement several times, aiming to make the forward and backward movement as pure as possible.

Once you have mastered this, add counter rotation from the shoulders. As you slide your top knee forward move your top shoulder backward fully, opening your chest towards the ceiling. Slowly reverse the movement, drawing the top knee back towards the hip and allowing the top shoulder to rotate fully forward. Make the movements slow, smooth and easy. Repeat ten times each side.

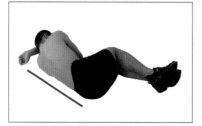

169

Notes from the Clipboard

An elite badminton player with recurrent hip pain was assessed and found to have poor trunk and pelvic stability. He was an immensely strong looking player with highly developed quadriceps and hamstrings, and he regularly performed a heavy strength programme in the gym. He depended upon his adductor group to compensate for poor GMax/GMed activation, and had frequently presented with adductor strains in the past. His lack of central control had eventually taken its toll and he sustained a serious injury in his hip joint.

Despite his elite status, this player found the Stage 1+ squat extremely difficult even with a 1 kg weight. His hips would move sideways as the weight moved across his body and he was unable to control this. The basic Bridge helped him to find and activate his GMax in order to improve his pelvic control.

The player also found the basic Wall Press very difficult, as he had no appreciation of a neutral trunk position and no TrA activation to maintain control. His spine would sag into extension as he approached the wall. Ball Bouncing and Greyhound exercises taught him how to control his trunk with low effort.

Once the athlete had learned to secure his CLA and to activate his trunk and pelvic stabilisers, he was able to progress through Phases 2–4, integrating what he had learned into his on-court training so that new movement habits became his natural way of moving.

Stories like this are common: athletes are allowed to compensate, and if they are achieving success, their faults are interpreted as individual style. Small movements are rarely tested, bypassed in favour of exercises more in keeping with the athlete's elite status. Big dramatic movements are built on small elements, however, and if these elements are missing, problems will eventually emerge. In this case, a talented and high achieving athlete was rendered unable to train or compete for an extended period due to a long history of uncorrected motor control problems. Like so many other athletes, he benefited from the basic movements provided in Phase 1, and was able to progress through to Phase 4 by building his stability in a systematic manner.

Chapter 6: Building Fluent Movement
Phase 2: Integration

Central Longitudinal Axis (CLA) Control
Integrating the Trunk With the Upper Zone
Lower Body-Trunk Integration
Balance
Mobility

Having activated your key stabilisers, you need to coordinate your control zones to work effectively together. Features of this phase are:

1 The stabilising of one body part against the movement of another.

2 A higher level of challenge to CLA stability.

3 Control of body weight against gravity.

Remember your basic guidelines:

* Balloon posture.
* Relaxed face and jaw.
* Listening feet.
* Normal breathing.
* A performance objective of effortless control.

As mentioned in Chapter 5, the quality of each movement is the most important factor to consider. Once your system fatigues, it may be impossible to continue to perform an exercise correctly. Although a guide to the number of repetitions and sets is given for the exercises, you may need to adapt these to your ability. It is more productive to perform two sets of five repetitions and perform each one perfectly, than to perform ten repetitions with poor form. Unless otherwise specified, two sets of ten repetitions will be sufficient for each exercise.

If you decide to perform two sets of an exercise, use the break between the sets to perform a different exercise which uses different muscle groups. For example, a set of Over the Top which addresses anterior chain muscles can be alternated with a Suspension Bridge which addresses posterior chain muscles.

Central Longitudinal Axis (CLA) Control

Single Leg Bounce

This exercise has been used for many sports to train symmetry of weight distribution over each leg. It quickly exposes trunk instability and highlights control preferences between sides of the pelvis. This is equally important to correct whether your sport requires you to stand or sit. Details on ball size are provided in Chapter 5.

Sit on a ball with your feet and knees a little closer than hip-width apart and find the position where your weight is going straight through your sitting bones. Take both arms above your head, feeling the stomach draw inwards in response to the movement. Now move one foot forward until it lifts off the floor, keeping your weight evenly distributed across both sides of your pelvis.

Begin bouncing, making sure that you are landing directly onto your sitting bones. Your task is to maintain a constant neutral pelvic position as you bounce.

Reps	5 each side

What would a poor performance look like?

Your pelvis creeps forward on the ball so that your spine slumps.

Your pelvis moves sideways in the direction of the lifted leg.

Dynamic Control Progression for Seated Sports

Rowers, paddlers and riders need both stability and controlled mobility around their lumbo-pelvic areas. The stable Single Leg Bounce as illustrated above is extremely important for balance and symmetry but to further develop controlled mobility the following "displace and recover" exercise can be added.

Step 1

Before attempting this exercise, make sure that you are able to perform the pelvic side tilts as illustrated in Chapter 4. This ensures that you have the available range to work with.

Step 2

Begin a basic seated bounce with your arms vertical, and then tilt your pelvis for one bounce and recover to the centre for one bounce before tilting the pelvis the other way and recovering back to the centre.

Step 3

Now you can progress to the single leg version, aiming for consistent control.

Integration of the Upper Control Zone With the Trunk

1.0: Over the Top (OTT)

OTT is a key exercise for a number of reasons. It trains the shoulder and trunk as a functional partnership, and as it requires load bearing through the arms, helps to stimulate rotator cuff activity. As a trunk exercise, OTT trains stability in a lengthened trunk position, which reinforces the central axis.

Kneel behind the ball with your hands on it. Roll over the ball, walking with your hands on the floor until your thighs rest on the ball. Find your balloon posture by lengthening the back of your neck and allowing your lower abdominals to move up into the Greyhound position. Your head should be level with your spine, looking straight down at floor with the back of the neck long.

 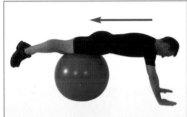 

Tip

Some people find it effective to point their toes and press them away from the crown of the head. This will often trigger an automatic response from the abdominals. Pull your body forward over your hands keeping this straight body line. Now push back the other way, making sure the back does not sag downwards. Repeat the forward and backward movement maintaining your position.

What would a poor performance look like?

- Your spine sags towards the floor, compressing your vertebrae. Focus on lengthening your spine by pressing the top of your head away from your tailbone. This helps you to draw your lower abdominals up with low effort to support the neutral spinal position.

- Your trunk bends as you pull forward. Focus on the movement being generated by your arms as you maintain a straight trunk instead of using hip flexors and superficial abdominals.

- Starting with the ball too far down your legs will make you use your hip flexors and superficial abdominals to maintain the spine's position against gravity. Start with the ball under your thigh.

- Your shoulders collapse or move towards your ears. Maintain your neutral head position, lengthen the back of your neck and lift your chest a little so that you feel stronger in your shoulders.

OTT Progressions

Once OTT is established, the following variations can be mixed into the set to achieve slightly different effects.

1.1: OTT Circles: Altering the Control Plane

 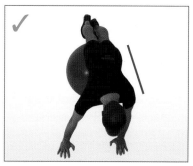 

Set up as for OTT 1.0. Keeping your body absolutely straight, move your trunk in a circle over your hands. Do not allow the pelvis and trunk to move out of line.

1.2: OTT Press-ups: Increased Upper Zone Control: Moving the Upper Limbs on a Stable Trunk

Set up as for OTT 1.0. Using the ball as a fulcrum, bend your elbows and tip your trunk downwards. As your head moves downwards, your feet will move upwards. Press straight up to the start position.

1.3: OTT Squat Thrust: Hip Mobility and Trunk Proprioception: Moving the Lower Limbs on a Stable Trunk

Set up as for OTT 1.0. Push backward, but as you pull forward, draw your stomach into your spine and bring your knees under your body. Take your legs back down to the start position.

The most important part of this exercise is the return to the start position. If your body awareness around your trunk area is not good, you will either stop short of the neutral start position with your hips slightly bent, or you will move past the neutral start position by relaxing your abdominals and letting your spine sag. As you come down, think about stretching the top of your head away from your feet so that you generate the right amount of trunk tension to control the movement.

 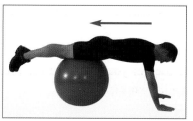 

1.4: OTT Twisting Squat Thrust: Increasing Lumbo-pelvic Control Through Rotation and Flexion

 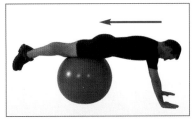 

Set up as for OTT 1.0. Push back first, but as you move forward bring your knees towards one shoulder. Return to the start position and repeat to the opposite side.

1.5: OTT Single Leg Squat Thrust: Increased Hip Control and Rotational Trunk Control

Set up as for OTT 1.0 and perform a normal straight squat thrust. On your next repetition, press back as you normally would but as you come forward use only one leg, allowing the other to straighten behind you. The supporting knee should come through straight in line with the hip joint. Do not let it drift towards your midline. This would indicate either inadequate trunk control or poor hip control.

1.6: OTT Scissors: Maintaining the Axis With Pelvic Rotation

Set up as for OTT 1.0. Press your right thigh down into the ball and pass it under your left thigh so that your pelvis turns to the left. Slowly reverse the movement and repeat it to the other side.

Upper Zone Stabiliser

This exercise was originally developed as part of the rehabilitation of an Olympic weight lifter. It has since been used as a training exercise for a variety of athletes who have high upper limb demands in their sport. It is interesting to note that an untrained person with normal upper limb to trunk integration would find this exercise relatively simple but an elite athlete with poor integration and well-developed compensatory strategies would struggle with it. The correlation between shoulder pain and poor integration is high.

Kneel on a chair with your hands on the ball. Position your knees under your hips and your hands under shoulders. Stay long through the back of your neck. Keep your weight through your hands and move the ball in small circles and back into the centre again. You should feel your abdominals contracting in response to the ball's movement.

What would a poor performance look like?

* Reducing the load on your arms by shifting your weight backward.
* Moving your shoulders towards your ears.
* Collapsing your chest so that your scapulae wing off your rib cage.

Perform 4 x 60 seconds sets.

○ Pull Backs

So far we have addressed integration of the upper and trunk zones in pushing motions. This exercise introduces integration for pulling motions.

Stand in balloon posture and soften your hips and knees. Your stretch band should be attached to a fixed point in front of you at the same height as your elbow. Grasp the stretch band with both hands and make sure you start with light tension on it. With relaxed shoulders and a long spine, pull the stretch band towards you with one hand, keeping your wrist straight as you pull. Allow your chest to broaden as you pull. Slowly release your arm forward and pull back with the other hand. If you are doing this correctly, you will feel your abdominals working to keep your trunk in alignment.

Progression

Perform the pull back in a split stance with one foot in front of the other.

Perform the pull back on single leg with the knee slightly bent. This movement can be performed using pulleys as an alternative.

Press-ups

Once you have achieved a controlled Wall Press, higher loads can be introduced by altering the body angle. The OTT press-up is a good bridge between the Wall Press and a press-up off the floor, as it assists you in keeping your trunk controlled. Once you can perform this exercise without difficulty, you can progress to the following exercises.

Press-ups off the floor are good general exercises which can be done anywhere. However, it is easy to do them poorly when you don't have basic trunk and scapula stability. Focus on maintaining a long neck and trunk throughout the movement.

Level 1

Take up a position on hands and knees and walk your hands out until your body forms a straight line from your knees through to your ears. Lengthen from the back of your neck down to the base of your spine and press your chest slightly away from the floor.

Keeping your trunk alignment controlled by drawing your lower belly upwards, bend your elbows and lower your chest to the floor.

Common errors

Bending your hips.

Dropping your head or tightening the back of your neck. Letting your lower back sag forward.

Level 2

Take up a plank position with your hands on a bench. Lengthen through the back of your neck, straighten your hips and draw your lower belly up to your spine.

Lift your chest a little by pressing the bench away from you. Bend your elbows and move your chest towards the bench without losing your trunk alignment. Keep the back of your neck long and in line with the rest of your body.

Level 3

For practical purposes, this level is listed here as a progression; however in terms of its actual level it would be categorised as a Phase 3 exercise. Lie on your stomach with your hands placed at shoulder level. A wide hand placement will target your chest muscles more, and a narrow hand placement will target your triceps more. Straighten your knees so that they lift off the ground and lengthen the back of your neck.

Lift your lower belly up towards your spine and press up off the floor so that your trunk hovers in a straight line just off the floor. Continue to press up until your elbows are straight. You should have a straight line from your ear through your shoulder, hip and knee to your ankle.

Lower yourself to hover just above the ground and repeat.

Lower Body-Trunk Integration

Lunge

The lunge is a fundamental movement for developing the lower body-trunk relationship. It is often included in training programmes and is commonly performed without adequate accuracy. As with any element of a strength and conditioning programme, you are not only aiming to strengthen a muscle but to strengthen a total pattern. There is no point in performing this exercise for repetitions and sets if the basic form is not established. You will not reap the benefits of the exercise.

When assessed carefully, fundamental control faults can be observed in athletes of all levels, even when they perform regular lunges in their routines. Depending upon their sport, these faults correlate with poor force generation, poor foot placement in running, injury, lack of symmetry and dynamic balance problems.

The listening foot, central axis control and GMax-GMed activation established in Phase 1 are necessary to perform an effective lunge. It may be necessary to start below the level of the basic lunge as outlined in the testing section in order to establish the correct pattern. Some athletes particularly struggle to generate GMax activity once the muscle moves out of inner range, especially if the muscle is working eccentrically, i.e. lengthening as it works. Decreasing the loading on the leg with the pre-lunge options below can help them to learn a correct pattern.

Pre-lunge Options

Some athletes are unable to perform even a basic static lunge correctly. If this is the case, they can develop better control through these pre-lunge options.

The Supported Lunge

Stand with a Swiss Ball supporting your lower back against a wall. Move one foot forward and the other back, with the back knee slightly bent and the heel off the ground. Make sure your pelvis is level and that your front knee remains straight in line with your hip and ankle.

As with the wall squat, you are aiming to take your sitting bones straight towards the floor by bending your hip and knee, stopping when your knee angle is 90 degrees. Your knee should not move past your ankle. If it does, start with your foot slightly further forward. Focus on maintaining tension in your GMax as you move.

What would a poor performance look like?
- Rolling your pelvis under the ball so that the sitting bones move backward instead of straight down.
- Failing to bend your hip sufficiently, so your hips move forward compared to your shoulders.

The Supported Single Leg Squat

Logically it would seem that this exercise is more advanced than the basic lunge; however athletes who are struggling to control the basic lunge have often mastered this exercise first.

Stand with one foot behind you resting on a chair, and take a hop forward with your supporting leg. Ensure that as you bend your front knee it maintains its alignment with your ankle and hip, that your sitting bones are moving straight to the floor and that your supporting hip does not creep sideways.

If your knee moves forward past your ankle, you either need to hop further forward, or focus more on a downward movement of your pelvis rather than a forward movement.

Basic Static Lunge

Stand with one foot in front of the other, hip-width apart. Raise your back heel. Put your arms straight out to the side. Keeping a vertical trunk, take your body straight to the floor.

Note: Your body weight should not be moving forward, so your knee will not end up in front of your ankle.

It may be helpful to imagine having a car headlight on the front of each hip. Keep your headlights level and facing straight forward.

Progression
Adding a variety of stimuli can improve control far more than simply repeating the same movement. Manipulating the influence of the eyes, inner ear and sensory systems and learning to control one body part while another moves, develop more transferable balance and stability.

Variations
- You can decrease your dependence on vision for balance and increase the role of sensory feedback from your body by performing the lunge with your eyes closed.
- You can increase the complexity of the lunge by adding another plane of movement to control, as follows:

Rotational Transverse Plane

Hold a light medicine ball or weight in your hands in the static lunge position, left leg forward. As you lower yourself to the floor, move the ball to one side by turning your shoulders. Keep your head looking straight ahead and keep your pelvis facing straight ahead. Don't let the knee move out of line.

- You can challenge your balance systems further by performing a rotational lunge and allowing your head and neck to turn with your shoulders as you move the ball across your body. Your pelvis and knee should remain straight.

Coronal Plane

Start with the medicine ball above your head. As you move down into your lunge, take the ball over your head to one side.

Start by keeping your trunk upright and simply moving the ball across, and as you become more comfortable, you can start to gently curve your upper spine sideways with the ball. Do not allow your hips to move in the opposite direction to the ball.

Stretch Band Lunge

A partner will loop a length of stretch band around your chest and stand to the side of you. As you perform your lunge, the partner will gently pull the band, and you must try to maintain your trunk in an upright position against this resistance. Your partner can change positions around you to vary the direction of resistance.

You can improve your trunk stability reactions by increasing your control of sudden changes in resistance. To achieve this, you will repeat the exercise outlined above with your partner increasing and decreasing the resistance through the band at random intervals.

Unstable surface

You can challenge your balance and stability by making your support surface unstable. This instability causes you to wobble, which in turn stimulates you to speed up your control responses in order to maintain your balance.

Place a wobble cushion under your front foot. Make sure that you keep your weight on the front foot as you perform the static lunge. It is tempting to shift your weight to the back foot. If your basic lunge is secure, you may choose to progress by moving onto the dynamic lunge.

Dynamic Lunge

Start with your feet together and your arms straight above your head. Having your arms above your head accentuates the trunk control demands of this exercise. It may be useful to hold a light pole to help you to monitor yourself.

Step forward into the lunge, maintaining a neutral spine, and knee/pelvic alignment. Your spine should not collapse either forward or backward.

Using your arms and trunk to push backward instead of using your legs. The alignment from your shoulders to your hip should stay vertical throughout the entire movement.

What would a poor performance look like?
- Sagging your back into a deeper curve as you move forward. This loss of your CLA puts your spine in a weak position.

Push strongly off the front foot to come back to the start position.

Collapsing forward with your arms and trunk.

Tipping your trunk to the side as you step forward. This can be due to pelvic or trunk stability problems. To keep your trunk upright and symmetrical, perform the lunge holding a light pole above your head with straight arms throughout the movement. Focus on keeping the pole level.

Variations
- Perform the dynamic lunge with your eyes closed to decrease your dependence on vision to keep your balance.
- Add a plane of movement. This can be performed in two ways for rotation.

Rotational Control

Method 1: Hold a light pole above your head with straight arms. As you step forward onto your left foot, turn the pole and your head to the left. Reverse the movement to come back to the start position.

Method 2: Hold a light medicine ball or weight in your hands. As you step forward onto your right foot, take the ball to the right. Keep your head looking straight ahead and keep your pelvis facing straight ahead. Don't let the knee move out of line.

Coronal Plane Control

Start with the pole first to learn the pattern and then use a medicine ball above your head. As you step forward, move the ball across to one side, making sure it does not pull your pelvis out of line.

As with the static lunge you can, (a) challenge your system further by turning your head as you perform a rotational dynamic lunge, (b) withstand external resistance applied by a training partner through a stretch band around your chest, and (c) maintain your control as your partner increases and decreases the resistance through the band at random intervals.

Control of increased surface instability
Stepping forward onto a wobble cushion may not be completely safe, as cushions tend to slide easily on the floor. However, if you have access to a Bosu unit; place it against a wall (ideally a mirrored wall) and lunge onto its surface. Aim to maintain your alignment for each repetition.

Step-ups

The step-up teaches you to control forces between your foot and your hip, and lays the foundations for strong propulsive action. This is essential for anyone who has to produce forces directed through one side at a time, e.g. running, jumping, Nordic skiing, and cycling.

Start with your foot on a low step. Put your hands on your hips and make sure that they are level. You may have to actively relax the hip on the working side to let it drop level with the other side. Press down into the step, feeling that an increase in pressure through the foot can be contained between the step and your hip as if it is a closed system. If you lose control of the pressure, your hip will move upwards or backwards, or your knee will move inwards.

Once you have felt this, with your trunk upright continue through the movement as if someone is picking you up from your tailbone until you are standing on the step with your hip and knee straight. Be aware of GMax squeezing your hip forward and up. GMax must actively straighten the hip for this exercise to be effective. If you tip your trunk forward, GMax does not have to activate, so keep your trunk upright.

Keeping your hips level, control the movement all the way back down.

The 'down' phase is as important as the up phase, as it trains *eccentric* control. You will feel your quadriceps contract easily, but you may have to feel the muscle of your GMax with your hand to make sure it is contributing to the movement. As you master this movement, you can increase the height of the step until it is the height of a normal weights bench. Then increase your speed to make the movement more explosive.

What would a poor performance look like?

| Trunk tipping forward. This enables you to avoid using GMax. | Knee straightening before the hip. This indicates an overdependence upon hamstrings. | The pelvis is not level throughout the movement. This flags a gluteal insufficiency. | The knee falls inwards. This is indicative of poor gluteal control of the femur. |

Space Invaders

This is a great exercise for building hip abductor strength and endurance. You should feel it most in GMed on the sides of your pelvis.

Tie a length of firm stretch band into a small loop and step into it. When starting this exercise you can place the loop just above your knees. As you become stronger, you can place the loop above your ankles. Stay upright with your hips and knees bent. Keeping your central axis vertical, step to the side. Slowly bring the other foot across, clearing the floor.

> Repeat x 10 in one direction and then x 10 in the opposite direction.
> Perform three sets in each direction.

What would a poor performance look like?

- Tipping the trunk sideways away from the direction of movement. This enables you to avoid using your GMed. You will not benefit from this exercise if you let your trunk tip. To avoid this problem, watch that your head and shoulders remain level throughout the movement.

- Shifting your hips backward. This changes the muscle group that produces the movement. Make sure that you keep your hips lined up under your shoulders.

- Allowing your knees to buckle inwards. Keep your knees in line with your hips and ankles.

Suspension Bridge

You must first establish a balance between the GMax and back extensor muscle groups before challenging the trunk in this exercise. Usually people concentrate so hard on keeping their hips up that they overuse their backs, which is not a useful pattern. If you need to start with your pelvis quite tilted in order to reduce your back's contribution, don't worry. Once your brain works out the new extension pattern against gravity, you will be able to move back into a more neutral spinal position. There is no point in performing the exercise in a neutral position if the pattern to maintain it is poor.

Start by sitting on a Swiss Ball. Keeping your lower belly in and maintaining a neutral head position, walk out with your feet until your head and shoulders are resting on the ball. Make sure your feet are directly underneath your knees, and that your hips, knees and ankles are in line.

Now feel the muscles in your lower back. If you have large ridges of tight muscle either side of your spine, it is likely that you are overusing your back muscles and under using your GMax. To rectify this, place your hands on your pelvis with your thumbs up and fingers down. Drop your hips slightly, and turn your pelvis back towards you as if it was a large wheel. Relax and then repeat this motion until you can feel your GMax creating the movement. Feel your back muscles again: the ridges should feel less

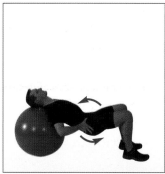

prominent. You are not trying to eliminate your back muscles altogether, but to create a balance between the two muscle groups. Your GMax should be doing most of the work, however.

Once you have achieved this basic position, there is a range of variations that can be included, each with a slightly different action.

Coordinating Foot Movements With Pelvic Stability

Move into the basic Suspension Bridge. Check your back muscles and position your pelvis to maximise your GMax activation. Lift your left heel and your right forefoot. Slowly switch your foot position so that you are performing alternate heel and toe raises. Maintain your hip position by squeezing your GMax.

Perform six alternating foot and heel lifts to form a set and then walk back up the ball to a seated position. Then walk back out into the Bridge position and repeat the set before trying another variation.

Pullover: Integrating the Arms With the Trunk and Pelvis

Move into the basic Suspension Bridge position with a light weight in your hands. Press the weight upwards and then slowly take it over your head, allowing your body to lengthen with your abdominals drawing in. Maintain your neutral trunk position and pull the weight back up to the starting position.

Adaptation: Take the weight over in a slightly diagonal direction, from one hip over to the opposite shoulder.

What would a poor performance look like?
* The most common error is to arch your back in response to the weight.

Sway

This extremely useful exercise teaches you to maintain your trunk alignment in the coronal plane and triggers GMax and GMed to accept control of the pelvis as you transfer your weight.

Move into the basic Suspension Bridge position. Now move your feet further apart so that you have a wide base. Take your arms straight out to the side.

Keeping your armpit and hip in line, move your body over the ball to one side. Pause for a count of three and return to the centre. Move to the other side.

What would a poor performance look like?
- Moving your chest and your pelvis separately. You must keep your armpit and hip in line to gain the benefit from the exercise.

Titanic

Titanic coordinates the relationship between back extensors and GMax, creating a sense of secure control around the lower back and pelvic area.

With your feet against the wall, place a ball under your pelvis. Allow yourself to bend forward over the ball with hips and knees bent.

Press up with your hands until your elbows are straight. Your shoulders will remain at this height. Make sure that your nose is facing the floor so that your head and neck are in neutral. Keeping your heels on the wall, press the crown of your head as far from your heels as you can. The movement is not *up*, but *out*.

This will straighten your hips and knees. Notice that this movement has pressed the front of your hips firmly forward into the ball, as if you were going to squash something between your hip and the ball.

Once you have this position, your back muscles should feel firm but not strained. Your GMax is responsible for keeping your hips in position.

Now stretch one arm forward, feeling your TrA pull upwards. Bring it back down and reach out with the other arm. This should feel the same on both sides.

> Five repetitions on each side would make a set. Perform two sets.
> To progress, hold both arms in front of you and count to 10.

● Floor Bridge

The Floor Bridge coordinates GMax with your back extensors to balance out your posterior chain and increases trunk control.

Lie on your back with a Swiss Ball under your legs. Keep your arms on the floor and make sure that the ball is as close to you as it can be. Press forward and down with your thighs so that you smoothly roll your hips up off the floor. The ball will roll slightly out away from you until

your hips and knees are straight. Relax your ribs slightly towards the floor to take any strain off your lower back muscles. Count to 10 and return to the floor.

This instruction contrasts with the usual method for performing this exercise, which is to lift your pelvis off the floor. If you try to forcefully lift your pelvis off the floor, you will feel your back muscles and hamstrings working hard. This is not the purpose of the exercise. You are trying to coordinate a better balance between your back muscles and GMax. For most people this means decreasing the amount of superficial back muscle used and increasing the amount of GMax.

To feel the difference, perform the exercise as a rolling action as first described. Feel your back muscles and GMax. Return to the start position. Now try to lift your pelvis strongly off the floor. Feel your back muscles and GMax. You will most likely find that the lifting technique uses a great deal more back muscle than the rolling technique, and this is not the pattern you are trying to achieve.

To progress the Floor Bridge, start with your arms up to the ceiling. Move into the Bridge position, and keep your trunk straight as you move one arm out to the side. Bring it back up and move the other arm. Different directions of arm movement will challenge your balance and stability. Move one arm over your head and bring it back up. Move an arm across your body starting from the opposite hip and crossing over and above your head. Add a small weight in one hand to challenge your control with an unbalanced load.

Balance

Wobble Cushion Steps

Stand on your left leg on the wobble cushion. Step forward into a partial lunge with the right leg, and then push yourself back to the start position on your left leg. The working leg is the one on the wobble cushion. Focus on quickly regaining stability and balance as you transfer your weight. Repeat this movement at different angles, adding a step to the side, backward, or diagonally.

● Compass Balance

Stand on one leg. Imagine that you are standing on a compass, with north in front of you and south behind you. Bending at the hip and knee and keeping your knee in line with your hip and ankle, bend to touch the floor with your hand in the north position, and stand up again. Try to keep your chest up as you bend at the hip and knee. Using the same hand, touch the floor at east, west and south, standing up between each movement. You should feel your GMax working to help you control your hip and thigh as you perform this exercise.

Standing Leg Swing Balance

Perform the standing leg swing functional mobility exercise from Phase 1, but this time as you swing your leg forward, move up onto your toe and keep your balance for a count of two. Make sure that your body remains straight, as it is easy to let your back sag in this position.

As you swing your leg back, let your heel come back to the floor.

Global Stability Plus Balance

Single Leg Balance With Medicine Ball Movements

Holding a medicine ball in both hands, stand on one leg with your knee and hip slightly bent. Move the medicine ball in the following variations:

1. Hold the ball straight above your head and move it in circles.

2. Start with the ball above your head. Move the ball through the shape indicated in red.

3. Keep your pelvis facing forward and rotate your upper body, moving the ball to the side.

195

Lift your knee a little higher and take it across your body so that your pelvis and chest rotate in opposite directions.

Bend your hip and knee and move the ball down to one side, then straighten your knee and push the ball up to the opposite side.

Balance Board Squats

Stand with your feet wide apart on a balance board. Keeping your trunk upright, sit down into your hips. Keep some tension in your GMax throughout the whole movement. Straighten back up again using your GMax to support the movement.

Mobility

Just as we are learning to develop stability relationships between different parts of the body to reflect the way the body normally functions, we can also develop mobility relationships. The following exercises lengthen chains of muscle rather than single muscles to integrate balance and stability with mobility. They are a challenging but enjoyable part of a cool-down.

Triangle Pose

Where should I feel it?

- Depending upon where you are most restricted, you may feel the stretch down the side of your trunk, or down the inner thigh of your front leg.

Step 1: Stand with your feet facing forward and wide apart. Draw yourself up into the balloon posture, which will lengthen your neck and help you to align your pelvis under your shoulders. Turn your right foot 90 degrees outwards. Turn your left foot slightly inwards. Your right heel should be in line with the arch of your left foot. Your pelvis and chest will face forward throughout the movement. Breathe in and raise both arms out to your sides with your palms down.

Step 2: Keep your chest open and as you breathe out, reach as far as you can to the right. Once you have reached your limit, tip your trunk sideways so that your left hand points to the ceiling and your right hand slides down the inside of your front leg. Keep lengthening through the top of your head. Breathe normally for 5 to 8 breaths. Inhale and come back up to the Step 1 position.

When you first try this pose, your hips may try to move backward as you tip your trunk. Try to keep them in line with the rest of your body. If your hips move backwards, your chest will tend to rotate towards the floor. Focus on the chest spiralling upwards.

Extended Warrior Pose

Where should I feel it?
- You will be stretching all the way from the shoulder to the hip, and you may also feel a pull in your inner thighs.

Step 1: Stand with your feet facing forward and wide apart. Draw yourself up into the balloon posture, which will lengthen your neck and help you to align your pelvis under your shoulders. Turn your right foot 90 degrees outwards. Turn your left foot slightly inwards. Your right heel should be in line with arch of your left foot. Breathe in and raise your arms out to your sides with your palms facing downwards.

Step 2: Breathe out and bend your front knee to 90 degrees, making sure that your knee does not fall inwards. Tip your trunk sideways, resting your right arm on your front leg and stretching your left arm over your head. Focus on your chest spiralling upwards and keep your hips forward to maintain your body alignment. Your left arm should remain level with your left ear.

Lengthen from your left fingertips to the outside of your left foot. Breathe normally for 5 to 8 breaths. The next step is a separate pose; however it is easily combined with the Extended Warrior.

Step 3: Rest your left forearm behind your back and slide your right arm down past the inside of your right knee. Press your left shoulder back and spiral your chest upwards. Use counter pressure through your right arm to prevent your right knee from falling inwards. This will feel like you are opening the right hip. Inhale and move back to the Step 1 position.

● Revolving Lunge

Where should I feel it?

* On your back leg you will feel the stretch on the front of the thigh, and you will feel the twist in your trunk.

Step 1: Step forward with your right foot and position yourself in a wide lunge with your front knee at 90 degrees. Both feet will point forward. Straighten your back knee and stretch both arms upwards.

Step 2: Turn your trunk to the right. Reach your right hand to the ceiling and your left hand to the floor, lengthening your body from the top of your head to your back heel. Breathe normally for 5 to 8 breaths. Breathe in and return to the Step 1 position.

● Hip and Spine Twist

Where should I feel it?

* This position will strongly stretch across the buttocks as well as mobilising your trunk.

● Mobilising the Hip

Step 1: Sit upright with your knees bent, ankles crossed and knees falling out to the side. Lift your left leg and cross it over your right leg so that the sole of the left foot is on the floor to the right of the right leg.

Step 2: Wrap your arms around your left knee and draw your spine and your leg together so that your spine lengthens all the way from the floor. Stay in this position for several breaths and then relax.

Mobilising the Spine

Step 1: Sit upright with your right leg straight. Lift your left leg and cross it over your right leg so that the sole of the left foot is on the floor to the right of the right leg.

Step 2: Lengthen your spine from the floor and turn your chest to the left, bringing your right arm to the outside of the left thigh. Bend your right elbow and point your hand to the ceiling. Use this arm to help you to keep lengthening and turning your chest.

Lengthening the Hip and Spinal Connection

Step 1: Sit upright with your knees bent, ankles crossed and knees falling out to the side. Lift your left leg and cross it over your right leg so that the sole of the left foot is on the floor to the right of the right leg.

Step 2: Lengthen your spine from the floor, and turn your chest to the left, bringing your right arm to the outside of the left thigh. Bend your right elbow and point your hand to the ceiling. Use this arm to help you to keep lengthening and turning your chest.

199

Chapter 7: Building Fluent Movement
Phase 3: Global Coordination

Global Coordination
Pulleys
Swiss Ball Exercises
Walking Drill
Handstands
Combination Stability / Mobility / Balance Sequences

Now that we have activated the balance and stability mechanisms and integrated the upper and lower control zones with the trunk, we can consolidate these skills with more global, whole body movements. Phase 3 exercises introduce one or more of the following features:

1 Whole body movement.

2 Dynamic rotational control.

3 Multidirectional movement.

4 Increased loading.

5 Moving between high and low body positions.

6 Pushing and pulling.

Remember your basic guidelines:

- Balloon posture.
- Neutral trunk is maintained with your lower abdominals drawing in.
- Pelvic and knee alignment controlled by your gluteal group.
- Normal breathing.
- Relaxed face and jaw.
- Performance objective of effortless control.

The cue for your hips and knees is now to imagine them as coiled springs, softly bending smoothly and elastically with the movements. As the loading starts to rise in the exercises, it is important to remember to have a relaxed face throughout the movements.

Global Coordination

Medicine Ball Clean

The purpose here is to learn kinetic chain coordination in the lower limb, trunk and upper limbs and also to develop a strong pattern for hip extension on a neutral trunk. Whether you have to power yourself forward or upwards, this pattern is essential. If you are planning on introducing power cleans into a training programme, this is an ideal movement to train the correct pattern.

Start with a medicine ball in your hands and your feet apart. Keeping your head and chest upright, squat down with your feet flat, using your GMax to control your hip angle. Quickly bring the medicine ball up your body until you are standing straight with your arms stretched upwards and the ball above your head.

When your arms are at full stretch, you should feel that your lower abdominals have scooped into the Greyhound position, and your GMax is squeezing your hip straight. This combination should make you feel very secure around your lower back area.

What would a poor performance look like?
- Moving the ball upwards with straight arms. This tends to stimulate you to bend your spine backwards instead of lengthening it upwards in neutral. Instead, focus on drawing the medicine ball up your body.
- Swinging your hips forward using momentum instead of using your GMax to straighten your hips. The movement should be upwards for your whole body, so don't focus on pushing your hips forward, as this increases your spinal back bending and doesn't target GMax.

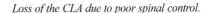

Loss of the CLA due to poor spinal control.

Variation

Once you have established this pattern it can be combined with a single leg drive. The exercise starts as above, but this time drive up onto one leg instead of two. Keep your balance for a moment and return to the start position. A repetition of this exercise would comprise one double leg clean, one on the left leg, and one on the right leg. You would then repeat this ten times to complete the set.

Progression of variation: greater explosiveness and balance

You will perform the single leg drive version of the medicine ball clean, but this time allow the drive to lift you off the ground to land on one leg. Maintain your balance for a moment before repeating onto the other side. To really challenge yourself, land only on your toes and keep your balance.

Medicine Ball Sweep

This exercise trains the same mechanisms as above but now adds extra lateral pelvic control.

Start with your feet together and a medicine ball in your hands. Take a step sideways to the left into a squat and move the ball down towards your left foot, keeping your head and chest up. Push back up and across strongly through your legs so that you end up standing on your right leg with your arms stretched above your head. Feel the Greyhound feeling in your abdominal area and a strong hip pressing the floor away. Pause and hold this position for a moment before repeating it to the other side.

Variation

Increased balance, and lateral pelvic control.

Perform the exercise above, but as you push back up and across, focus on exploding off the ground. Land on the one leg and pause to focus your balance in perfect alignment.

What would a poor performance look like?

- Dropping the chest and head forward to avoid the muscular effort of controlling a deep hip bend. To gain the benefit of through-range GMax activation, focus on taking your "tail" to the floor in the squatting phase.

- Failing to hold a straight body line from the medicine ball down your body to your supporting foot at the end of the movement. Make sure that you

feel the weight of the ball dropping directly through your trunk to your foot: if you watch yourself in the mirror, an imaginary line from the ball to the floor should not fall either side of your foot.

Medicine Ball Spiral

Before performing this exercise, warm-up with the total body rotation movement listed in Phase 1. This will help you to rotate your pelvis over your foot smoothly and safely.

Stand with a medicine ball in your hands and your feet apart. Soften your hips and knees and lengthen your spine. Turn your body to the left, allowing your right foot to pivot and your pelvis to turn over your left foot. Reverse the motion and turn to the right.

Once this motion is established, deepen the hip and knee bend as you turn to the left and straighten your legs as you turn to the right. Your spine should maintain the same shape throughout the movement. If you can control this stage, add greater contrast with your arm movements moving the medicine ball downwards as you lower your body and sweeping it upwards as you lengthen yourself. Focus on maintaining a neutral spine throughout the movement.

Loss of Spinal Control

What would a poor performance look like?

- Dropping the chest and head forward to avoid the muscular effort of controlling a deep hip bend. To gain the benefit of through-range GMax activation, focus on taking your "tail" to the floor in the downward phase of the movement.

- Keeping the back heel fixed to the floor. Remember to release the heel as you turn.

- Allowing the spine to collapse into an arch when the arms reach upwards.

Pulleys

Pulleys offer a great deal of versatility for whole body integrated movement. The exercises can be adapted to emphasise any plane of movement and can combine high-low, left-right, push-pull and rotational motion. They involve shoulder, pelvic and trunk stability. Height adjustable pulleys are ideal, as they can be positioned appropriately for the proportions of different athletes. If you do not have access to a pulley system, the movements can be learned using stretch band at first, although it should be remembered that with elastic equipment, the resistance becomes greater at the end of the movement whereas pulleys can deliver more consist resistance throughout the movement. Do not start with high resistance. This will simply teach you how to brace yourself using excessive effort. You should select a resistance level that is challenging but allows you to remain fluid in your movement.

Straight Pulley Push

Stand with the pulley behind you set at shoulder height and the handle in your right hand. Lift your elbow so that it is level with your hand. Start with your feet together and your hips and knees slightly bent. The free hand will be stretched out in front of you. Your movement will involve the opposite arm and leg. Maintaining a neutral trunk position by drawing

your lower abdominals in, step forward with your left leg and push your right arm forward strongly. Your left arm will pull backwards. Your pelvis and knee should be aligned and your trunk central.

What would a poor pattern look like?

- Relaxing your abdominals and allowing your spine to collapse into a deeper curve. Maintain a firm trunk throughout the movement.
- Allowing your pelvis to tip sideways. Aim for a level pelvis throughout the movement.
- Allowing your knee to drift inwards. Use GMax to control your knee angle.

● Trunk Incline Pulley Push

Some sports require a neutral trunk in a forward tilted position. A sprinter driving out of the blocks or a sprint canoeist reaching forward to catch the water represent this body position. The pulley push can be adapted for this by using the same technique but the movement objective of driving the trunk out of the pelvis. This cue is helpful in preventing collapse of the trunk in this angled position.

Start with the pulley set a hole below shoulder height. As you drive forward, you are aiming for a straight line from your hand through your body to your back foot. To achieve such a position you need your TrA to be tucked up in the Greyhound position.

● Trunk Rotation Pulley Push

Start with your feet at a 45-degree angle from the pulley column. The pulley is set at shoulder height. Take the pulley in the hand closest to the column; place this hand on your chest with your elbow horizontally in line with it. Bend your hips and knees so that they feel like loaded springs.

Keeping your trunk long, light but firm, drive forward onto your front leg, turning your pelvis and pivoting your back foot so that both feet are facing in the direction of the push. Turn your chest as you move and punch through with your arm. Your focus should be in that order: legs, pelvis, chest and arm.

Control the movement back to the start position.

Pulley Pull

Set the pulley midway between hip and shoulder height. Stand in a static lunge position with your left leg and right arm forward and the pulley in your right hand. Your left arm is pulled back with the elbow bent. Without turning your hips, pull the handle straight back towards you, switching arm positions.

Progression
Perform the same movement standing only on your left leg, with the hip and knee slightly bent.

Pulley Pull Drive

Developing strong hip extension.

Start in the lunge position as above with the opposite arm stretched forward. As you pull back with your arm, drive your front hip forward and upwards using a strong GMax squeeze. Your end position is standing tall and upright over your front leg with your knee and hip straight.

Trunk Incline Pulley Pull

To integrate upper limb pulling with a lengthened trunk position.

Set the pulley at head height. Start in a static lunge position with your trunk inclined forward and both arms stretched overhead. Your body will be straight line from your fingertips to your back heel. Make sure that your knee is in line with your ankle and that you have engaged your front GMax. The pulley will be in one hand. Maintaining a straight body alignment, pull your arm straight down, feeling the connection between your arm pull and your abdominals.

Cross Body Pulls

Stand at 90 degrees to the pulley with your left shoulder closest to it and your feet slightly apart. Your hips and knees should be slightly bent. The pulley should be set as high as it can be. Take the pulley with both hands and lengthen your body to prepare for the movement.

You will pull down and across to the right side of your body. Keep your trunk feeling long throughout the movement. You will lose the benefit if you allow your body to compress as you pull down.

Variation

Once you have established this movement, start with your feet together and hips and knees straight. Lift your right knee as you pull down. Keep the front of your body long and open, resisting the temptation to overuse your superficial abdominals.

Lunge-based Variations

Standing Stretch Band Leg Drive

To develop strong propulsive movement of the body over the foot.

Start in the static lunge position with opposite arm and leg forward. A partner will have a length of stretch band around the front of your hips to provide resistance for you to push your hips into. Lengthen your trunk. The movement muscle to focus on is GMax. Use it to drive your front hip forward and up onto the stance leg, lifting the opposite knee and switching

the arm position. Hold this position for a moment and then repeat. Make sure you do not hold the position with your knee bent, as this makes it easy to balance with a combination of hamstring and quadriceps rather than using GMax.

Standing Knee Lift Drive

To coordinate strong hip flexion with stable pelvic support

A partner will loop a length of stretch band around your ankle and hold it with light tension close to the floor. Take up a static lunge position with this leg backwards.

Drive forward onto a straightened front leg and bring your back knee through to hip height. You should end up with your trunk erect with your stomach in, and your stance hip and knee straight with your GMax working. When you first start this exercise, perform one movement and pause in the knee lift position. Once you become proficient at it, repeat it at increased speed without the pause. You must make sure that your leg returns to the same spot behind you each time.

Compass Lunges

To develop multidirectional control from the pelvis to the foot, and dynamic balance for the trunk.

Stand with your feet together and imagine that you are in the centre of a compass with north in front of you. All of the movements will be performed with one leg as the moving leg no matter which direction you move in. Allow your fixed foot to pivot naturally as you introduce side and angled movement. Relax your arms. To increase the demand on your trunk stability, the sequence can be performed with your arms stretched above your head.

The North Lunge is a straightforward dynamic lunge as outlined in Phase 2.

To perform the South Lunge, take a large step backwards and drop your back knee towards the floor. Keep your trunk vertical.

To perform the East Lunge with the right leg, keep both feet facing forward and take a large step to the right side, dropping your body into a wide squat position. Keep your trunk vertical, as it easy to tip forward in this position. Focus on opening at the hips.

To perform the West Lunge with the right leg, pivot on your left foot, bring your right leg across your body and step into a normal lunge. Push strongly through your front foot and pivot on your left foot to come back to the start.

To perform the Northwest Lunge with the right leg, step diagonally forward across your body to the left, allowing your back foot to pivot.

To perform the Northeast Lunge with the right leg, step diagonally forward to the right, allowing your left heel to lift and turn with the movement. Your feet will be pointing slightly away from each other. This will keep your pelvis facing relatively forward so that your hips open.

To perform the Southeast Lunge, step diagonally backwards to the right, allowing the hips to open. Your back knee will be pointing diagonally backwards and your front knee will be pointing forward.

Variations
- Whichever leg is moving will not touch the ground in between lunges. This means that as you transfer your weight back to the start, you will be performing a single leg balance between each movement.
- Perform the entire sequence with eyes closed.
- Have a partner toss a ball in each direction so that you must react and control the lunge when slightly distracted.

Progressive Lunges

These movements are often performed in warm-ups with little attention to form. They should not be taken so lightly. If you cannot perform a basic dynamic lunge with perfect form, you cannot control progressive lunges. Poor movement habits can develop if this is not addressed. The aim is to hold your form through a series of steady, rhythmic alternating deep lunges across a space.

Perform a series of alternating progressive lunges with your arms above your head. You should be able to maintain a steady neutral trunk, which does not tip forward, backwards or sideways. Your pelvis should remain level and your knee always in line with your hip and ankle.

Rotations

Start with a medicine ball in your hands and your feet together. As you step forward with your right leg, move the ball to the right, turning your shoulders with it but keeping your head facing forward. Step straight through onto your left leg, moving the ball to the left and turning your shoulders to the left.

Figure 8s

Start with your medicine ball in your hands and your feet together. As you step forward with your right leg, loop the medicine ball down to the right and around in a circle so that as you prepare to step forward on your left foot, it crosses the centre of your body ready to loop down to the left as you step forward. The shape of one complete left and right sequence looks like a figure 8 on its side.

Trunk Inclines

As you step forward, incline your trunk so that you have a straight line from your hands to your back foot. Think about lengthening your trunk so that it feels streamlined.

Drive forward onto your front leg and pull your arms down strongly as your trunk moves vertically.

You must focus on bringing the hip forward under the trunk to achieve a

vertical line. If you focus on straightening the trunk, it is most likely that you will arch your back as you recover.

Swiss Ball Exercises

Phase 3 exercises increase global body coordination and higher global control loads. Your performance objective is still effortless control. Release as much tension as you can while maintaining your alignment, and continue to breathe normally.

Swiss Ball Pendulum

To train trunk rotation with pelvic stability.

Adopt the suspension bridge position. Your shoulders and head will be supported on the ball and your feet positioned slightly wider than hip width apart and directly under your knees.

Bring your hands together above your chest. Keeping your elbows and shoulders locked in position, turn your shoulders and arms to the right side, pushing the ball under you in the opposite direction. Keep trying to drive the right side of your pelvis up with your GMax, as it is most common to collapse this side.

Control the rotation back to the start position and perform the turn in the opposite direction.

Losing the fixed point by dropping the hips.

Swiss Ball Body Spin

To train smooth pelvic rotation with control of trunk neutral.

Step 1

Start with the ball under your hips and your feet apart against a wall. Lift your lower abdominals a little, push your shoulders up with your hands, and squeeze your hips forward into the ball. This position emphasises a balance between back muscles and GMax to maintain the trunk position.

Turn your left foot slightly outwards. Place your right hand on the floor and your left hand on your left hip. Using your right arm to help you, turn your hips to the left, allowing your feet to pivot in response to the movement. Your whole body should be facing to the left. Return to the start position and repeat the movement in the other direction.

Step 2

Start in the same position as above. Turn your left foot slightly outwards. Place your left hand on your left hip and your right hand behind your head. Drive the right side of your pelvis into the ball and slide it under your body so that your pelvis turns to the left. Allow your feet to pivot as you move. Keep your trunk straight, and control the motion back to the start position.

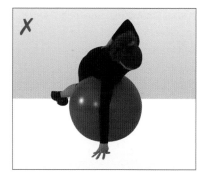 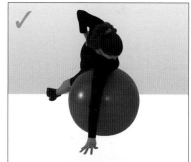

Swiss Ball Press-up

To introduce a higher load global stability challenge for the shoulder girdle and trunk.

Start in a kneeling position with your hands on the ball. Draw yourself up into a balloon posture. This alignment must be maintained no matter what angle your trunk is positioned in.

You may initially need to place the ball against a wall. Tip forward so that your weight is supported by the ball. Keeping the back of your neck long and your hips straight, bend your elbows to bring your chest towards the ball, and then straighten them.

What would a poor pattern look like?
- Dropping your head or tightening the back of your neck.
- Bending your hips.

- Letting your lower back sag towards the ball.
- Bunching your shoulders towards your ears.

All of the errors involve compressing or shortening the body. Focus on lengthening from the top of your head to your tail to achieve the position which will most effectively activate the correct muscles for the movement.

Incline Plank Knee Drive

Higher load trunk stability challenge with a smooth hip flexion pattern.

Support your body with your hands on a bench and your feet on the floor. Straighten your body by lengthening from the back of your neck to the base of your spine and drawing your lower belly up. Lift your chest slightly by pressing away with your hands to make sure that you are engaging the muscles around your scapula.

Without moving your trunk, bring one knee under your body in a straight line. Your body should remain completely still apart from this leg. Return it to the floor and repeat with the other side. Focus your awareness on feeling long, strong and light through your centre, with clean smooth leg motion.

What would an incorrect movement look like?
* Your spine should not bend as you bring your knee in, or arch as you straighten your leg back out.

The Twisted Floor Bridge

This exercise trains you to maintain a strong axis around which to rotate your pelvis.

With your arms out to the side on the floor, move up into the Floor Bridge position. Lift one leg and pass it over the other one, allowing your pelvis to turn in the direction of movement. Slowly return it to the start position. Repeat in the other direction, trying to maintain a straight trunk as you rotate.

What would an incorrect movement look like?
* If you lose control of your central longitudinal axis, your back will collapse into an arch or a side bend. Your pelvis cannot cleanly rotate around the axis. You are no longer in lumbar neutral, and no longer training the muscles that protect your spine during strong rotation such as in a kicking a football.

Walking Drill

Walking drills are commonly used by track athletes in their warm-ups, but are useful for many athletes to train symmetry, balance and stability through the supporting leg. You are aiming for perfect balance over your stance foot.

Start with both arms stretched above your head, and your feet together. Step forward, contacting the floor with your heel. Roll over the foot up onto your toe and press up, lengthening your body through to your fingertips as you draw your other knee up to waist height. Pause in perfect balance, and repeat with the other side.

What would a poor pattern look like?
- Allowing the hands to drift to one side. This indicates a body alignment problem associated with a stability issue. It causes a collapse on one side of the body, which in turn prevents the hip stabilisers from functioning properly. If you are not sure whether your hands are drifting, hold a light pole in your hands as you perform the drill. The pole should remain horizontal throughout the movement. If it tips downwards on one side, focus on pressing that side upwards as you move.

- Failing to drive up onto the toes powerfully and in balance.

- Keeping knee or hip bent. You should be working muscles to extend your joints from your feet, through your ankles, knees and hips.

Handstands

Higher Level Upper Limb Loading: the Handstand

Just as the press up is a useful body weight strengthening exercise with the arms positioned forward of the body, the handstand can be used to strengthen with the arms in an elevated position. Lower trapezius and serratus anterior are generally active if the position is performed well.

Preliminary Level

This level helps you to become accustomed to supporting yourself in an inverted position. Kneel on a bench and place both hands on the floor with your head hanging down. Press yourself away from the floor to stabilise your shoulders. Keeping one arm firm, lift the other for a count of 5 before switching sides.

Basic Level

This level demands greater trunk control, and allows you to become more comfortable supporting your body weight with your arms.

Facing away from a wall, place your hands on the floor and walk your feet up the wall. Lengthen your body and firm up your trunk as you press yourself away from the floor. Sustain the position for as long as you feel comfortable and then walk back down the wall.

Standard Level

This level requires full shoulder range and normal strength.

Facing the wall, place your hands on the floor and flick your legs up so that your heels rest on the wall. Lengthen your body and firm up your trunk as you press yourself away from the floor. Sustain the position for as long as you feel comfortable and then return to the start position.

Advanced Level

Once you have the strength to maintain a full handstand, you can introduce an inverted press up. Maintain your firm trunk position in the handstand, and start with small elbow bending and straightening movements. The amount of movement can be increased as you become stronger. Do not try to go for a large range of motion at first – bending the elbows is easy but straightening them may not be!

Combination Stability / Mobility / Balance Sequences

Aeroplane Sequence

Step forward with your left leg into a lunge.

Drive your body weight forward onto the left leg, straightening your hip and knee and drawing your right knee up.

Maintain this position and move up onto the toes of your supporting leg, keeping your balance.

Bring your heel back down, and with your hands behind your head turn left and right with your shoulders without moving your pelvis.

Then move your arms to the side and press your right knee outwards while keeping your pelvis facing forward.

Bring your knee back across your body so that your pelvis rotates but your chest is still facing forward. Bring your leg back to the front and tip your trunk forward as you press your heel out behind you. You should have a straight line from your head to your heel.

Starting with your arms out to the side, turn your chest so that your left arm is pointing to the floor and your right arm is pointing to the ceiling.

Turn your chest in the opposite direction. Recover to a straight position and in one motion, bring your trunk back to vertical with your knee held high in front of you. Return to standing with your feet together.

○ Star Sequence

Lie face down on the floor with your hands under your shoulders and your elbows tucked in. Your toes will be turned under.

Straighten your knees so that they lift off the ground and draw your lower abdominals up towards your spine.

Keeping your elbows in, press up so that your body hovers in a straight line just above the floor. Count to 5. Now press fully upwards into a plank position, keeping the back of your neck long and your hips straight. Count to 5.

Maintaining the support in your right arm, turn your body onto its side with your left arm up towards the ceiling. This is the star position. Keep your hips up and your shoulder pressed away from your ear. Do not let your hips drift backwards. Count to 5.

Lift your top leg and count to 5.

Keeping your balance, circle your top leg up and back and allow your pelvis to rotate so that your toes can touch the floor behind you. Stretch your top arm over your head so that your whole body lengthens. Count to 5.

Reverse the movements, working back from star to plank, to floor press.

Chapter 8: Building Fluent Movement
Phase 4: Dynamic Control

Medicine Ball Exercises
Upper Body Loading
Dynamic Control
Swiss Ball Exercises
Full Flexion Pattern Development
Stability Reactions
Mobility

The characteristics of Phase 4 are:

- Control of movement at increased speed.
- Control of movement when distracted.
- General global stability conditioning.

Now that you have activated the systems, integrated them with each other so that your upper and lower body connect through your trunk, and learned to control different planes of motion, these skills need to evolve from conscious focus to automatic response.

In order to do this, you will be distracted with a catching task or a speed demand to control. You don't have the same time available to prepare for each movement, and some of your focus will be diverted from yourself to your task. Now is the time that the movement and postural habits that you have learned must move from the main focus to the underpinning foundation for movement that they should be.

This is also the time to introduce general conditioning exercises for global stability and control of the trunk as it moves out of the neutral position. These higher loaded exercises require both local and global stabiliser activity.

Phase 4: Dynamic Control
Medicine Ball Exercises

Once you have established the medicine ball techniques, you can use them as intensely as you like. They are relatively low load exercises compared with weight training, so they can be used in high repetition sets.

The aim is to integrate the legs, trunk and arms. You are therefore aiming for fluid well-coordinated movements. Many athletes over-stress the muscles of their shoulders because they do not transfer the power of their legs and trunk to their arms. Others over-stress muscles around their hips or the joints of their lower backs because they use small movements which are often missed in dynamic movements. These exercises work on improving a variety of common patterns.

Side Squat Tosses

Side squat tosses encourage elastic, explosive multi-joint movement in the legs, central axis control and consistent GMax activation in both the eccentric phase (the muscle working as it lengthens) and the concentric phase (the muscle working as it shortens).

Begin standing with the medicine ball in both hands. Toss the ball up and to the side, and side skip to catch it in a deep wide squat. Absorb the motion in your hips, keeping your trunk upright. Spring back up as you toss the ball in the other direction. Repeat the side to side movement with a steady rhythm 10–15 times.

You might start with small ball tosses, but as you gain confidence, challenge yourself to toss the ball higher and wider.

What would a poor pattern look like?
* Many athletes do not use their GMax effectively, so they do not bend their hips sufficiently. They bend their hips to a certain point and then tilt their trunks forward when they are trying to lower their centre of gravity. If they do this, they overtrain their hamstring and adductor muscles, and these muscles do not provide sufficient support for the hip. To avoid this, focus on suppleness in the hips to allow you to bend smoothly. This helps you to keep your trunk upright and puts GMax in a position where it can more effectively work.

Toss and Stretch

This adaptation of the side squat toss increases the demand on your dynamic trunk control. It also requires coordination of the feet with the pelvis in response to the movement to encourage fluid, natural control.

Begin standing with the medicine ball in both hands. Toss the ball up and to the side. Side skip to catch the ball and take a further step with your outside leg into a deep side lunge. Allow the heel of your back foot to lift and pivot so that your pelvis can turn as you catch the ball and push it away from you in the direction of movement. Your spine should be neutral in shape, and you should feel a line of tensile connection between your back foot through your trunk to your hands.

Pull the ball back in to your centre and toss it into the air in the opposite direction. Side skip and step to catch and reach in the opposite direction.

Once you understand the elements of this movement, try to make it as smooth and continuous as possible. Don't use a medicine ball that is too heavy to start with, and maintain a neutral spine throughout the movement.

What would a poor pattern look like?
* This is a smooth, integrated movement from the feet to the hands. Poor performance is usually the result of a failure to release the back foot and turn the pelvis in the direction of movement. This effectively blocks the movement and causes the spine to bend and the arms to disconnect from the rest of the movement.

   Allow your lower body to turn naturally and focus on really stretching your arms and trunk "out of your pelvis".

Overhead Tosses

Overhead Tosses provide an increased trunk control challenge, and integrate upper body action on a stable trunk and pelvis. It is relevant for any athlete involved in over arm activities, whether it is a footballer taking a throw in or a volleyballer serving.

Stand with your feet together in front of a wall with a medicine ball in your hands. Soften at your hips and knees.

The biggest challenge with this exercise is maintaining a neutral trunk. As you take the ball over your head, make sure that your back doesn't bend backwards with it. You should feel your lower abdominals drawing in to support your spine as you raise the ball.

Step forward with one foot and firmly toss the ball against the wall. Focus on "standing up" to the movement. As you release the ball, your front hip should stay forward and the trunk will move past it as you release the ball.

What would a poor pattern look like?

Many athletes lose the benefit of the exercise by allowing the hips to move backwards as their trunks move forward. They are effectively collapsing their trunk, losing their fixed point for force production and decreasing their power. Stand up tall as you throw and keep a forward focus for your whole body.

Variation

*   To add diagonal motion, start with the medicine ball over your left shoulder and toss it firmly at the wall when you step through with your right foot. Switch to the opposite diagonal.

Quick Rotations

Quick Rotations require a strong central axis, a stable pelvis and an accurate rotation motion. Your challenge is to use your local stabilisers to maintain an upright trunk while your oblique abdominals generate force.

Holding a medicine ball, stand side on to a wall with feet apart and hips and knees softly bent. Your trunk position should be relaxed and upright. Keeping your pelvis still, move your medicine ball away from the wall, allowing your shoulders to turn and your trunk to "wind up". Quickly rotate your trunk back towards the wall and release the ball.

Catch the ball as it rebounds and follow its momentum back into rotation away from the wall. Make sure that your trunk doesn't tilt forward. Your pelvis will remain in a consistent position throughout the movement. Quick Rotations can also be performed in a static lunge position.

What would a poor pattern look like?

- Poor technique will show up as a tendency to allow the rotation to pull the spine into forward or backward bending. Aim to keep your trunk upright and try to keep the ball's movement parallel with the floor.

Follow Through Rotations

This exercise integrates pelvic rotation and weight transference into the rotational movement.

Holding a medicine ball, stand side on to a wall with feet apart and hips and knees softly bent. Your trunk position should be relaxed and upright.

Swing the medicine ball away from the wall, allowing your weight to transfer onto your back leg and your pelvis to turn slightly away from the wall.

As you swing the ball through strongly, allow your weight to transfer onto your front foot and your pelvis to turn towards the wall. As you catch the ball, allow yourself to rotate away from the wall again.

What would a poor pattern look like?

- Poor technique will show up as inadequate hip bending and a tendency to allow the rotation to pull the spine into forward or backward bending. Aim to keep your trunk upright and try to keep the ball's movement parallel with the floor.

Stepping Rotations

Having worked on isolated trunk rotation control and pelvic integration, the lower body can be added to complete the movement chain.

Stand side on to the wall a little further away than for the previous exercise. Start with your feet together. You can vary your arm position. Arm options are:

Arms start low and rise to waist height as you rotate to release the ball.

Arms start at shoulder height with the palms facing towards the wall.

Arms are maintained at waist height throughout the movement.

Side step strongly towards the wall to initiate the throwing movement. Continue to rotate the pelvis and trunk over your front foot before releasing the ball. Make sure you release your back heel in order to let your pelvis rotate freely. One side will feel natural and the other side will not. Practice a few movements without the medicine ball to make sure the movement sequence is established before loading it.

What would a poor pattern look like?

* If you don't allow your back heel to release and turn as you move, your movement becomes blocked and you will try to throw the ball using your arm instead of using the momentum generated from your lower body and trunk. Releasing the ball should feel like a whip cracking. It should not feel like you have to use a great deal of shoulder strength.

Lunge Bounces

This exercise increases force production and focuses on integrating your arm action with your trunk and lower body. Start with your feet together and a medicine ball in your hands. As you begin to step forward into a lunge, raise the ball above your head keeping your trunk neutral. As your front foot contacts the floor, firmly throw the ball into the floor.

What would a poor pattern look like?

- Allowing your spine to arch as you take the ball over your head means that you have lost trunk control and disconnected your arms from your trunk and lower body.

Standing Quick Throws

This exercise coordinates the trunk and the upper limbs with a light plyometric stimulus.

Stand with knees and hips softly bent and lower belly drawn in to help you to maintain a neutral spine. Remember to keep the back of your neck long in the balloon position.

Take a light medicine ball at chest level and throw it at the wall with both hands. Catch and repeat rapidly. Focus on feeling your abdominals controlling your spine.

Progression

- Perform the same exercise on single leg, maintaining a firm pelvis and trunk. Keep your pelvis level and your knee in line at all times.

What would a poor pattern look like?

- Your trunk should remain upright during this movement. Some athletes try to stabilise with their back muscles instead of the abdominals by pushing their hips out behind them and deepening the curve in their spine.

Upper Body Loading

Plyometric Press-ups

Plyo Press-ups can be introduced at a variety of resistance levels.

Level 1

For young athletes and those who do not have sufficient scapular stability and upper body strength to perform full press-ups with good form, a standing Plyo Press-up can be performed to increase the speed of stabilising reactions.

First you need to be able to perform a good standing Wall Press. Then ask a partner to place a hand on your back between your scapulae. This will give the partner a marker for where to keep the hand throughout the exercise. You will perform your Wall Press but as you move back out to the start position, the partner will provide a barrier to your movement, pushing you back to the wall each time. You must keep your form regardless of the speed you select. Your trunk must remain neutral, your head and neck relaxed, your chest open and your shoulders down.

What would poor technique look like?
- The pelvis is moving separately to the chest because you have lost your trunk stability.
- Your shoulders are creeping towards your ears.

Level 2

Take up a press-up position with your hands on a bench. Lengthen through the back of your neck, straighten your hips and draw your lower belly up to your spine. Lift your chest a little by pressing your hands away from you. You must be able to perform an incline press with good form before attempting the plyo version. To do this, simply bend your elbows and move your chest towards the bench without losing your trunk alignment. Keep the back of your neck long and in line with the rest of your body. Once you can do this, increase the speed and force of the upward press so that your hands lift off the bench between repetitions. Your trunk should stay in neutral throughout the movement.

What would poor technique look like?
- Your hips are higher than your chest because they are bent.
- Your hips are sagging below the line of your body because you are not using your abdominals.
- Your shoulders are creeping up towards your ears.

Level 3

To perform the full Plyo Press-up, you should be able to perform a full press-up with good form. This means that your head is held in a straight line with your spine and with your nose pointing to the floor, your chest is open and your neck long, your hips are straight and your lower abdomen is drawn up towards the spine. Once you can do this, push forcefully off the floor so that your hands lift off.

Spiders

This exercise targets shoulder stability and trunk stability.

Perform your press-up to the left of a low step or block. Then place your right hand on the block and perform a press-up. Place both hands on the block and perform a press-up. Drop the right hand to the floor beside the block and perform a press-up.

Focus on keeping your head and neck in line with your trunk at all times throughout the movement. Maintain straight trunk alignment.

Dynamic Control

● Multi-directional Catching Lunges

This exercise introduces distraction, so the control you have developed in the previous phases must now become more automatic.

Stand with your feet together. Decide which leg you will use to lunge onto. Have a partner toss a tennis ball so that you must lunge to catch the ball, and push back up to stand on your other leg for balance.

Maintain a long strong trunk position no matter where the ball is thrown. It is easy to collapse your trunk for low balls, but try instead to deepen the bend in your hips and knees to maintain a better trunk position. You are aiming to challenge your body to control larger ranges of motion, and to be strong at different muscle lengths.

Poor performance
- Failure to bend at the hip and knee.
- Repeat with the ball being thrown at different angles and depths.

Progression
- Perform the same exercise with your supporting leg on a wobble cushion or foam pad to increase the balance challenge.

● Pendulum Lunges

This exercise introduces the new skill of controlling the body weight over a pivoting foot.

Start with your feet together facing a partner. Your left foot will be your main lunging leg for the first set. Your partner will throw a ball to your right side. You need to pivot on your right foot and rotate your pelvis into a lunge to catch it. Throw the ball back as you push back out of the lunge and pivot on your right foot to catch the ball in a lunge on your left side.

○ Multi-directional Jump and Land

Control of landings requires dynamic balance, pelvic stability and trunk control. If your trunk shifts off line each time you land, it will increase the stress on your lower limb joints. You will therefore aim to keep your trunk in a relaxed upright position for each landing.

Before performing this exercise, you must have established an elastic, controlled landing on both feet. Try to minimise the sound of your landing to encourage your hips and knees to bend and absorb impact.

Start with your feet slightly apart. Your aim is to create an elastic jump with quiet landings. Jump upwards and land on one leg, softly absorbing the landing force through your hips and knees. Make sure that your trunk is central and upright and that your knee and pelvic alignment is straight. Hold your balance for a moment.

Once you can control a soft, light and elastic single leg landing, vary the direction of your jump so that you have to control forward, sideways and angular momentum with stability, alignment and balance. Hold each landing for a count of 5 before repeating.

Once you have mastered this, you can vary it in two ways. Research has indicated that vision has an important role in landings [102], but athletes are often visually distracted at the time of landing. You can increase the balance challenge by performing the jump with your eyes closed, or add distraction by having a partner toss you a ball to catch just before you land.

Side Leaps

The relationship between pelvic stability and trunk position has an effect on change of direction speed. Athletes can overshoot with their trunks as they try to control lateral momentum, allowing their shoulders to move beyond the pelvis as they land with the outside foot. This puts the hips in a poor position to push from and makes quick change of direction difficult. Athletes who change direction effectively start counter moving their trunks slightly before their outside foot even contacts the ground.

GMed and GMax activation give you the pelvic foundation to organise your trunk for effective direction change. Now that your GMed is activated, it needs to learn to support both a strong sideways push, and also to control lateral momentum.

Stand on one leg with your body upright. Soften your hips and knees and leap up and out to the side, aiming to lengthen all the way from the trunk down to your toes on your push off side. Land softly on the opposite leg, making sure that your trunk does not tip past your pelvis, that your knee is aligned and your pelvis level.

Immediately push back in the other direction, aiming for the feeling of being a rubber ball bouncing as you absorb the landing and immediately take off again.

Once you can do this, mark two lines a metre or more apart depending upon your height and leap lightly on a forward diagonal, progressing up the lines. Repeat the exercise moving backwards. You can add a jump height element as well as jump breadth by placing hurdles between the lines.

Mini Trampoline Leaps

Your stability will be tested further by jumping onto a slightly unstable surface in this exercise. Make sure that your mini trampoline is secured and will not slip. Stand far enough away from it that you will need to leap rather than step onto it. Ensure that you can perform the basic movement before adding distraction. You will jump from three directions.

1 Start with a straight leap from behind the mini trampoline. As you land, soften your knee to absorb the force and keep your pelvis level, your knee aligned and your trunk central. When your form is perfect, ask someone to throw a ball to you just before you land. They can throw it slightly to the side, or make you reach high or low to catch it.

2 Stand to the side of the mini trampoline. Push strongly up and across from your outside leg and land with the other leg on the mini trampoline. Your landing should be soft and controlled with no overshooting of your trunk. Once you can do this, add the catching task.

3 Start midway between the first two start positions with both feet facing forward. Push strongly off the outside foot and land with the other foot pointing in the direction of movement. Your trunk should not collapse forward as you absorb the landing into your hip and knee. Once this is achieved with good form, add the catching task.

Low-High Balance

This exercise combines stability, balance and control in the pelvis and lower limb with mobility and control in the trunk.

Stand on one leg. Have a partner toss a ball for you to catch high and to the side or low and to the side. Keep good alignment of your knee and pelvis, bending smoothly at the hip and knee to catch low balls.

Progress by performing the exercise on a foam pad or a mini trampoline to add the challenge of a mildly less stable supporting surface.

Box Jump onto Single Leg

This exercise combines an explosive jump with stability, balance and momentum control. Prior to performing the single leg version, make sure that you can perform a jump landing on two feet on the box. Make sure you absorb the landing and forward momentum by landing lightly with soft springy hips and knees.

You will jump off both feet and land on one foot on the box, absorbing the landing elastically in your hips and knees and maintaining trunk, knee and pelvic alignment. To generate more power from your legs, perform the movement with your hands behind your head.

Stair Bounding

Having mastered the basic step-up, you can now progress to rapid alternating stair bounds. Depending upon your height, you will climb two or three stairs at a time.

Imagine a ball bearing bouncing off a piece of glass – it sharply "pings" off the surface. This is how you will contact each step. Your aim is to be as light and fast off each step as you can. You should feel elastic and powerful.

Keep your trunk upright and push strongly through your legs to propel you up the stairs.

Bending forward will decrease the effectiveness of the exercise.

Swiss Ball Exercises

Phase 4 exercises continue to increase global body coordination and higher global control loads. Do not allow yourself to make it look or feel difficult. Your performance objective is still effortless control. Release as much tension as you can while maintaining your alignment and continue to breathe normally.

Swiss Ball Side Raises

This exercise aims to strengthen the trunk's side flexors and coordinate them with hip stability.

Lie sideways over a Swiss Ball with your feet on a wall. Place your uppermost foot forward, and your lower foot back on the wall. Arrange your body so that it is directly on its side and draw your lower abdominals in.

Without letting your lower hip slide forward or backward, lower your body sideways over the ball so that your trunk is curved downwards. Keeping your body in this plane, side bend your trunk back up again so that it is curved upwards.

What would poor technique look like?

- It is easy to allow your hips to bend so that your hips move backwards on the ball. Try and keep a straight body line.

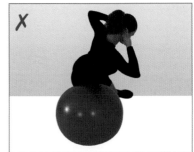

Swiss Ball Full Press-up

If you have not tried this exercise before, place the ball against the wall. Once you are familiar with it, you can move the ball away from the wall.

Support your weight in a press-up position with your hands in a comfortable position on the ball. Keep your head position neutral and your hips straight with your lower abdominals in. Bend your elbows and move your chest towards the ball. Press back out again.

Progression

- Perform the same movement with one leg lifted behind you.

What would poor technique look like?

- Dropping your head.
- Bending your hips.
- Dropping your hips so that your back sags.
- Letting your shoulders creep towards your ears.

Swiss Ball Elbow Circles

Support your weight on the ball with your elbows and forearms parallel and take up a plank position. Maintaining a neutral head and trunk posture and drawing your lower abdominals upwards, move the ball in circles using only your arms.

The same exercise can be performed with straight arms. This is called a Ramp. If the Ramp is too easy, perform it with one leg lifted from the floor.

What would poor technique look like?
- Dropping your head.
- Bending your hips.
- Dropping your hips so that your back sags.
- Letting your shoulders creep towards your ears.

Elbow Support Knee Drive

Once you can perform the Phase 3 Incline Plank Knee Drive without difficulty, you can increase your global stability demand by introducing a Swiss Ball. Place your elbows and forearms on the ball so that they are directly under your shoulders and parallel to each other. Straighten your body out with your feet in line with your hips. Lengthen from the back of your neck to the base of your spine, drawing your lower body up. Lift your chest slightly to create a strong shoulder position. Without moving your trunk or the ball, bring your knee under your body in a straight line. Do not lift your hips as your knee moves under your body.

Single Leg Squat

Start in the basic Wall Squat position with the ball behind the curve of your lower back. Make sure your feet are slightly forward, and positioned closer than hip-width apart. Bend your knees and hips slightly.

Focus on the GMax of the side that is going to support you. Lift the heel of the other foot off the floor so that you only have light toe contact, making sure you can support the position with your hips level and your knee in line with your ankle. You may need a small amount of toe support to keep your alignment. It is better to do this than to perform full single leg squats with poor form. If you are able to maintain your alignment, take the supporting toe off the floor and continue the squat movement. Do not move past 90 degrees at the knee.

Swiss Ball Hamstring Curl

This exercise trains your symmetry and control of a central body line, concentric and eccentric hamstring strength, and trunk stability.

Start on your back with the Swiss Ball under the soles of your feet. Your arms will be on the floor to increase your base of support.

Press your feet down into the ball to lift your hips. Your GMax will work to keep your hips up. Roll the ball out away from you until your legs are straight. Aim for a straight movement. Keeping your hips up, pull the ball back towards you again. Once you can achieve 10 of these without difficulty, cross your arms over your chest and repeat the movement. You should focus on a straight movement and straight body line.

What would an incorrect movement look like?
- If you are not using your GMax, your hips will move up and down as your legs move in and out. Try to keep a consistent hip height.

Kneeling Ball Balance

This exercise targets trunk and hip stability.

Put your hands and the front of your lower legs on the ball, and rock forward until your feet come off the floor. Bring your knees underneath you and straighten your hips so that your trunk is upright.

Use your GMax to maintain a straight hip position, and the balloon posture cue. Do not hook your feet onto the ball for support.

Variations

- Take both arms over your head. Move one arm down to the side and back up and repeat with the other side.
- Take both arms out in front of you. Move one to the side and move it back and repeat with the other side.

- Take both arms to the side and turn your shoulders one way and then the other.

- Throw and catch a ball against a wall or with another person.

- Work in pairs. Link arms with a partner who is also kneeling on a ball. Both of you lengthen your bodies so that your hips are straight. Keeping your arms straight, pull one of your partner's arms towards you and push the other away. This will create a rotational pressure on your partner's trunk. Your partner's job is to resist this pressure and create a counter pressure.

You can also work on side bending control by pressing one arm down and pushing the other arm up. Your partner resists this pressure and provides a counter pressure. In both of these exercises, you should feel connected from your shoulders to your knees. If you try to resist the pressure with your arms rather than your whole body, you will lose control of your legs on the ball.

Full Flexion Pattern Development

These exercises work on coordination of the trunk and hip flexor group. Until Phase 4, the hip flexors have been trained to work against a neutral trunk. This pattern has been used because the trunk flexors such as rectus abdominis are often overactive and the deep stabilisers such as transversus abdominis which maintain a neutral trunk are often underactive. For activities such as running or cross-country skiing, this pattern will provide poor support for the pelvis and spine against hip flexion.

For activities which require a trunk and hip flexion combination movement; e.g. diving or gymnastics, a lack of TrA activity creates a flexion pattern where the movement muscles are not acting on a stable foundation. The flexion pattern is therefore not complete, as a component is missing. Activating TrA has therefore been a priority in order to construct a complete flexion pattern. The following exercises now integrate TrA, rectus abdominis, and hip flexors into the full flexion pattern.

The following exercises have been used as "core" exercises for many years, but having followed Phases 1–3, you will see that these movements represent only one pattern of several which need to be addressed in a balanced stability programme. If powerful trunk flexion is not a component of your sport, the time you spend on stability training should not be overly biased towards movements of this type at the expense of other more relevant positions. These are not priority movements for athletes with lower back pain. If you are suffering from lower back pain, seek the advice of a trained therapist before adding these exercises to your programme.

○ Basic Curl-ups

These exercises can be made far more effective if you focus on keeping your lower abdomen in throughout the movement, and you use equal focus on the up and the down phase of the movement.

Lie with your knees bent and your feet flat on the floor. Your hands are on the front of your hips. Keeping your lower abdominals in and your head and neck relaxed, slide your hands up your thighs to curl your trunk of the floor. Keep your lower abdominals in all the way back down again.

To add an oblique element, slide your hand up your opposite thigh as you curl. To increase the loading of the exercise, place your hands level with your ears. It is easier to have your elbows pointing forward, and harder to have them pointing sideways.

Toe Touch Sit-ups

Begin as for the exercise above. As you curl up, lift one leg and reach with your opposite hand to touch it. Try to keep your leg as straight as possible. Put your foot back to floor as you return to the start position, controlling your trunk by keeping your lower abdominals in.

Ball Bounce Sit-ups

Lie down facing a wall with a Swiss Ball in both hands and your knees bent.

Take the ball over your head, lengthening your spine along the floor so that your abdomen drops towards your spine.

Keeping your lower abdominals in, rapidly pull the ball forward and throw it hard against the wall. Catch it as it rebounds and continue to move back to the floor again, controlling the motion by keeping your lower abdominals in.

Extended Lever Swiss Ball Sit-ups

The sit up movement is often performed from the floor, which only allows development of trunk curling control from neutral. Sports such as cricket and gymnastics require an athlete to use the abdominals through a larger range of motion.

Sit on a Swiss Ball and walk yourself out until your spine is curved over the ball. Your head and shoulders will be supported by your arm, which is folded behind your neck. Place the other hand on your lower abdomen, to make sure that you keep it drawn in towards your spine to create a stable platform for the movement.

To create the movement, curl your upper body towards your lower body. Make sure that your spine peels off the ball joint by joint on the way up and reconnects with it joint by joint on the way back down.

◉ Straight Leg Curl-ups

The straight leg curl up trains a higher level of spinal flexion control than the basic curl-up. Straight leg curl-ups have been frowned upon for many years, and there is a prevailing belief that they are dangerous for the lower back. This belief is certainly well-founded if the movement is performed without a well-functioning TrA, and at speeds that exceed your control capabilities. However, as you have worked your way to this point, you should have the necessary spinal control to perform this exercise without difficulty.

Should I do this exercise if I have a back problem?
* If you are currently experiencing lower back pain, you are unlikely to possess the control necessary for this exercise. Prioritise exercises from Phases 1–3 to develop this control.

Lie flat on the floor with the fingertips of one hand resting lightly on your lower abdomen below the level of your umbilicus.

Starting from your head, curl one segment of your spine at a time off the floor until you are sitting up. Your lower abdomen should have remained flat throughout the motion.

To reverse the action, focus on controlling the movement from your lower abdomen, placing one segment at a time back on the floor until you are lying flat again. The movement should be very smooth, and you should not miss any segment as you curl and uncurl.

◉ Double Toe Touch

If you can perform the Straight Leg Curl-up, you can try the Double Toe Touch.

Lie with your knees bent and your feet flat on the floor. Your hands are on the front of your hips. Keeping your lower abdominals in and your head and neck relaxed, curl up as you lift both feet from the floor. Touch your toes and uncurl as you place your feet back on the floor.

A diver or gymnast will be able to perform this exercise as a V-sit with straight legs and straight arms throughout the entire movement.

First level – short lever arms.

This is not an exercise for novices. You do need to have securely established your TrA in the previous phases before attempting this exercise.

Second level – long lever arms.

Should I do this exercise if I have a back problem?

* If you are currently experiencing lower back pain, you are unlikely to possess the control necessary for this exercise. Prioritise exercises from Phases 1–3 to develop this control.

Stability Reactions

Ball Follow

In Chapter 3, the Ball Follow was introduced as a method for assessing whole body movement. The exercise stimulates the need to react accurately with good mobility and whole body stability. It can be varied by increasing the pressure between the two athletes.

Hold a Swiss Ball between you using one hand each. Your feet will be apart. Increase the pressure on the ball. One of you will lead the movement and the other will follow. The leader will attempt to throw the follower off balance, varying the movement and forcing the follower to react. Use the largest range of motion and the most creative combinations of movement that you can. Progress with increased speed and increased pressure.

Wrestle Walking

Wrestle Walking stimulates trunk bracing reactions to sudden pressure. There are two positions that can be used.

1. Trunk Pressures

One athlete will walk or jog in a straight line. This is the focus athlete. A partner will apply varying pressure at random intervals by pushing sideways into their pelvis and trunk. The pressure does not have to be heavy. The focus athlete tries to maintain a straight line of movement.

2. Arm Pressures

This variation is for sports like football where a player needs to keep another player away from their trunk as they move. The focus athlete will bend his elbow and lift his arm to just below shoulder height. His focus is to keep pushing his elbow away from him. The partner will deliver pressure though the arm, trying to push the elbow towards the focus athlete's body thus pushing him off balance easily.

Push Jumps

Athletes in sports where jumping is involved need to be adaptable in their landings. Basketballers and footballers are often contacted in the air. They may land awkwardly. This may increase their injury risk, or influence their ability to move quickly after landing. Push Jumps should be started off both legs. The focus athlete will jump and try to land in the same spot. The partner will apply a sideways pressure through the hips or trunk when the focus athlete is in the air. It is harder for the focus athlete to control a trunk push than a pelvic push, so you may choose to mix these up.

Variation: Jump and Go

- You can increase the complexity of the task by asking the focus athlete to move quickly to a marker directly after the Push Jump. He must control his landing and immediately move to a target or new task, so there is an element of distraction for the landing task as he thinks about the next movement. Drills can be constructed where the Push Jump starts a sequence which may involve acceleration, change of direction, catching or kicking.

Variation: Catch and Go

- A handball or basketball player can be pushed further by performing the Push Jump while catching a ball. The greater distraction requires greater landing control. Vary the direction of the throw to vary the task.

Change of Direction

This drill ensures that you are equally happy moving off both legs and turning in both directions. If you can overcome a strong dominance in turning coordination, you can minimise the twisting knee stress caused by a poor turn in your non-dominant direction. Phase 3 introduced the relationship between foot movement and body movement. This drill further develops that relationship.

Sprint forward until commanded to brake and back pedal as quickly as possible. To brake well you will keep your knees elastic and shift your weight back on your final two steps so that you are not using pressure through your toes to stop your momentum. The weight will be distributed over a wider surface area of your sole.

As you back pedal, you will receive a command to turn to your right and sprint towards a target. On the next run through, turn to your left and sprint towards a target.

You may need to run through these drills slowly at first to feel the difference between left and right. Is there a difference in footwork, or the turning of your pelvis? Try to make them as similar as you can and then increase the speed.

Mobility

● Cork Screw: Chest Opening Spinal Twist

As this phase has introduced higher level arm loading and greater global stabiliser activity in the trunk, this exercise lengthens the muscular chain from the shoulder to the hip.

Lie on your back on the floor with your knees bent and feet flat on the floor. Your arms will be flat on the floor level with your shoulders with the palms turned upwards. Cross your right knee over your left knee. Move your left foot slightly to the right. Keeping your right shoulder on the floor, slowly allow your knees to fall to the left. Focus on breathing into your lower ribs so that you gain maximum lengthening. If you allow your right shoulder to lift, you will lose the benefit of the stretch.

Correctly rotating around a secure spine

Spine incorrectly allowed to sag

Once you have relaxed into this position for several breaths, slide your right arm up towards your head and let it rest on the floor. Continue to breathe into your lower ribs for several breath cycles before releasing the stretch and returning to the start position.

● Chicken Wings: Chest Opening With Shoulder Internal Rotation

Stand in your balloon posture and put both hands behind your back with one hand resting on the palm of the other. Maintaining a neutral lumbar spine by drawing your lower abdomen in a little, open your chest and press your elbows back. If this is easy, grasp your elbows. Maintain your neutral spine and open your chest. Hold this position for a few breath cycles and reverse your arm position so that the other arm is on top.

Maintain a neutral spine and head position.

Incorrect spinal position.

Tail Up

This exercise lengthens the hamstrings in partnership with pelvic mobility.

Stand with your feet no more than hip width apart in front of a chair. Place both hands on the seat of the chair. Imagine where your tail bone is, and tilt it upwards towards the ceiling so that the inwards curve of your spine deepens. Repeat this movement several times and sustain the final movement for several breaths.

If you have good hamstring flexibility, you will need to place your hands on a lower support in order to achieve a stretch.

Variation

* You can add pelvic rotation to the Tail Up stretch. Start in the basic Tail Up position. Keeping your tailbone tilted to the ceiling, soften one knee which will drop the pelvis on that side. This will intensify the feeling in your straight leg. Straighten the bent knee and repeat on the other side.

  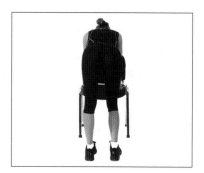

Hip Ranger

This exercise gently mobilises your hips into flexion and extension. Take your time with this one and let yourself relax into the position. Start from a kneeling position on the floor. Slide one leg straight out behind you and fold your body down over your front knee. Breathe and allow yourself to sink into your hip joint. Perform five breath cycles as your hip moves further into flexion. Now you will work the other hip into extension. Keep your legs in the same position, and straighten up your trunk. If you can keep your balance, place both hands on your front knee to help you to straighten. If you need more support, keep one hand on your knee and the fingertips of the other on the floor. If you need more support, use a book to prop yourself up. Perform five breath cycles and swap legs.

Programme Summary

The four phases are intended to provide a sensible progression for increasingly dynamic control. The proportion of each phase that you eventually use in your programme will depend upon the demands of your sport.

A balanced programme is likely to incorporate elements from each phase. Phase 1 elements can be retained for preactivation prior to training, or in the cool-down period for maintenance. Some sports will have very few Phase 4 exercises in their programme, as Phase 2 and 3 elements are more relevant to their needs but dynamic, multidirectional sports will incorporate many of the Phase 4 elements.

Chapter 9: Stability Across the Training Programme

Stability Principles for Warm-ups and Mobility
Body Weight Training
Elastic Resistance Exercises
Stability in the Gym Environment
Static Stretches

As we have learned so far, stability, in combination with balance, functional mobility, proprioception and symmetry fosters and maintains ideal joint mechanics and movement patterns. Specific stability exercises are designed to trigger and reinforce stabiliser muscle activation. They also help to reduce the limitation of mobility and alteration of joint mechanics that occur through over activity and excess tension in the global muscle groups. This focused work is beneficial, but only if it transfers into efficient functional movement. Specific stability exercises can therefore only have an impact if the principles of effective movement are applied and reinforced in all areas of training.

The rules outlined for stability training are the same for any other aspect of the training programme.

- Balloon posture establishes the critical head on neck position, no matter whether you are standing, running, squatting or performing press-ups. Allowing your neck to collapse so that your head is pulled back, or your chin pulled upward or forward will compromise your shoulder mechanics, decrease the effectiveness of your hip muscles and make it difficult to switch on your deep abdominals.
- Relax your face and jaw.
- Breathe normally.
- Keep the back of your neck long to ensure that your shoulders are not pulled towards your ears.
- Keep your chest open to prevent shoulder stress and overdependence upon pectorals for support.
- Maintain a firm central axis: don't let your trunk collapse.
- Maintain a listening foot. If it becomes rigid, it indicates poor body orientation over the foot and poor balance.
- Your pelvis remains level and your knee is in line with your hip and ankle.
- Release any tension you don't need.
- Aim for purity of movement. Know what you are trying to achieve with any exercise you are engaged in and make sure you commit to quality performance.

This chapter highlights some of the common errors and misunderstandings that can occur in other areas of the training programme.

Stability Principles for Warm-ups and Mobility

A warm-up will incorporate several elements in order to prepare the body for action.

One of the activities during a warm-up is to take the joints and muscles through their full range with rhythmic, repeated movements. This is not just a muscular activity but an opportunity to warm-up the neuromuscular patterns that will be needed for the sporting activity, reinforcing the sequencing of the muscles and joints in the kinetic chain. If you don't pay attention to your movement at this time, you can reinforce poor movement habits and miss some of the benefits of the warm-up. Even if you aren't paying attention, your nervous system is, and it is recording the way you move. Don't feed your nervous system a poor movement when you warm-up if you are trying to improve your technique in other areas of training.

The following exercises commonly appear in warm-up or cool-down routines but are usually performed poorly. Once you start to apply the stability principles to these movements, it is easy to recognise the errors and identify them in other movements that you may use in your warm-up.

High Knee Lift

This movement combines ankle mobility with hip mobility and provides the opportunity to wake up the neuromuscular patterns for clean hip flexion on the movement side and stability on the support side. It also encourages balance and precise body weight placement over the forefoot.

Step forward onto your left heel and roll up onto your toes, driving the right knee upwards. Your balloon posture is your best focus for this motion, as it reminds you to bring your knee up to your trunk, instead of your trunk collapsing towards your knee. This reinforces a sound hip flexion pattern on a stable trunk.

Poor form: trunk is collapsing towards the leg.

At the top of the movement, aim for a straight line in your supporting leg from your toe through your knee and hip to your shoulder. Pause in this balanced position for a moment and then continue. To further reinforce balance and symmetry, perform this as a walking drill with both arms stretched over your head. You should be able to maintain a straight horizontal line between your armpits, and a vertical central axis. You should feel as though you are perfectly aligned over your forefoot.

If you collapse slightly to one side, shortening the side of your trunk or moving your hands to one side, this usually indicates that you are trying to use your latissimus dorsi to help stabilise your trunk. This will throw off your balance and make you overuse your groin muscles to maintain control. This problem is quite common and often associated with groin injuries and poor gluteal activation on the support side.

Variation 1

• Perform the knee raise, and as you balance on your supporting leg, straighten out your other knee before stepping forward. Focus on really stretching your arms and trunk "out of your pelvis".

Variation 2

• Perform the knee raise with a trunk twist.

Heel Flicks

Maintaining your balloon posture, flick your heels up at the back to lengthen your quadriceps. You are aiming to maintain a straight line down the front of your body when you perform this exercise. Remember to lengthen through the back of your neck to help your trunk to straighten and your lower abdominals to draw inwards.

The most common error for this motion is allowing your spine to arch into extension. When you do this, you allow your pelvis to tip forward, losing your neutral trunk position, bending your hips and failing to properly lengthen the quadriceps.

Poor form: hip bending.

Side Skips

Side Skips address adduction-abduction mobility in the hips, and also trigger GMed to push off effectively. The most common error in this exercise is to use the trunk to generate the movement, which makes it appear as if it waves from side to side. This decreases the exercise's effect on mobility and activation.

Keep your central axis straight and firm as you reach with one leg and push with the other.

Poor form: trunk rocking from side to side.

Progressive Lunges

The correct form for lunges still applies in the warm-up. Allowing yourself to collapse your lumbar spine into extension and let your knee drift inside your ankle fails to activate correct neuromuscular patterns and does not fully lengthen the hip flexor muscles. Allowing your trunk to tip forward and backwards as you move indicates that you are not using your GMax adequately.

Maintain a firm vertical central axis throughout the movement, and pay attention to GMax as you push out of your lunge.

Variation

* Progressive lunges with a twist. Start with both arms out to the side. As you step forward onto your left leg, turn your upper body to the left. Your arms should stay parallel.

Stride Openers

This movement aims to mobilise both the front and back of the hips and give a sensation of length to the hip motion.

The basic movement entails placing one foot on a bench and performing a deep lunge onto it, keeping the back foot facing forward and the trunk neutral. Then push your hips back, keeping your chest up and focusing on pressing your tailbones backwards.

The common errors are to collapse the trunk into extension on the way forward and into flexion on the way backwards.

Wood Chops and Spiral Movements

These movements involve the joints from the feet to the shoulders, warming-up rotational mobility and control.

A basic spiral is the less complex of the movements and is helpful to establish rotation of the pelvis over the fixed foot as well as a sense of rotating around a firm central axis. It also plays a kinaesthetic role in differentiating between the pelvis and the thorax. Once the pelvis has reached its limit, the thorax continues to move into its full available range, so you should be aware of your pelvis and shoulders moving at slightly different times.

To benefit from this exercise, start with balloon posture to establish your central axis and draw your lower belly inwards.

Turn your body to one side, transferring the weight onto this foot. Allow your other foot to turn in the direction of movement so that the pelvis is free to continue moving over the fixed foot. Allow your shoulders to keep turning freely and let your arms swing. As you reverse the movement, be aware that it is your abdominals that are maintaining the central axis for rotation. The common errors associated with this movement are loss of control of the spine so that it deepens its curve, and insufficient pelvic rotation.

The Wood Chop adds another dimension to this movement by incorporating an up and down element. The same factors apply as for the spiral, but this time as you turn you will bend your hips and knees, keeping your body upright. The most common error is to bend your back instead of your legs. As you reverse the movement, you will straighten your legs and move your arms up and across. The most common error is to bend your spine instead of your hips.

Leg Swings

Stand on one leg and lift your body up over your supporting hip to activate GMed. Stay tall and swing the other leg fully back and forth, allowing your arms to move normally. Your trunk should stay vertical and your leg should swing in a straight line. Your pelvis should remain in a constant position throughout the movement.

The common error associated with this exercise is movement of the lower back. It should stay in a consistent position throughout the exercise.

The movements included in a warm-up depend upon the sport and its demands. A warm-up will become increasingly specific to the sport, starting with general movements and activation exercises and ending with sports specific drills.

Examples of this include an Olympic weight lifter who performs balance board squats to activate her GMax before warming up her lifts with the bar, and an international sprinter who incorporates wobble cushion balance exercises, Greyhound and Superman prior to his walking drills and dynamic movements to make sure that his stabiliser system is fired up for his track session. The coach of a junior ski squad found that his athletes showed more control on their early runs on the slopes if they added Swiss Ball balancing on hands and knees and in kneeling to their warm-up. A world-class triathlete finds that she runs technically better if she performs pre-activation exercises that trigger the balloon posture and GMax and GMed as part of the warm-up prior to a running session.

Body Weight Training

Body weight exercises are perceived to be safe, simple and effective elements to include in circuit training. For this reason, they are often given to young athletes or make up part of a circuit for adult athletes to perform with intensity and speed. Once you start to recognise the fundamentals of good form, you realise as you observe the performance of these exercises that often they are not reinforcing desired functional patterns, but simply reinforcing poor ones.

Junior athletes performing full body weight press-ups rarely demonstrate scapular stability or even trunk stability. They do become stronger at press-ups with practice, but may develop muscle imbalances and poor patterning to achieve this. If the total pattern is poor, i.e. the contribution of stabilisers and mobilisers is unbalanced, transfer of improved press-up strength to a specific sporting activity is diminished. You may need to start on a low load exercise like the Wall Press to develop the stable pattern, and use other more supported exercises for strength. As you master the pattern, you can progressively load the movement so that the entire pattern strengthens safely and effectively.

A sensible progression route for Press-ups would be the Wall Press ➝ Single Leg Wall Press ➝ OTT Press-up ➝ Incline Press-up ➝ Kneeling Press-up ➝ Full Press-up.

Repetitive lunges or step-ups may be a low load, relative to weight training, but speed and number of repetitions can accentuate poor mechanics. The initial objective is not how many repetitions can you do but how well you do them. You want to condition the pattern not just the muscles. Once you have consolidated this form, you can increase speed or endurance.

Body weight exercises can be very effective as long as you understand the form with which they should be performed. There is no doubt that you are likely to have the strength in your mobility muscles to perform a movement, and that body weight may be a fraction of what these muscles are capable of lifting, but if the smaller stabilisers cannot withstand the load and maintain a stable pattern, you will create a situation of increasing imbalance.

Elastic Resistance Exercises

Stretch-band exercises are often given by coaches to young athletes for arm strengthening, particularly with the aim of improving rotator cuff performance. This is so seldom challenged that it has become standard practice especially in sports such as tennis. However, without a good appreciation of correct shoulder mechanics, these exercises are more likely to cause problems than solve them.

As we learned in Chapter 2, shoulder mechanics depend on a variety of factors. The shoulder joint should be able to rotate around a stable axis. That is, the head of the humerus, (or ball of the ball-and-socket joint), should not drift back and forth in response to rotational movement. In order to have a stable axis, the scapula, which provides the socket of the ball-and-socket joint, must be securely positioned throughout the movement. This often depends upon having an independently stable trunk and pelvis, so that the shoulder is not pulled into a poor position due to body positioning errors.

Unfortunately, stretch-band exercises are often given to young children with none of these elements in place. The amount of resistance at the hand end is greater than their ability to stabilise, causing them to recruit alternative muscle groups in order to perform the movement. The most common of these is pectoralis major, which pulls the shoulder forward. The axis for shoulder rotation is lost, and athletes learn to stabilise their arms superficially from the front surface of their chests rather than effectively training the rotator cuff. This pattern is reinforced with repetition, and can lead to loss of mobility and a weak, ineffective rotator cuff.

The argument from a tennis point of view is that the amount of resistance is less than that which is applied when they hit a tennis ball. The answer to this is that a groundstroke in tennis is generated by the sum of all moving body parts from the feet through the trunk to the arm. It is not merely a function of upper body strength. The situation is worsened by individuals who believe that tying the stretch band to a tennis racket and performing arm movements makes the exercise sports specific. It is more likely to break down the coordination pattern throughout the kinetic chain, as the young athlete engages the resistance at the hand before moving the body, a reversal of the normal movement. Regardless of varying opinions on the benefits of stretch-band exercises, they will continue to be used for shoulder training by many coaches in many sports. Because of this, a simple process has been provided below for commonly used exercises to make sure that future biomechanical problems are not caused.

1 Basic tests such as Wall Press, Superman and Diamond should be performed to gain an impression of basic stability around the trunk and scapula. Also test shoulder internal rotation.

2 Basic pelvic and trunk stability should be established.

3 Basic isolated scapular stability and rotator cuff activation should be in place. Exercises like Diamonds, Superman and Over the Top should improve scapular control. Exercises that load the arms, such as Wall Press and Over the Top also help to activate the rotator cuff muscles.

4 Practicing shoulder internal rotation as outlined in Chapter 3 helps to establish the rotational axis.

5 With this foundation established, resistance from the hand can be introduced. The athlete should start in the "balloon" posture to activate the trunk stabilisers and place the shoulder in neutral.

6 For active internal rotation in a neutral position, the elbow should be bent to 90 degrees so that the forearm is horizontal and the wrist is straight. A tennis ball can be held lightly between the elbow and the body to prevent the arm drifting out of position. Step away from the stretch band's fixed point allowing the working arm to rotate outwards to its limit. This is the start position.

7 Athletes can place their free hand over the front of their shoulder to ensure that it does not drift forward during the movement. Keeping the wrist straight, use the lightest resistance to train the pattern and only progress within the limits of the athlete's ability to maintain the pattern.

For external rotation in neutral, the first four steps should be in place. The athlete will hold the stretch band between his hands, and start with the forearms horizontal, wrists straight and facing to the floor, and balloon posture to activate his stabilisers globally and open the chest. Again, the tennis ball can be lightly held between elbow and body.

Keeping the wrists parallel with the floor, move one away from the other. The shoulder itself should not move, and the wrists should not turn upwards. As the wrist returns to the start position, the shoulder should not be dragged forward.

Poor form: wrist turning.

Rotational exercises are often taken from neutral into 90 degrees at the shoulder for greater relevance to sporting movements. This is far more difficult to control, and in young athletes should only be done under supervision.

The first four steps should be in place. Then, without resistance, the pattern should be practiced. The athlete takes his shoulder up to 90 degrees with the elbow bent. He places his hand across the front of his shoulder to the underside of his arm. This will help to keep the shoulder and arm in place. It is common practice to rest the arm on a table to maintain a consistent elbow position, but this can allow the athlete to overuse latissimus dorsi by pulling down into the table, and as this is a common patterning dysfunction it has been avoided by having the athlete self-monitor the arm position.

The athlete then rotates the arm fully from external to internal rotation, maintaining a consistent shoulder position. The shoulder should not drift forward into his hand.

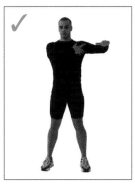

*Loss of the shoulder
as a fixed point.*

Athletes can progress their control with a low load but higher speed by throwing and catching a tennis ball in this position. They can also progress at higher load and low speed by introducing light elastic resistance.

Elastic Resistance for the Lower Limb

Similar principles apply for exercises prescribed for the lower limb. With the band around their ankles, athletes are asked to pull the band in a variety of directions, but the usefulness of these exercises depends entirely on the set up and maintenance of pelvic and trunk stability throughout the movement. The basic principles are:

1 Test single knee raise and lunge to gain an impression of the athlete's pelvic stability and body alignment.

2 If these are poor, start with Phase 1 activation exercises such as the Bridge, Greyhound and Clam to build foundation stability.

3 Once the athlete has gained some basic pelvic control, the resistance can be added. Start with balloon posture to increase stabiliser activation in the trunk.

4 When shifting the weight onto one leg, lift and position the body over the supporting hip to make sure that GMed will activate appropriately.

5 When moving a leg against stretch band resistance, keep a straight line down the body to the foot. It may be helpful to keep the arms above the head to prevent collapse of your trunk. The pelvis should remain in a secure position, and shouldn't tip forward, backward or sideways.

Loss of trunk control.   *Loss of pelvic control.*

Stability in the Gym Environment

This book focuses on establishing effective neuromuscular patterns for stability and freedom of movement. These patterns should provide a foundation for strength and power training but fundamental errors in exercise selection and performance can lead to imbalance and poor transfer of strength gains to performance.

Single Leg Vs Double Leg Activities in the Weights Room

There is a tendency to assume that weights performed on single leg will develop more stability than performing the same exercise on two legs. This is not always the case.

If an athlete uses excessive foot, ankle and lower leg muscle activity to maintain single leg balance, performing weights on a single leg will amplify the problem and create a rigid, non-listening foot. The specific exercise may seem to improve: however that improvement will not transfer into a functional change. They are more likely to become increasingly functionally rigid, instead of dynamically stable.

If you are planning on adding single leg weights exercises to your programme, make sure that you focus on maintaining a relaxed foot and ankle and that you draw your body up over your hip to activate your GMax and GMed effectively.

Notes from the Clipboard

A 27-year-old female professional golfer presented with both technical and injury problems. She had pain in the lower back and shins which was not resolving. She also lacked power and was trying to address this by increasing her time in the weights room.

The striking thing about this player was the high degree of tension in superficial muscles like her back extensors and rectus abdominis, as well as distal muscle groups such as those in her lower legs and feet. She had correspondingly low tone in her more central muscles such as GMax and TrA. This level of imbalance required even higher total body tension in order to control a golf swing. This made it impossible for her to achieve the sequential rotation from her feet through her pelvis and trunk that was necessary to generate power in her swing.

The player had been given single leg bicep and deltoid exercises to do by her trainer, with the aim of improving stability and balance. The degree of muscle tension in her feet and lower legs as she performed these exercises demonstrated a primary and habitual poor stabilising strategy. Selecting the position which most amplified this poor strategy and then loading it could only worsen the problem.

The player's strength and conditioning coach was very receptive to this information and adjusted the gym programme so that central stability could be developed as well as effective weight transference. All initial exercises were done in bilateral weight bearing. Her remedial programme involved listening foot exercises to improve ankle and foot dissociation as well as rotation mobility drills to improve her movement sequencing. The shin and lower back pain resolved and the player was able to make technical adjustments more easily.

Conversely, if a sport requires powerful alternating leg movement, limiting the gym programme to bilateral activities may be missing a key component. If you are a cyclist, for example, the amount of effective force that you are able to exert through the pedal is dependent upon the stability of your pelvis to support your leg muscles in alternating patterns. A cyclist with strong leg muscles but poor pelvic and trunk stability can only access a proportion of his strength, as some of it will be dissipated through loss of a fixed point for muscles to pull from. Bilateral squats can build muscular strength in sports relevant *muscles* effectively, but they do not address the accessibility of this strength when stability is challenged. Unilateral activities such as lunges, step-ups and single leg squats should be included in the programme to ensure that a sports-relevant *pattern* is trained.

Purity and Purpose of Movement

The effectiveness of an exercise is easily lost if the essential movement is not well understood. Among the most common offenders against this principle are:

Calf raises. These should be performed with a stable, well aligned ankle, but athletes with a poor pattern will allow the ankle to collapse outwards as they push upwards, displacing their weight onto the outer joints of the forefoot. A pattern like this in a runner or jumper can give rise to posterior shin splints, a painful sensation on the inner aspect of the tibia.

Good form: straight ankles.

Poor form: the ankles are collapsing outwards.

Squats. Athletes are sometimes taught to over emphasise their lumbar curve when they squat. This cue can be misinterpreted. As they focus on keeping the lumbar curve, they move their hips backwards as they squat instead of focusing on lowering their hips towards the floor. Their trunk continues to move downwards with a deep curve after the hips have stopped bending. This has the effect of loading the back extensors, proximal hamstrings and quadriceps, but the GMax can become underactive. Squats should target strength in the knee and hip extensors in a coordinated pattern. It is common to see athletes missing out on transferable strength because they are strengthening the knee extensors and back extensors instead.

The spine is maintained in the athlete's neutral position.

The athlete is over accentuating his lumbar curve.

The athlete is moving his spine instead of bending at the hips.

● Power Cleans

The power clean movement should be a smooth and coordinated multi-joint movement. Two common problems occur. The first is a sequencing problem. Athletes are so focused on driving up onto their toes and moving the bar upwards quickly that they have achieved this position before the hips have fully straightened. If this is the case, an important hip extension element of the pattern has been missed. An athlete who does this looks as if they are slightly bent at the hip when the bar is at shoulder height.

The second common error is a conceptual problem. Because you start with your hips and knees bent, the hips seem to need to move forward in order to straighten, and your head seems to need to move backwards. While this is true in a sense, working from this conceptual framework can lead you to drive your head back and displace your whole pelvis forward, causing you to over extend your lower back. The athlete who does this looks to be bending backwards excessively as they raise the bar.

From an alternative point of view, a power clean is like releasing the lid from a jack in the box. As you squat into your start position, it is like someone closing the lid and compressing your springs. You will drive upwards as your "springs" release, so that your hips, knees and ankles all unfold and straighten with coordinated timing. If you are lifting a heavy weight, your shoulders may move slightly backwards as you drive upwards, but there is no sudden backwards bending movement concentrated in the lower back.

If this coordination is difficult, try it without the bar first. Focus on compressing your springs first by bending your hips, knees and ankles. Release explosively by launching yourself straight up like an arrow, making sure that your trunk doesn't lose balance forward, backward or sideways.

The athlete is driving straight up.

The bar has been pulled up before the legs have straightened.

The athlete is over-bending the spine.

Forward Plate Raises

Use of momentum and poor patterning lead to a trunk stability problem with this exercise. When performed poorly, athletes start with too heavy a weight, so they initiate the movement with legs and trunk in order to start the plate moving. Athletes will end up in a position where the back is deeply bent backwards, and the arms do not reach their full range of motion.

The movement should be simple. Hold a weight plate in both hands in front of you. Stand with hips and knees bent and your trunk upright. Raise the plate above your head, and bring it back down again. Your trunk should remain in a consistent position throughout the movement.

Bicep Curls

This exercise falls victim to use of momentum instead of strength. You see the athlete's body shifting forward and backward with the movement, or the shoulder rolling forward every time the weight is lifted.

To avoid this error, use a basic system. Start in an upright posture. Your body will not move, and your shoulder will not move. The only movement will be elbow bending as you raise the weight to your shoulder. The same system can apply to many resistance exercises. Work out what should be moving first. Eliminate movement from all other body parts.

Upright Row

Although the target muscle for this exercise is the lateral deltoid of the shoulder, a poorly performed upright row will tend instead to work upper trapezius, the muscle running across the top of your shoulder and up the side of your neck.

Using the same system as you did in bicep curls, start in an upright position with your arms straight in front of you. The only movement should be your elbow moving upwards to shoulder height. You should not see your shoulders moving towards your ears.

Good isolated shoulder movement.

Loss of the shoulder as a fixed point.

There are many other examples of poorly performed exercises in the gym setting. However, if you adhere to the principle of a neutral spinal position, a neutral shoulder posture and precise movement in the joints directly involved for the muscles you are trying to target, you will avoid most of the problems which occur.

Stability and the Periodised Programme

A periodised training programme precisely outlines the timing of strength, power and speed development to best prepare the athlete for competition. Rigid adherence to set programmes can have a detrimental effect, however. The power phase presents the most trouble, as athletes may be asked to perform explosive movements which exceed their ability to compensate. If their control is inadequately developed for the task, injury is inevitable. Bounding drills are common offenders because they are perceived as body weight exercises, which are not considered to be potentially harmful. As previously discussed, poorly controlled body weight exercises at speed or high repetition are as potentially problematic as any weights exercise. If you are prepared to be flexible, however, periodisation targets can be met while still developing optimal patterns, as outlined in the example below.

Notes from the Clipboard

A 15-year-old male sprinter showing exceptional potential was brought in for screening. He was found to have extremely poor trunk and pelvic stability. Due to his age, his coach was programming body weight exercises, and according to the periodised programme the athlete was due to begin a power development phase. This athlete did not have sufficient pelvic stability to control a static lunge, and a dynamic lunge amplified his poor trunk control. Among the exercises proposed by his coach were alternating deep split jumps (jumping on the spot from a deep lunge on the left to a deep lunge on the right). When it was explained that the athlete could not perform the simplest version of this without collapse, the coach interpreted this as not being able to start the power development phase. This was not true. It simply required thinking about it in a structured way with movement quality as the key design component.

The modified programme was designed to meet competitive and developmental needs. Power work was done bilaterally, with both legs together. Broad jumping, box jumping and medicine ball cleans all addressed power development. While this was happening, control of unilateral activities was being trained in order to lay down the stability foundations for strength and eventually power work which would safely and effectively support the athlete's physical and technical development. Activation of the trunk and pelvic stabilisers followed by controlled weight bearing activities such as the supported Single Leg Squat, Lunges, Step-ups, Wall Press and Over the Top on the Swiss Ball established control patterns. Once these patterns were established, the athlete could confidently progress into more dynamic tasks without fear of later breakdown or technical plateau.

Static Stretches

Static stretches may appear as part of a flexibility development and maintenance programme. As a general principle, long sustained static stretches should not be performed directly prior to competition or dynamic training, so they do not appear as part of the warm-up. As with the dynamic flexibility exercises used in a warm-up, they are susceptible to performance errors. The following commonly performed stretches are regular offenders.

Quadricep Stretches

The key concept for any stretch is to take one end of the muscle away from the other end. That is, the origin and insertion move away from each other. The common error in this popular stretch is to allow the origin of the muscle to move towards the insertion by letting the pelvis tilt forward. This collapses the lumbar spine into extension and allows the hip to bend, decreasing the stretch on the muscle.

For an effective stretch, use balloon posture with your lower belly drawn in, keep your knees together and squeeze your GMax.

Quadricep stretch with the trunk in a stable position.   *Loss of trunk stability.*

Hip Flexor Stretches

This stretch suffers a similar fate to the previous one, in that the pelvis is often allowed to tip forward and the lumbar spine to sag into extension.

To perform it well, start in a half kneeling position, draw your body up into a balloon posture and tilt your pelvis as if you are tucking your tail under. For a greater lengthening effect through the whole side, maintain this pelvic position and stretch the arm up, allowing the ribs to lift on the supporting side.

Hamstring Stretches

There are many ways to lengthen hamstrings, but the effectiveness of the stretch is often lost through inaccurate movement. The effectiveness of lying on your back with one leg straightening towards the ceiling is greatly reduced if you have the other leg bent, as this allows the pelvis to tip backwards, taking the origin towards the insertion of the muscle.

To correct this, press one leg straight into the floor and press the other one to the ceiling (or the wall behind you if you are very flexible).

If you are trying to stretch hamstrings by putting your foot on a bench, do not try and touch your toes or put your head on your knee as this will stress the spine more than the hamstring muscles. Instead, make sure that your feet and pelvis are facing forward and simply move your tailbone backwards while keeping your head and chest up. This tilts the pelvis so that the origin of the hamstring muscle is moved away from the insertion without stressing the spine.

Supine Buttock Stretches

Athletes can often be seen repetitively manipulating their backs as they attempt to stretch the muscles in their buttocks. Regardless of which buttock muscle you are trying to stretch, focus on the hip, not the spine.

Piriformis Stretch

Piriformis is a deep muscle which links your thigh with the sacrum, the triangular bone at the base of your spine. It is quite specific to stretch, but can bring relief from stiffness in the lower back as well as the hip.

Lie on your back with both legs straight. Raise one knee until your hip is at 90 degrees. Move it across your body until it is in line with your navel. Grasp your shin with your opposite hand, and place your other hand on the outside of your knee. Gently guide the whole leg in the direction of your opposite shoulder. Both sides of your pelvis should stay on the floor.

General Buttock Stretch

Lie on your back with your knees bent. Rest the ankle of your left leg on your right thigh. This creates a hole for you to reach your left arm through. Raise your legs and clasp your fingers behind your right thigh, continuing to draw the legs gently towards you. Focus on keeping your pelvis on the floor so that your hips are able to stretch more effectively.

Shoulder Stretches

Stretches for the front of the shoulder can be difficult to perform safely and effectively. Swimmers in particular can be seen performing a risky version, which involves bracing a hand on a doorway or wall and turning the body away from it. This tends to force the ball of the shoulder forward in its socket, stressing the deep structures, which help to control the shoulder joint, and not providing a productive muscular stretch. The risks outweigh the benefits in this stretch. The following bilateral stretch is safe and effective if performed with trunk stability.

There are three positions for pectoral stretching.

Stage 1: Pectoralis minor.

Stand with one foot in front of the other in a doorway with your hands level with your shoulders. Tuck your elbows into your sides and do not let them move backwards. Keep your trunk neutral by drawing in your lower belly and shift your weight towards your front foot. Keep the elbows forward and allow the chest to open.

Poor form: the elbows have drifted backwards.

Stage 2: Pectoralis major.

Move your arms up the doorway so that your elbows are level with your shoulders. Keep your lower belly in to prevent your spine from sagging into extension and shift your weight onto your front foot.

Stage 3: Pectoralis major.

Slide your arms up the doorway so that your elbows are at head level. Repeat the same movement.

If you do not have a doorway, you can modify this procedure as follows:

Step 1

Stretch both arms up above your head and turn your palms away from each other. Keeping your lower belly drawn in to maintain your spinal position, pull both elbows down and back, opening the chest.

Step 2

Place the whole forearm against a wall or other available equipment. Make sure that your body is positioned level with the arm and then turn your head and trunk away from the arm without leaning forward. The same procedure can be used with the arm positioned slightly higher.

Latissimus Dorsi Stretches

The common error for this stretch is allowing the pelvis to slide out sideways as you bend your trunk in the opposite direction. This fails to fulfil the origin and insertion rule of stretching, as it offloads the muscle by making the origin moveable instead of fixed.

To avoid this, stand with both arms over your head and a neutral spine. Grasp one of your wrists, and pull that arm upwards towards the ceiling. Maintaining this position, move the arm towards your head and allow yourself to tip into the stretch, feeling the ribs of that side lifting and opening.

Latissimus Dorsi Stretches With the Swiss Ball

Step 1

Kneel on the floor with both hands on a Swiss Ball. Sit back onto your heels and push the ball as far from you as you can. Relax your chest down towards the floor.

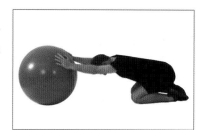

Step 2

Kneel on the floor with your hands on the Swiss Ball. Move your right hand so that it crosses over your left hand. Sit back onto your heels and make sure that your hips stay central. Push the ball away from you and roll it to the left, feeling your right side lengthen. Do not allow your hips to countermove out to the right.

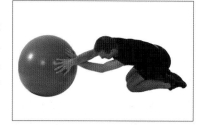

Correct pelvic positioning.

Loss of a fixed point: the pelvis has drifted sideways.

Posterior Shoulder Stretches

Athletes can often be seen performing these stretches with the shoulder collapsed upwards towards the ear. When this happens, they miss the tight muscles on the back of their shoulder and pull their scapula around instead.

To perform the stretch, start in balloon posture and raise one arm in front of you with the elbow bent and hand pointing to the ceiling. Keeping your shoulder relaxed down, move the arm across your body, guiding it with your other hand. Repeat the movement but this time start with your forearm horizontal to the floor. Focus on keeping your shoulder down.

Loss of a fixed point: the shoulder has shifted upwards.

Tricep Stretches

The key to good performance of this exercise is the position of the lumbar spine. The common error is to collapse the trunk into extension in an attempt to pull the elbow back further. Athletes also try to pull the arm behind the head and miss the tricep stretch altogether.

Start in balloon posture with your lower belly drawn in and maintain this spinal position throughout the exercise. Lift your arm to the ceiling, and drop your hand so that it lands on the scapula of the same side. Using your other hands to help, aim to point your elbow directly upwards towards the ceiling.

Chapter Summary

Stability concepts should be carried throughout the training programme. In order to do this, you will ideally have:

1 An understanding of the correct muscular patterns and actions for the exercise.

2 An ability to detect a movement dysfunction or error.

3 An understanding that stability principles apply to all types of training and are necessary for correct performance of any movement.

4 An appreciation that a stability programme should be multi-modal (use a variety of exercises, movements, and equipment), multi-planar (use a variety of movement directions), proprioceptive (use a variety of high and low level exercises to stimulate awareness and control), and diversified (challenge your body with unfamiliar movements and different objectives).

Chapter 10: Stability Training for Children

Developing Sound Movement for the Future
Planning a Session
Awareness and Activation in a Simple Context
Moving Well
Sample Session

Developing Sound Movement for the Future

Developing sound movement habits can equip children with the physical foundations for more effective sports skill acquisition. There is also evidence to support the effect of awareness, balance and control exercises on preventing injuries in young athletes [30,91]. It is important to include a variety of general movement activities in children's physical programmes; however, specific elements like balance, stability and body awareness can also be identified and addressed very early. These elements can make it easier for a child to develop new skills and can also affect speed, agility, balance and dissociative movement.

Planning a Session

A well-planned functional stability session will incorporate two processes. The children will learn new skills and will also learn how to self-monitor. By teaching new movements using a consistent procedure and increasing their self-awareness and familiarity with body parts, it is possible to teach children how to assess their own performance by interpreting intrinsic feedback. This allows them to problem solve by making adjustments to their own movement to achieve a new outcome.

There are several simple guidelines to follow when planning stability sessions for children.

* Be relevant. Have an objective in mind for the drills and games to ensure that all major elements are covered.
* Keep it simple. Teach in a structured way which is easy to understand, monitor and progress.
* Be consistent. Each time the drill is performed, reinforce the purpose and quality that you are aiming for.
* Don't rush. Allow children to consolidate basic movement skills before introducing complexity. A child's ability to lunge for a drop shot in tennis is unlikely to improve through sheer repetition if he cannot perform a basic lunge with no additional distraction or demand.
* Once a skill has been consolidated, introduce contextual interference to diversify the skill. Initially this may be as simple as having to do two things at once, such as lunging and catching a ball at the same time, but it can be expanded to provide a variety of different situations in which to use the established skill. This promotes greater transference of the skill [36]. Remember however that the skill must be established before applying contextual interference principles.
* Minimise augmented feedback. Constant feedback on the quality of children's performance blocks their ability to assess their own movement. Teach using a structure that helps children to assess themselves.

- Following on from this, foster children's ability to feed back on their own performance. Asking which body part they feel is working the most, or which body part is moving the most can help to sharpen awareness. If they can work in pairs, giving the task to feed back to each other can increase learning. For example, ask them to look out for spine shape or knee alignment as their partners perform a task.

- Create fun sessions by striking a balance between game style exercises and form development exercises.

Make It Easy to 'Get It Right'

When starting this type of work with children, it is important to establish and reinforce consistent checkpoints so that they easily learn correct technique and can apply it in the widest possible variety of situations.

It is easy for children to appreciate the "Balloon" postural cue, just as they can quickly tell the difference between an "arrow spine" (good spinal alignment), a "banana spine" (an excessively curved spinal shape), a "noodle spine" (wobbly and inconsistent spinal position) and a "duck tail" (sticking their bottoms out behind them).

Children also understand that "knocking knees" are not correct in any exercise. If a tiny train was to run down their leg, it would run fastest on a straight track, not one with a big bend in the middle where their knee has collapsed inwards.

Turtles provide an image for heads and necks. It is easy for children to realise that they are "pulling their heads into their shell", and work out how to bring their heads "back out of their shells". Describing turtles is more effective and elicits a better neuromuscular effect than asking them to "pull their shoulders down".

Engage Learning Through Structure

Category 1 exercises benefit from being taught in a structured way. Each exercise can be broken down into a checklist so that children become aware of themselves and accurate in reproducing a movement. That checklist should include:

1 An accurate starting position.

2 A sequence of checks moving from one end of the body to the other, using the "rules". Keep these instructions consistent and resist the temptation to give too many additional instructions.

3 Which body parts should be "doing the work".

Depending upon your setting and the ages of children you are working with, it can also be useful to explain what the exercise has to do with their sport. For example, pelvic stability exercises can be for changing direction quickly or better running and jumping; trunk stability exercises help you to keep an arrow spine so you can slip through the water when you swim or maintain your position in a tennis serve. Balance exercises can help you to kick a ball, and a Superman exercise can build stronger shoulders. Children can be quite receptive to this approach. For example, a fourteen-year-old tennis player was developing progressively worse posture, and did not respond to being told to "stand up and pull your shoulders back" by his parents and his coach. He didn't care when they told him that improving his posture would improve his appearance or prevent a future injury. What changed him immediately was being told how it was affecting his forehand.

Once children have learned the basics of an exercise, start asking them for information regarding checkpoints of the exercise. When you suggest a certain exercise, ask, "What is important to remember about this one?" By doing this you are engaging the child in a process, rather than just teaching an exercise. You also make it possible for the child to practice independently, rather than depending on your instruction.

Example

Children performing a Suspension Bridge should be able to respond to the question, "What is important to remember about this one?" with:

1 Head and shoulders on the ball.

2 Feet under knees.

3 No knocking knees.

4 Shrink the mountain ranges.

This response demonstrates that they know the set-up position for the exercise.

"Where should you be feeling it?" "Glutes!" (A response which is usually accompanied by them slapping their own glutes). You miss a huge opportunity in developing body awareness and understanding in the children if you don't teach in a structured way, and if you don't engage their minds actively. It does not detract from their pleasure. Instead it seems to give them a sense of pride and purpose about what they are doing.

Natural Movement in Fun Ways

Sessions should be structured to provide variety, fun, and learning. Very dynamic drills should be done early, with quieter more concentrated work done towards the end of a session. As well as stability and balance, elements of coordination, footwork and general movement should be included.

Balance in the session will influence success. A session will generally be divided into: (a) exercises which allow time to focus inwards on body parts, building body awareness and learning to activate key muscles, and (b) fun drills, which integrate this learning into more generalised functional movement patterns. Basic movement foundations such as running, jumping and throwing, control of momentum and body orientation will be key elements in a session for integration.

It is tempting to try new drills with children every session; however too much variation initially will hinder motor learning. Basic skills need to be consolidated before diversification or interference is introduced. Constantly changing the drills can be distracting and make it difficult for the children to see whether they have made progress.

To avoid this problem, decide on your movement priorities for a certain number of sessions. Keep 75% of the session reasonably constant, and introduce new drills to fill the other 25%. The children become confident with the consistent elements and can progress steadily. The new elements provide new challenges, prevent staleness and increase skill transference.

.

Notes from the Clipboard

A ten-year-old tennis player was evaluated for basic balance and stability, as well as tested for speed, agility, vertical jump and filmed to assess tennis specific movement. On his basic foundations testing he had exceptionally poor balance, an inability to vertically orientate his trunk, poor pelvic and leg control and no scapular stability. On static lunge testing, balance was only maintained if he squeezed his arms into his sides, and even then his trunk tipped to the left. Other tests showed that he was slow to generate speed, had significant difference in agility from left to right, low vertical jump height and fundamental problems with tennis technique.

The player attended a group programme designed to provide a multi-modal collection of movement experiences twice a week, and as he enjoyed the exercises he chose to do additional practice. Six months later he won the national clay court championship in his age group, his asymmetries had markedly reduced, and his improved speed, agility, balance and control continue to support his technical development.

Initial testing: Low complexity. Poor performance of a basic static lunge.

Six months later: High complexity control. Maintaining a stable lunge while sliding on clay and mimicking shot preparation.

Stability training for children can be divided into two categories.

1. Awareness and Activation in a Simple Context

This category of exercises keeps the activities simple and focuses on developing awareness of control, movement of one body part on another and how different muscles feel.

Feedback from coaches has indicated that this type of exercise helps them to teach technique more effectively, as the children have developed better general awareness of themselves both consciously and unconsciously. These exercises give a child the opportunity to focus on intrinsic feedback.

Concepts which should be covered in this category include:

- Balloon posture.
- The difference in feeling between a neutral (arrow) spine and an unstable (noodle) spine.
- Knee alignment.
- Feeling the difference between a "shoulders up" and a "shoulders relaxed" position.
- Feeling the gluteal, abdominal, and midback muscles working.
- Listening to the feet.
- Basic balance.
- Rotational movement of the chest on the pelvis.
- Rotational movement of the pelvis on the chest.
- Rotational movement of the pelvis over the foot.
- Transferring weight.
- Pivoting the foot.

2. Moving Well

Teaching children how to move effectively helps to develop good functional motor patterns. A variety of cues can be used to improve performance. These include a limited amount of augmented feedback for explicit learning about the task and for implicit learning, directing the child's attention to sensory stimuli such as the sound of a foot strike as it hits the ground, the feeling or sound of the rhythm of a movement to promote symmetry and consistency, and differentiating the lightness or heaviness of the movement.

Concepts covered in this category are:

- Keeping the body balanced over moving feet.
- Rhythmic control.
- Jumping and landing.
- Dynamic balance.
- Momentum control in different directions.

Exercise Options

As with adults, children can benefit from a combination of focused stability exercises and fun dynamic stability games. These should be combined with mobility exercises such as those listed in previous chapters. Stability without mobility will not be used functionally.

Many of the exercises and progressions listed in Phases 1 and 2 are applicable to children, but may need a small degree of adaptation depending upon the age of the child.

A number of the Phase 1 and Phase 2 exercises in Chapters 5–8 are adapted below for children.

Category 1: Awareness and Activation in a Simple Context

Ball Bouncing

Coaching Objective

To train dynamic postural stability, central axis control, activate transversus abdominis and multifidus.

Step 1: Increasing awareness of pelvic position
The children will be sitting on the ball with feet flat on the floor and their hands under their sitting bones. Ask the children to sit more on their right sitting bone, and then sit more on their left sitting bone. Then ask them to sit evenly on both sitting bones.

Ask them to slump and feel how they have rolled off the back of the bones. Their sitting bones are now pointing forward.

Then ask them to really sit up straight and feel how this rolls them over the front of the bones. Their bones are now pointing backwards.

Then ask them to sit so their weight goes straight down on the bones. Their bones are now pointing downwards.

This is the position that they will aim to maintain throughout the exercise.

Step 2: The movement
The children will take their arms over their heads so that they are straight and firm. They should feel their abdominals come in as they stretch upwards. Now they can start their bouncing, keeping their bodies straight and landing accurately on both sitting bones.

Variations
Keeping the trunk straight but moving one arm down to the side and back up as they bounce.

Placing hands behind the head, and turning the chest for one bounce and back to the middle for one bounce.

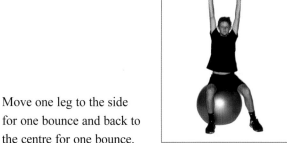

Move one leg to the side for one bounce and back to the centre for one bounce.

Progression

* Land evenly through both sides when supported only on one leg. Add the arm and trunk variations.

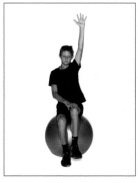

Touching the opposite knee without collapsing the trunk.

Touching the opposite foot without collapsing the trunk.

 Question for the Children

* *Are you landing on both sitting bones, or do you land on one more than the other?*

Ball Circles

 Coaching Objective

Increase awareness of abdominals.

The children lie on their backs with their knees bent and feet flat on the floor. They have a small Swiss Ball in their hands.

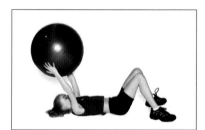

Ask them to take a big breath in and then let it all out and relax. Once they have done this, ask them to take the ball in a circle over their body, and tell you what they feel in their stomachs. Perform the circles for 30 seconds.

> 🙂 *Question for the Children*
> * *Is the feeling always the same or does it move around your stomach?*
>   *The sensation should move in response to the ball's movement.*

 Greyhound

This is an easy exercise for children to master, and can be taught very simply.

 Coaching Objective

Increase awareness of the neutral spine and the deep abdominals.

The children lie on their backs with their knees bent, their feet on the floor and their arms up towards the ceiling. As they take their arms over their heads they slide one foot out along the floor, making their spine stretch and melt along the floor. They focus on staying long and thin in the middle and bring their arms and leg back to the start position.

Note: Feeling long and thin in the middle is not the same as "pull your stomach in". It is just a way to maintain the trunk sensation and position that occurred naturally in response to arm movement.

> 🙂 *Question for the Children*
> * *Which body parts do you feel working?*

Ball Over Head

This is a progression from Greyhounds. Start in the same position with the children holding a ball. This time the ball will move back overhead in the same way as they previously moved only their arms. They need to focus on making their spine lengthen along the floor like melting toffee. When they do this, ask them to notice whether their stomach has changed or moved. It should have dropped down towards their spine.

To bring the ball up, ask them to focus on keeping their lower belly down towards their spine to lift the ball back up again.

Progression

* As the ball moves overhead, ask the children to slide one foot out so that they are as long and thin in the middle as they can be. Ask them to stay thin in the middle and bring the ball and the leg back in again. Their pelvis should remain level throughout the movement.

> 😊 *Question for the Children*
> * *Ask them whether they can feel the floor under their hips on both sides equally. If not, imagine squashing something under the side that lifts.*

Superman

The technique for this exercise is the same as for the adult version. However, it is fun for the children to balance a water bottle on their midback. This is an easy way for them to find out whether their bodies are straight and their scapular muscles are working.

Coaching Objective

To coordinate the pelvis, trunk and upper body and increase awareness in all three zones while activating muscles at low threshold. The rotator cuff must activate to keep the chest parallel to the floor.

The children start on hands and knees with head and neck in straight alignment. Hands should be positioned under shoulders, and knees under hips so that they feel like a strong wooden table. Their lower belly is drawn upwards.

They press straight out with one heel keeping their pelvis level and feeling strong through their support hip so that it does not sag out to the side. Stretch out with the opposite fingertips so that there is a straight line from fingers to heel. Their chest and pelvis should be parallel to the floor. If the chest tips or the scapula on the supporting side lifts off the rib cage, ask them to press their chest away from the floor a little bit more to make their shoulder feel strong. Once they are in position, balance a water bottle on their midback. If they can keep this balance, they can try moving their free arm out to the side and underneath their body without dropping the bottle. The next progression is to swap from one diagonal to the other without dropping the bottle.

Superman With a Partner

One child will perform the Superman and the other child will gently push him or her in different directions to challenge them. To prevent overpushing, tell them that if someone falls over it is because the pusher has pushed too hard, not because the other person isn't very stable!

Floor Bridge
Coaching Objective

To activate GMax in inner range without overusing back muscles; sagittal and rotational trunk control.

The children lie on their back with a Swiss Ball under the legs as close to their body as possible. Their arms are on the floor, so they have a big base of support. They will straighten their legs by pushing the ball away from them and allowing the hips to lift so that their body is in a straight line from shoulders to toes. Their knees should be straight, and they should be squeezing their GMax to keep their hips up.

Check to make sure that the children are not just pushing their abdomens upwards, as this will trigger hamstrings and back extensors instead of GMax. They will look like their body is domed upwards instead of straight, as it should be. Have them poke their own GMax and compare its firmness to their back muscles. If their back muscles are firmer than their GMax, have them drop their ribs a little until their body is straight.

If you have several children in a group, put them in a line where they can pass a ball over or roll a ball under their body to the next person, or play over and under, where a ball is passed under one person and over the next.

Progression
- Arm movements in all directions: overhead, out to the side, across the body.
- Making circles with a water bottle in the hands for a little resistance.

Question for the Children
- *Which muscle do you feel the most? If they say it is their back, you know that they have arched their spine upwards. If they say it is their hamstrings, check that their knees are straight; otherwise they will try to lift themselves with knee flexion instead of hip extension.*

Suspension Bridge

This exercise is also performed in exactly the same way as for adults. The cues must be very consistent for children, but they quickly learn to perform this exercise well.

The children start by sitting on a Swiss Ball. Keeping their lower bellies in and not poking their chins out, they walk out with their feet until their head and shoulders are resting on the ball. They must make sure their feet are directly underneath their knees, and that their hips, knees, and ankles are in line.

Ask them to feel the muscles in their lower back. If they have ridges of rigid muscle either side of their spine, these are "mountain ranges". In between the mountains there will be a valley where the spine is. If they have big mountains and a deep valley, they will not be using their GMax effectively, and overusing their back muscles.

To correct this, have them put their hands on their pelvis with their thumbs up and fingers down. They drop their hips slightly to take their hip flexors off stretch, and turn their pelvis back towards them like a big wheel. Ask them to check that their mountains are smaller.

The variations given in Phase 2 apply for children also.

Question for the Children
- *Which muscle do you feel the most? If they say it is their backs, ask them to lower their body a little and turn their "wheel" (pelvis) back towards them. If they say it is their hamstrings, make sure their feet have not crept in front of their knees.*

● Titanic
○ Coaching Objective

To encourage coordinated balance responses; minimise rigidity as a balance strategy; enable independent arm movement.

The children start with a Swiss Ball under their stomachs and their feet against the wall. Their knees and hips are bent and their hands are positioned beside their shoulders with their elbows bent. Keeping their noses pointing to the floor, they will push out strongly and stretch their arms out in front of them so that their knees and hips are straight. Their feet should stay flat on the wall, and their spine should not curve upwards.

● Bouncing Ball Balance
○ Coaching Objective

To encourage coordinated balance responses; minimise rigidity as a balance strategy; dissociation of the arm.

Major system objective
Sensory motor and vestibular components of the balance system, trunk, and lower limb stability.

The children stand on one leg and bounce the ball from hand to hand across the body, and as far around their body as they can reach. They then bounce it as far forward as they can, as far to the side as they can, and under their other leg.

Basic Static Balance
Coaching Objective

Increase the children's awareness of their feet, and improve components of the balance system, trunk, and lower limb stability.

Ask the children to stand on one leg in their balloon posture with their arms in the air. Ask them to push their body up away from the floor to activate their hip stabilisers. Challenge them by asking them to move their arms or free leg in any specific direction. Then ask them to shut their eyes. This will make them wobbly, but you do not want them to become rigid as they attempt to control their position, so ask them to focus on making their feet wider and softer. Challenge them again with arm or leg movements.

Simple Star
Coaching Objective

Global stability for the hip, trunk, and shoulder.

Start with the children sitting on the floor with their legs straight. To perform a right star, they will turn onto the right side with their body weight supported on their right hand. They will then straighten their body and reach for the ceiling with their left hands. Their hips should be in line with their body.

They will then turn their body so that their left hand comes to the floor, and they are supporting themselves on their hands and feet before turning themselves into a left star.

Other suitable Category 1 stability exercises for children include the following exercises as listed in Phase 1:

Diamonds

Sphinx

Clams
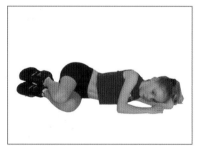

Hip Pops and Hip Swivels

Wall Press and Wall Squat

Over the Top   Pull Backs

Lunges

Rotational Movement Sequencing
Counter Body Rotation

The ability to rotate the upper and lower body in opposite directions is essential for the development of a number of sporting movements. The following drills give different options for experiencing rotation.

1 Start with the children standing with their arms crossed over their chests and their knees bent. Explain that their trunk has a top part and a bottom part. Keeping their knees facing forward, ask them to turn their top part from side to side.

2 Then with their hands on the wall, ask them to turn their lower body from side to side without moving their feet. If they can do this, repeat the movement with arms crossed over the chest.

3 Place the hands back on the wall and turn the lower body by jumping and turning the feet from side to side. Their shoulders should remain parallel to the wall.

4 Without the wall, counter body rotation is added by "twisting" the trunk so that the feet and arms go in opposite directions without the feet moving.

5 Add a jumping twist where the arms swing one way while the feet turn the other way.

The whole sequence can be linked together as a dance with the children performing four repetitions of each movement one after the other. This introduces coordination and rhythm in addition to the motion.

Pelvic Rotation Over the Fixed Foot

The combination of pelvic rotation and weight transference is necessary for tennis players, golfers, footballers and baseballers, but some children (and adults) have a mobility awareness block around this area of their bodies. For example, a ten-year-old tennis player was struggling with his backhand and could not work out how to perform this movement. Once he discovered his ability to transfer his weight onto his front foot and rotate his pelvis, it was very easy for him to overcome the movement block in his stroke.

Ask the children to stand up with their arms relaxed. They are going to turn their body to the left, allowing their right heel to lift so that their foot can pivot and their pelvis can freely rotate over their left foot. Letting their arms swing freely, they will turn to the right, lifting their left heel to allow their pelvis to rotate. Increase their awareness by asking which way their weight is moving when they rotate.

Rotate and Freeze Game

Once the children have established their pelvic rotation and weight transference, set a tempo for them all to move in together. Intermittently ask them to freeze at the point of maximum rotation and keep their balance.

Hoop Throwing

Hoop throwing is a fun way to explore pelvic rotation, weight transference and balance. Children can often be observed transferring their weight backwards instead of forward as they learn to throw, kick or swing. This exercise provides an opportunity to learn forward weight transference, which in turn improves other movement skills.

Each child holds a large plastic hoop with hands on opposite sides of the hoop. To encourage effective trunk rotation, both hands are used. The hoop will be held parallel to the floor. The aim is to toss the hoop as far as possible towards the other end of the room.

They will stand with their feet apart at a 90-degree angle from the throwing direction. They will start by swinging the hoop across their body by turning their shoulders,

feeling how their weight is shifting from foot to foot. Then make them aware of releasing the back heel to enable greater rotation. Once they have practised this, let them complete the movement and toss the hoop as far as they can. They must "freeze" in the release position and tell you which foot their weight is on. Some children lack the control to keep their body moving forward into the movement, so they topple backwards as they release the hoop. When they try again, encourage them to stand tall on their front leg after they have tossed the hoop. Children who do not effectively integrate their arm movement with their body movement may also have a poor result on their first attempt. They will try too hard and overuse their arm, and this results in poor distance or direction of the throw. These children respond best to a slow, relaxed hoop release after the practise swings, with the emphasis on how smooth their movement is rather than how hard they throw.

○ Forward Weight Transference With Rotation

Weight transference and pelvic rotation are important components of the throwing action [29]. Poor throwers emphasise arm movement in the throw and minimise the rotational dissociation of the pelvis and shoulders that provide the drive for the action. The pelvis and shoulders tend to move in the same plane. The following movements can be part of the dynamic warm-up, or can be used to precede throwing practise to stimulate awareness of body rotation.

To adapt the previous movements to prepare for throwing practise, the children will start with one foot forward. They will use the same principles of transferring weight, rotating the pelvis and pivoting the back foot, but this time they are moving forward instead of sideways.

Step 1: Right-handed children stand with their left foot pointing forward, right foot at 45 degrees to it and arms out to the side. They turn their body to the right, and as they transfer weight onto the front foot, they will turn their body to the left, looking forward throughout the motion. This warm-up movement emphasises the body drive element of throwing without the distraction of arm movement.

Step 2: Throwing is commonly taught with the throwing hand starting behind the ear, but this can encourage some children to delay the release of the ball and use elbow straightening to generate the movement once their chests are facing the target. Children who do this stop their shoulders rotating as soon as the ball is released and frequently tip their bodies forward to absorb the force instead.

For children with this problem, start with the elbow at 90 degrees instead, tennis ball in the right hand with the same foot position as above. They will rotate back into right rotation as for step 1, but as they transfer their weight onto their front foot they will release the ball. Let them do this as quickly as they like. Increased rotational body speed can cause their shoulder to move into more external rotation initially, which is a more natural cocking position.

Step 3: Start with feet together 45 degrees from the target direction, and step forward into the rotational throwing action.

For coordination and symmetry, repeat the same activity sequence using the non-dominant side.

Around the World

The children stand back to back with a small gap between them, and one holds the ball. They will pass it around to the other child, allowing the trail foot to release and the pelvis to rotate over the stance leg. They will then turn in the opposite direction to receive the ball as it comes around.

There are several focus points:

- The balloon posture will be maintained to make sure that the abdominals continue to work.
- The trail foot is allowed to release to avoid stress on the knee.
- The pelvis rotates freely over the stance leg.

Once the children can perform this exercise, they can try a low to high version, receiving the ball low and passing it back high and vice-versa.

○ Big Ball Side Throws
○ Coaching Objective

To teach a strong trunk rotation around a strong central axis with weight transference.
Major body part focus: upright trunk.

Both children stand facing the same way, at least 3m apart. One child has the ball in his hands. This child will swing the ball across his body to the other child, transferring his weight onto his inside foot and allowing his pelvis to turn. There should be no low to high movement: the ball should move in a level line.

Category 2: Moving Well

○ Knee Taps

Recovering from a quick movement to be able to move again quickly.

○ Coaching Objective

To teach good body posture by encouraging hip and knee bending, coordination of the arms with the leg and trunk position, strength through range in the quadriceps and gluteus maximus, balance, and contrasting high intensity reactive work with controlled balance challenge. *Major muscle group focus:* gluteus maximus, gluteus medius.

Children work in pairs. The objective for each child is to tap the other child's knees, and to avoid being touched themselves. They must keep their heads up and bottoms down as they try to reach forward. After 20 seconds, stop the drill and ask all of the children to stand on one leg with their arms above their heads. If they are just learning they can have their eyes open, but will eventually have their eyes closed. Ask them to move one arm at a time, the other leg, and turn their trunks to challenge their balance. Start the drill again.

Side Step Game
Coaching Objective

To improve change of direction effectiveness, coronal plane trunk control, forward momentum control, and balance. *Major muscle group focus:* gluteus medius.

The objective for each child is to react to an auditory cue to change directions as quickly as possible, to win a race to the front of the court, control their forward momentum and be able to keep balance successfully.

Children are in a line beside each other. They start a side to side step movement until a clap is heard and they move in the opposite direction. A double clap means that they keep going in the same direction but face away from you. A triple clap or shout means that wherever they are, they must turn and run towards you, pick up a tennis ball without falling forward and stand on one leg with the ball held up over their heads.

Rabbits and Spiders

This exercise stimulates stability around the shoulder girdle through weight bearing as well as hip mobility.

Rabbits: Place a collection of hoops on the floor. The children crouch down with their weight on their hands and feet. To move like rabbits, they will move both hands together into a hoop followed by both feet together.

Spiders: The children will support themselves on hands and feet, with the knees off the ground. You will give them instructions to scuttle like spiders in any combination of directions, using their hands and feet. This time the hands move independently and the feet move independently.

Combining games: Line tennis balls up along the floor. The children need to perform rabbits or spiders to get to a ball, pick it up and run across a finish line.

● Landing on Lily Pads

Good jumping and landing technique should be taught as part of a general development programme for children. Effective techniques include trying to land without making a loud noise, and learning to jump without overdependence on arms. This will lay the foundations for plyometric training, which has been found to be effective in improving athletic performance in prepubescent children [19].

Coordinated jumping doesn't necessarily develop spontaneously. When screening a netball team for functional motor patterning it was noted that a large number of the players had poor vertical jump height. When asked to jump with their arms eliminated from the movement by placing their hands on their heads they had minimal takeoff. When asked which body parts were most important for jumping, an alarming number thought it was their arms.

When asked to jump from standing, children will often swing their arms and use this momentum to help them off the ground. If arm swinging is more dominant than using their hips, knees, and ankles, this strategy sweeps them into a weak spinal extension position in the air as their arms move upwards and backwards over their heads. A poor jumping pattern can make children appear to have increased muscle tension in their arms, neck and back, and decreased tone in the legs when they are in the air. Frog jumps emphasise the sequencing of ankle, knee and hip extension for jumping, and develop an awareness of the leg muscles pushing upwards.

For every jump there must be a landing, so this is taught as part of the same drill. If you were a frog landing on a lily pad, you would know that you could not land heavily or unbalanced. You would need springy knees, hips and ankles to absorb the landing, and you would need to land softly and lightly. You therefore have an imagery cue of your frog's bendy elastic legs and an auditory cue to land quietly.

● Coaching Objective

To stimulate correct movement sequence for jumping and landing.

Children start with their knees bent, hands touching the ground in front of them and their heads up to watch you. They will leap in the air and land on the spot with both feet, absorbing their landing with springy legs. Once they can do this, they can leap up and sideways, forward or at angles into hoops placed on the floor.

Variation
Place hoops in a zigzag on the floor. Ask the children to frog jump keeping their feet facing forward.

Leaping Frogs
Coaching Objective

To stimulate correct activation chain for jumping, pelvic stability and trunk orientation, and momentum control. To develop dynamic pelvic and lower limb stability, balance and control of the central axis of the trunk for controlled landings.

Major muscle group focus: gluteus maximus and gluteus medius for pelvic control.

Children start with their hands touching the ground in front of them and their heads up to watch you. They jump at a 45-degree angle forward and land to hold their balance on their outside leg. They should "land with springs" in their hips, knees and ankles so that the landing is soft and light.

Variation
Vary the direction of the leap.

Racing Frogs
Coaching Objective

To train efficient orientation of trunk over pelvis, lateral pelvic control, dynamic balance, and equal push off from each foot.

Major muscle group focus: gluteus medius.

Children's objective is to keep balance, and win a race to the other side of a tennis court or exercise space.

Children line up behind one another and squat down with their hands on the ground in front of them. They will jump up and across to land on a line with their right (outside) foot and keep their balance until you clap. They will react quickly to the sound and race to a line of tennis balls on their left, check their forward momentum by dropping their hips, pick up a ball and hold it above their heads while standing on one leg for balance.

○ Jump and Turn
○ Coaching Objective

To manage body orientation in the air, to control rotational momentum.

Stand in a ready position with hips and knees slightly bent. Jump and turn in the air to 90 degrees from the start position. Return by jumping back to face the front.

You are looking for the pelvis to face straight ahead, and the knees to land parallel to each other. Poor rotational knee control is a mechanism for serious knee injury in adult multidirectional sports, and in this drill will appear as the knees continuing to move in the rotational direction after landing.

Once 90 degrees has been mastered in each direction, introduce 180-degree turns. If control is good, a game can be played mixing directions and making the children think and remember degrees e.g. 90 degrees right and back to the front, 180 degrees left and back to the front, 90 degrees left and back to the front.

○ Jump and Roll
○ Coaching Objective

To develop agility, coordination, and whole body movement.

Use a length of elastic to create a jump. The children will use a high knee stepping action to jump over the elastic, then drop to the floor and perform a log roll under the elastic. They will repeat this movement down the full length of the elastic.

Variation

- *Jumping spiders.* Children jump over the elastic in the same fashion as for jump and roll, but instead of rolling under the elastic they must drop onto hands and feet and slide under without touching the floor with their knees or the bands with their backs.

Side Leaps
Coaching Objective

To use the muscles of the hip area effectively for lateral drive.

Make a V-shape with the elastic at a low height. The children will start at the narrowest end on the outside of the left arm of the V. They will push off their left foot to land in the middle of the V with their right foot, following quickly with the left foot to take off again and jump over the right arm of the V, landing on their right foot. They will reverse the movement, moving sideways and slightly forward, so that each crossing is a little wider. You are encouraging them to push more powerfully each time so that they jump further.

Big Ball Bounces
Coaching Objective

To integrate upper limb movement with trunk stability.

Major muscle group focus: abdominals.

Children are taught to take the ball high overhead maintaining an arrow spine. Staying tall, keeping their lower abdominals in and aiming for a spot 30 cm in front of them, they then try and bounce the ball as high as they can.

An alternative movement is to teach children to take a step forward as they bounce the ball.

Overhead Ball Toss

This exercise is best performed after the big ball bounce.

Coaching Objective

To integrate upper limb movement and trunk stability.

Major muscle group focus: abdominals.

Children take a football-sized ball overhead while keeping an arrow spine. They step forward and perform the overhead throw with both hands, making sure that they stay tall. Stronger children can throw a Swiss Ball.

Awareness pointer

Children will commonly collapse at the hips as they try to throw further. Ask them to tell you whether their hips move forward or backwards as they throw. When they can tell you this, ask them whether they get taller or shorter when their hips move backwards. Then ask them to see if they can stay tall and throw the ball.

Side Foot Touch and Reach
Coaching Objective

Gluteus maximus activation in outer range, and gluteus medius controlling the pelvis.

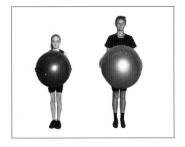

Children stand with feet together. They step to the right, and keeping their body as upright as they can, reach over to touch their right foot. They then push off that foot and shift their weight over to the left foot, and they keep their balance with their left arm stretched up. This can be progressed to holding a Swiss Ball in both hands to perform the movement.

Dynamic Rotations
Coaching Objective

To integrate body rotation with footwork, stimulate use of the trunk to initiate and control rotation and increase awareness of the pelvis.

Major muscle group focus: abdominals.

Children's objective is to turn as quickly as possible. Start with children in a circle. Before they start, have them put their hands on the front of their pelvis, so that they know which body part to focus on. By turning the pelvis, the movement will be sharp and the trunk muscles will activate. If you do not give them some awareness of the pelvis first, the children will focus on their foot or the shoulders to generate the movement.

They will have their hips and knees slightly bent in a "ready" position. They will move their right foot across their body, turning as they do this. Do it slowly first so that they have time to notice their pelvis turning. Once they have this idea, they will perform the movement as fast as they can, then reverse the movement and repeat it to the left. There are two variations to this exercise. Both activate the trunk muscles.

First variation: The shoulders and hips will move together, as they would to prepare for a tennis volley for example.

Second variation: The shoulders will stay facing forward with the arms out to the side, allowing the pelvis to rotate freely. This works more on dissociation of the pelvis from the trunk, as would happen when kicking a football. This version is also good to work on counter body rotation symmetry, which is important for any running related activity as explained in Chapter 1, and dissociation of upper body on lower body as is relevant to throwing, tennis forehands and golf swings.

◉ Fast Feet: Forward and Backward
◉ Coaching Objective

To develop trunk control and lower limb movements, which will support future footwork drills.

Children stand on one side of a line, so that they can step forward and backwards over it. Staying bouncy on their toes, they will use a two beat timing to move right and left foot over the line, and right and left foot back over to the start position. They must keep their body positioned over their feet rather than allowing their feet to shift underneath their body. Start slowly, and gradually increase speed as the children move up the line.

Teaching notes

1 A toe-in pattern is common in children, so start slowly and focus on straight feet moving forward and backward. As they become more proficient, they can increase their speed.

2 Have them clap out the rhythm on their thighs first so that they can become familiar with a regular beat. Keep the beat for them as they practise by clapping it for them.

3 To keep their body orientated over their feet in a dynamic position, aim for a soundless performance. If a scuff or squeak is heard, it means that the child is allowing body position to drift backwards with respect to their feet. When this happens, the training effect on their hip and knee flexion motion is diminished.

◉ Fast Feet: Side to Side

This pattern works on a triple beat, so rhythm and symmetry are emphasised.

Children stand with the line on their right side. Before trying the drill, have them clap out the rhythm on their legs. It will be: *1-2-3, 1-2-3, 1-2-3, 1-2-3*.

They will step over the line with their right foot, and then step onto left and right before stepping back onto the left foot and stepping right and left. Once the pattern is learned, make it bouncy and sharp, silent and soft.

Teaching notes

Children with particular dominance on one side or poor trunk stability and hip flexor strength will tend to lose their rhythm. You may need to clap it out for them as they perform the drill.

Karate Punches
Coaching Objective

To develop a sense of firm trunk and pelvic control against upper limb movements.

Major muscle group focus: abdominals.

Stand in balloon posture with hips and knees softly bent in the ready position. One arm is straight in front at shoulder height, and the other is bent at the elbow and pulled back.

Switch arm positions as quickly as possible, making sure that the arms are moving through the whole range. The most common error is to move the arms only from the chest. You will see the arms moving in and out from the chest, rather than sweeping back past their sides.

Remember to maintain long necks and abdominals tucked in. Perform a 30 second burst, have a short rest and repeat.

To increase the challenge and also the fun, the same drill can be performed on a wobble cushion once the basic exercise has been mastered.

Robot Steps
Coaching Objective

Establish pelvic and knee control as well as dynamic balance.

The children should already have mastered the basic lunge. They will step forward into a left lunge with their arms out to the side, keeping their knee straight and their body in balloon posture. They will step straight through into a right lunge maintaining the same form. There should be no foot touches on the floor as each leg moves forward.

Double Ball Game

Coaching Objective

Multi-directional agility, reactions, coordination and cooperation.

The children will work in pairs. One child will hold two tennis balls. They will toss a ball so that the other child can catch it on the first bounce. As that ball is returned to them, they toss the other ball to another position, far enough away that their partners must try hard to get to it on the first bounce, but not so far that it is impossible. They will mix up the ball tosses between left and right, forward and backward.

Ball Follow With Both Hands on the Ball

The ball follow as described in Phase 4 can be used with children. It can be modified to start with by having both of each child's hands on the ball. Ask them to perform big movements slowly at first with their eyes closed in order to focus their attention on sensory feedback. It can be made more difficult by performing the exercise on one foot for a greater balance challenge.

Throwing and Catching Coordination Drills

While it is tempting to only use the dominant arm for throwing drills, coordination, movement adaptability and body awareness can be enhanced by integrating right and left sides of the body. When throwing with their non-dominant arm for the first time, ask the children first to feel how they throw with their dominant arm, and compare it with how the throwing action feels on their non-dominant side.

Give Sensory Awareness Cues. Examples: Does your weight move when you throw normally? Does it do the same thing on your other side? See if you can make both sides feel the same. Why do you think one arm feels different? See if you can work out how to make it feel the same.

Drill 1: Two children face each other, each with a tennis ball. They will start by bouncing their ball to the other person, throwing it with their right hand and catching it with their left hand. Both children will throw and catch simultaneously, which speeds up their reactions. Once they have managed to achieve this, they will throw with their left hand and catch with their right hand.

Drill 2: One child will throw the ball to the other with the right hand. The other child will bounce the ball to the other with the right hand. Both will catch with the left hand. After several cycles they will switch hands, throwing with their left and catching with their right. After several cycles, the "bouncer" will become the "thrower", and vice-versa.

Drill 3: Both children will throw the ball. They will start with a right armed throw and a left armed catch, and then switch to a left armed throw and right hand catch.

Sample Session

Warm-up

- General movement to raise heart rate and prepare the body for action.
- Dynamic flexibility.
- Fast feet.
- Knee tap and balance.

Main Body of the Session

- Side Step Game.
- Racing Frogs.
- Double Ball Game.
- Basic Lunges with arms out to the side.
- Landing on Lily Pads.
- Jump and Roll.
- Spiders.
- Simple Star.
- Big Ball Bounces.
- Side Foot Touch and Reach.
- Karate Punches.
- Bouncing Ball Balance.
- Weight transference with pelvic rotations.
- Throwing practice with a partner:
  - a) Throwing alternately with dominant arm and non-dominant arm for coordination and symmetry.
  - b) Throwing with one arm and catching with the other.
  - c) Each child has a ball, and one throws the ball to their partner while the other bounces the ball to their partner.
  - d) Normal throwing.
- Ball following.

End of the Session

- Seated Ball Bouncing.
- Greyhounds.
- Superman balancing a water bottle on the back.
- Diamonds.
- Floor Bridge with the Swiss Ball.
- Wall Press with the Swiss Ball.
- Over the Top.
- Basic Bridge passing a tennis ball under and over the body.

Finish by learning some correct stretching techniques. Many of the exercises from Phases 1–4 are suitable for children, but they must be progressively developed. The lunge development sequence is particularly important, as it is easy to pass over the more static levels in favour of fun dynamic drills. This can eventually let children down, as they may not develop the foundation pelvic control that will help them with sporting technique development. The key is to mix up the less exciting but very important exercises with the fun games acting as a reward. For this reason, Basic Lunges are listed before Landing on Lily Pads, and Side Foot Touch and Reach precedes Karate Punches and Big Ball Bounces, which are often favourites.

Mini trampolines, balance boards and wobble cushions all add interest and fun to a session, but once again, add them as variations or progressions once the basic skills have been established.

Chapter 11: Sample Programmes

The four phases contain a collection of broadly applicable exercises. For convenience, a collection of exercises relevant to a variety of sports has been provided below as a guideline to streamlining a programme. This does not mean that these are the only exercises from the four Phases which are relevant to the sport. They have simply been prioritised for clarity.

Programmes of this nature are intended to be performed in a complementary fashion with the rest of the training and testing programme. For each sport, there are additional specific muscle length tests and joint mobility tests that sports medicine professionals can apply.

1 Running

For efficiency and speed, runners need to eliminate any unnecessary sideways or up and down movements. Their bodies need to be able to smoothly and symmetrically counter rotate around a secure central longitudinal axis. This will require balance and mobility as well as trunk and pelvic stability. The runner must be trained to maintain a neutral spinal position with low effort so as not to interfere with their breathing pattern and spinal rotational mobility.

The runner is aiming for short foot contact times on the ground, and this will require good pelvic stability to prevent coronal or sideways collapse of the hip. Ineffective gluteal action can also cause collapse in the sagittal plane, where the hip and knee bend too much on impact, dropping the runner's body on each step and increasing muscular load. In sprinters, this problem makes them appear as though their body is always behind their feet, rather than their feet propelling their body forward. In any runner, it can predispose the knee, Achilles tendon, hip flexors and lower back to injury.

Priority tests

- Static balance with eyes open and eyes closed to check the sensory feedback from each foot and that the CLA is maintained centrally in single leg stance.

- Lunge to check mid to inner range GMax, lateral pelvic stability and trunk control.

- Standing knee lift to check for hip and pelvic stability.

- Seated knee lift on Swiss Ball to check the trunk control component of the CLA.

- Standing leg swing to check for a secure CLA and pelvic stability.

Priority exercises
Phase 1:
- All trunk and lower limb activation exercises
- Breathing technique
- Listening foot mobilisation
- Counter body rotation mobility exercise

Phase 2:
- Single Leg Seated Bounce
- OTT
- Lunges
- Step-ups
- Space Invaders
- Sway
- Balance

Phase 3:
- Medicine Ball Sweep
- Medicine Ball Spiral
- Pulley Pull Drive
- Cross Body Pulls
- Standing Stretch Band Drive
- Standing Knee Lift Drive
- Aeroplane Sequence
- Walking Drills

Phase 4:
- Side Squat Tosses with Medicine Ball
- Follow Through Rotations with Medicine Ball
- Stair Bounding
- Side Leaps

2 Golf

The golfer needs to ensure that he or she has no blocks to joint rotation from the foot all the way through the spine and shoulder. A firm CLA to support trunk rotation, good stabilisers of the pelvis, and dynamic balance are also necessary. If any of these factors are compromised, a golfer can be vulnerable to lower back, wrist, knee or shoulder injuries.

Priority tests
- Static balance to check for sensory feedback from the feet.
- Static lunge to check for hip support from GMax and a centrally balanced trunk.
- Single knee lift to check for pelvic and trunk stability.
- Seated hamstring test to check for spinal proprioception and hamstring length.
- Total body rotation to check for hip and spinal rotation.
- Seated trunk rotation to check for trunk rotation.
- Lumbo-pelvic mobility.
- Listening foot to check for lower leg mobility.
- Diamonds to check for external rotation at the shoulder.
- Superman to check integration of upper, central and lower control zones.

Priority exercises
Phase 1:
- Listening foot mobility
- All Phase 1 exercises are relevant

Phase 2:
- OTT Twisting Squat Thrust
- Lunge
- Sway
- Titanic
- Balance
- Any of the Phase 2 mobility poses

Phase 3:
- Medicine Ball Clean
- Medicine Ball Sweep
- Medicine Ball Spiral
- Pulley Push
- Rotational Pulley Push
- Rotational Lunges with a Medicine Ball
- Swiss Ball Pendulum
- Swiss Ball Body Spin
- Aeroplane Sequence

Phase 4:
- Side Tosses with Medicine Ball
- Medicine Ball Follow Through Rotations
- Kneeling Ball Balance with arm movements and trunk rotations
- Swiss Ball Side Raises
- Pendulum Lunges
- Cork Screw

3 Equestrian

The equestrian athlete requires a secure CLA through effective stability, symmetry, lumbo-pelvic and hip mobility and balance. When not on the horse, movement and posture habits influence and reinforce sense of body orientation and weight distribution, and this affects rider position when mounted. Testing on the ground can therefore identify the habits which may be affecting the riding position. Similarly, training off the horse to correct these imbalances can improve the position, posture and mobility of the rider.

Priority tests
- Static Balance
- Static Lunge
- Seated Knee Lift on Ball
- Standing Knee Lift
- Superman
- Lumbo-pelvic mobility in all directions
- Seated Forward Tilt to assess control of the neutral spine
- Mini Squat to assess the trunk's response to hip bending

Priority exercises
Phase 1:
- Any Phase 1 exercise
- Lumbo-pelvic mobility exercises
- Listening foot mobility

Phase 2:
- Single Leg Bounce
- OTT
- Pull Backs
- Sway
- Titanic

Phase 3:
- Medicine Ball Sweep
- Medicine Ball Spiral
- Pulley Push
- Pulley Pull

Phase 4:
- Kneeling Ball Balance
- Basic Curl-ups
- Tail Up Stretch
- Cork Screw

4 Football – Handball – Basketball

Dynamic multidirectional sports require good control of momentum in all directions, the ability to drive powerfully from the lower body, the ability to withstand contact from other players and well controlled jumps and landings. These types of sport sustain high rates of knee, ankle and back injuries if dynamic balance and stability are not adequate.

Priority tests

- All of the foundation tests
- Jumping and Landing
- Side Hops
- Rotational Jumps
- Minisquat

Priority exercises

Phase 1:

- Any of the Phase 1 exercises

Phase 2:

- OTT
- Pull Backs
- Lunges
- Step-ups
- Space Invaders
- Bridges
- Titanic
- Balance
- Any of the mobility poses
- Leg Swing
- Lunge Progressions: test with catching tasks
- Add Shoulder Internal Rotation Test for handball and basketball

Phase 3:

- Any Phase 3 exercise

Phase 4:

- Any Phase 4 exercise

⑤ Cross-country Skiing

These athletes require a strong neutral trunk position combined with powerful hip drive. Without attention to detail in their dynamic posture, they can easily overuse their back muscles to keep their pelvis secure, increasing their risk of lower back pain and decreasing their hip drive.

Priority tests
- All of the basic tests
- Forward Trunk Inclination
- Standing Leg Swing

Priority exercises
Phase 1:
- Any Phase 1 exercise
- Lumbo-pelvic mobility

Phase 2:
- OTT
- Pull Backs
- Lunges
- Step-ups
- Space Invaders
- Bridges
- Titanic
- Balance

Phase 3:
- Pulley Push
- Pulley Pull
- Medicine Ball Clean
- Medicine Ball Sweep
- Trunk Incline Pulley Push
- Pulley Pull Drive

Phase 4:
- Side Squat Tosses
- Overhead Tosses
- Stair Bounding
- Side Leaps

⑥ Cycling

Small asymmetries and deviations out of the sagittal plane can affect efficiency and power in cyclists. They should be trained to keep the pelvis in a consistent position by accessing the gluteal group, and learn how to flex the hip without side bending the spine. They should also learn how to keep the knee aligned with their hip.

A secure trunk using low effort abdominal activity will allow these athletes to breathe normally as they cycle. Compressing the body in a sprint situation will give a short-term blast of power, but the same strategy cannot be sustained in long road races. Road racers and triathletes should develop independent trunk control so that they are not over dependent upon their arms for stability, and so that they do not restrict their rib cage expansion by overusing oblique abdominals.

Priority tests
- The basic assessment
- Step-up

Priority exercises
Phase 1:
- Seated Knee Lift
- Greyhound
- Bridge
- Clam
- Superman

Phase 2:
- Step-ups
- OTT
- Titanic
- Space Invaders
- Bridges
- Lunges

Phase 3:
- Medicine Ball Sweep
- Pulley Push
- Progressive Lunges
- Incline Plank Knee Drive

Phase 4:
- Swiss Ball Elbow Circles
- Elbow Support Knee Drive
- Hip Ranger

7 Rowing

Three common complaints associated with rowing are lower back pain, knee pain and stress fractures of the ribs [60]. Full and coordinated joint motion throughout the kinetic chain is necessary to prevent over-stress in some areas due to poor mobility in others. For example, poor hip bending mobility can cause rowers to compensate by bending excessively in the spine and knees to reach their catch position, or they may over reach with their arms to strain for a little extra range. If these body parts are repetitively loaded in positions just beyond their safe zone, the whole kinetic chain is compromised and injury is likely to occur.

Rowers will often be told to "keep their chest up" in order to avoid collapse of this kind, but if they do not have sufficient hip joint mobility, or they lack sufficient trunk and pelvic control, this will not be achievable. The ability to control the relationship between the pelvis and the spine is critical in order to achieve an effective drive but is also essential to minimise lower back stress.

Priority tests

- Basic tests
- Forward trunk inclination
- Supine hip flexion

Priority exercises
Phase 1:

As for the other sports, Phase 1 exercises are used to activate the trunk, pelvic and scapular stabilisers, develop awareness of the neutral spine and introduce joint mobility relationships.

- Ball Bouncing
- Greyhound and Progressions
- Seated Knee Lift
- Basic Bridge
- Hip Pops
- Hip Swivels
- Diamond
- Sphinx
- Wall Press
- Straight Up Hamstring Mobility
- Wind-up Stretch
- Total Body Rotation. Although this movement is not a feature of the rowing motion, its role is to remove myofascial restrictions which may influence joint mobility.

Phase 2:

Phase 2 exercises develop stability relationships, and stable mobility.

- Single Leg Bounce with pelvic tilt to improve lumbo-pelvic control and coordination
- OTT and OTT Squat Thrust
- Upper Zone Stabiliser
- Pull Backs
- Lunges
- Titanic
- Step-ups
- All of the Phase 2 mobility exercises

Phase 3:

The Phase 3 exercises emphasise a strong drive while maintaining good trunk control.

- Medicine Ball Clean
- Medicine Ball Sweep
- Pulley Push – Incline Pulley Push
- Pulley Pull
- Pulley Pull Drive
- Progressive Lunges
- Incline Plank Knee Drive

Phase 4:

Many Phase 4 exercises can be used to balance the forces around the trunk and pelvis. Mixing up the direction of movement and introducing non-rowing movements can help to counteract imbalances and overuse in only one direction.

- Tail-up
- Hip Ranger
- Side Squat Tosses
- Toss and Stretch
- Overhead Tosses

- Quick Rotations
- Stair Bounding
- Swiss Ball Side Raises
- Swiss Ball Full Press-up
- Swiss Ball Elbow Circles
- Elbow Support Knee Drive
- Single Leg Squat
- Swiss Ball Hamstring Curl
- Toe Touch Sit-ups
- Ball Bounce Sit-ups

8 Swimming

Lower back pain and shoulder pain are frequent complaints among swimmers. When examined, swimmers with lower back pain often demonstrate over active erector spinae muscles (superficial long back muscles), inadequate control over the junction between the lower spine and the pelvis, and poor trunk and pelvic stabiliser activation.

Shoulder problems can come from a variety of sources, but there are some common features. The trunk is often not stable enough to provide a foundation to support the pull. The scapula is often not dynamically stable, and the glenohumeral (ball-and-socket) joint is subjected to muscle imbalances. The other important thing to remember is that you are testing both for swimming and for dry land training. It is not unusual for a swimmer to be uninjured until he or she takes up strength training in the gym.

Priority tests
- Double Arm Raise
- Seated Hamstring Test
- Static Lunge
- Standing Knee Lift
- Seated Knee Lift on the Ball
- Total Body Rotation
- Diamonds
- Wall Press
- Superman
- Double Arm Floor Press
- Standing Leg Swing
- Active Shoulder Internal Rotation (Windscreen Wiper)

Priority exercises
Phase 1:
- Ball Bouncing
- Greyhound and Progressions
- Seated Knee Lift
- Basic Bridge
- Hip Pops
- Hand Slides
- Diamond
- Windscreen Wiper
- Sphinx
- Wall Press
- Superman
- Star Hold
- Straight Up Hamstring Mobility
- Floor Presses
- Standing Leg Swing

Phase 2:
- Over the Top
- OTT Circles
- OTT Press-ups
- Upper Zone Stabiliser
- Pull Backs
- Supported Lunge
- Supported Single Leg Squat
- Static Lunge and Progressions
- Pullover
- Sway
- Titanic
- Floor Bridge
- Press-ups: Levels 1–3
- Triangle Pose
- Extended Warrior Pose
- Revolving Lunge
- Hip and Spine Twist

Phase 3:
- Medicine Ball Sweep
- Straight Pulley Push
- Pulley Pull
- Swiss Ball Body Spin
- Swiss Ball Press-up
- Handstand: Preliminary, Basic, Standard, Advanced
- Star Sequence

Phase 4:
- Side Squat Tosses
- Toss and Stretch
- Overhead Tosses
- Plyometric Press-ups: Levels 1–3
- Swiss Ball Side Raises
- Swiss Ball Full Press-up
- Basic Curl-ups
- Toe Touch Sit-ups
- Ball Bounce Sit-ups
- Cork Screw: Chest Opening Spinal Twist
- Chicken Wings: Chest Opening With Shoulder Internal Rotation
- Tail-up

9 Tennis

For effective stroke production, the tennis player needs great integration from the feet through the legs, pelvis, trunk and arms. Rotational mobility of the pelvis, over the hips, and the shoulders over the pelvis should be unrestricted. Pelvic and trunk control needs to be dynamic to allow that rotation mobility to provide a foundation for power. Without pelvic and trunk stability the shoulder becomes vulnerable as explained in Chapter 2, but the shoulder is also prone to its own muscle imbalances. To prevent injury and maximise technical proficiency, the lower, central and upper zones must all be managed.

Priority tests
- All of the foundation tests
- Jumping and Landing
- Side Hops
- Lunge Progressions: test with catching tasks
- Windscreen Wiper
- Double Arm Floor Press
- Momentum Control

Priority exercises
Phase 1:
- Any Phase 1 exercise to establish basic activation and balance in all three zones.

Phase 2:
- Over the Top
- OTT Circles
- OTT Twisting Squat Thrust
- OTT Scissors
- Upper Zone Stabiliser
- Pull Backs
- Dynamic Lunge and Progressions
- Step-ups
- Space Invaders
- Pullover
- Sway
- Titanic
- Floor Bridge
- Press-ups: Levels 1–3
- Wobble Cushion Steps
- Compass Balance
- Global Stability Plus Balance
- Triangle Pose
- Extended Warrior Pose
- Revolving Lunge
- Hip and Spine Twist

Phase 3:
- Medicine Ball Clean
- Medicine Ball Sweep
- Medicine Ball Spiral
- Straight Pulley Push
- Trunk Rotation Pulley Push
- Pulley Pull
- Compass Lunges
- Swiss Ball Body Spin
- Handstand: Preliminary, Basic, Standard, Advanced
- Aeroplane Sequence
- Star Sequence

Phase 4:
- Any of the Phase 4 exercises can apply to tennis conditioning.

310

⑩ Flatwater or "Sprint" Kayak

This is a sport where accurate, symmetrical repetition of a skill at speed is challenged by the changing elements of wind and water. It requires sensory perception and rapid neuromuscular adjustments in order to maintain efficient, powerful form.

The paddler needs good central control, shoulder stability, and mobility through hamstrings, pelvis and thorax. Training regimens, which focus solely on "core strengthening", can restrict rotation if the paddler does not have sufficient mobility through the legs, spine and shoulders. Rotational restriction, whether it is caused by actual muscular tightness or secondary mobility loss due to "bracing" in order to cope with loss of control on the water, will cause unwelcome movements as the body tries to compensate, especially around the shoulder and lower back.

The list below shows how you can adapt relevant exercises into tests as the formal tests in order to gain insight into paddling specific movement potential.

Priority tests

- Seated Thoracic Mobility
- Lumbopelvic Mobility. All of this set of movements sitting on the ball are relevant. Test 5.1 examines whether you can move your spine into the correct sitting position, 5.2 tests whether you 'give" more to one side than the other, and 5.3 Pelvic Rotational Mobility, looks at the available motion for the actual paddling action
- Trunk Inclination
- Straight Up Hamstring Mobility (see page 164), pressing the foot out to the point that corresponds to maximum knee extension in your kayak. Rotate into the Wind Up stretch. If this can be performed well, move into Straight Up Mobility and add Trunk Inclination. Finally, rotate in this position
- Seated Knee Lift on the Ball to test coronal plane spinal control
- Diamonds for scapula and shoulder stability

The exercises are aimed at creating a secure CLA, the available mobility to rotate thorax and pelvis around this axis, the anterior chain patterning to enable rotational torque generation without "bracing", and a relaxed, effective shoulder position. Phase three exercises emphasise coordination from legs through to arms.

Priority exercises
Phase 1:

- Knee Creepers and Thigh Slides, ensuring that CLA remains straight and shoulders and hips remain level
- Diamonds
- Scapular awareness and mobility (see page 166)
- Basic bouncing with side arm movements, ensuring that hips remain level and spine does not bend sideways.
- Seated Knee Lift, maintaining pelvis and thorax in direct alignment
- Straight Up Mobility, progressing to wind-up stretch
- Greyhound
- Floor Presses

Phase 2:

- Over the Top Circles: controlling this movement helps to prevent sideways trunk bending
- Single Leg Bounce: ensuring that hips do not drift sideways with respect to thorax
- Pull Backs: modified so that as the arm pulls back, the whole chest turns with it, keeping pelvis facing forward
- Step-ups: for development of force control from foot through to pelvis
- Compass Balance: to ensure that mobility is fully available even when balance is challenged
- Lunges with thorax rotation
- Upper Zone Stabiliser
- Revolving Lunge
- Hip and Spine Twists

Phase 3:

- Pulley Pull, maintaining relaxed shoulders
- Medicine Ball Sweep, Clean and Spiral for coordination of upper and lower body
- Swiss Ball Pendulum

Phase 4:

- Corkscrew
- Kneeling Ball Balance with thorax rotation
- Quick Rotations
- Swiss Ball Side Raises
- Tail Up
- Toss and Stretch
- Side Squat Tosses

Sample Group Session for a Professional Football Club

This is an example of a training session provided for a professional football team. Initially the players found even simple exercises challenging, and quite a few experienced post-exercise soreness in the first week or so. However, as their stability and movement patterns improved, the injury rate in the team significantly reduced and players reported feeling more confident about their bodies.

Warm-up:
- Ball Following
- Knee Tap and Balance
- Star Sequence
- Whole Body Rotation Mobility Exercise

Dynamic stability:
- Lunges
- Basic
- With added rotation and eyes closed
- Multidirectional with and without ball catch

Jumping:
- Single Leg Landing
- Leap Sideways onto one leg and balance
- Double Leg Landings with partner resistance
- Outside Leg Landings with partner resistance

Medicine ball:
- Medicine Ball Clean
- Medicine Ball Sweep
- Medicine Ball Toss and Stretch
- Medicine Ball Follow Through Rotations
- Medicine Ball Overhead Toss

Stretch band:
- Space Invaders
- Lunges with Stretch Band Resistance From Partner

Swiss ball:
- Titanic
- Over the Top
- Wall Squat with diagonal Medicine Ball movement
- Suspension Bridge – Sway
- Twisted Floor Bridge

Balance:
- Eyes closed balance with trunk side bend, rotation and forward tilting
- Aeroplane Sequence

Focused stability-mobility:
- Greyhound
- Clam
- Counter Body Rotation Exercise
- Hip and Spine Twist
- Triangle Pose
- Extended Warrior Pose
- Revolving Lunge

Chapter 12: Notes from the Clipboard: Rehabilitation Pathways

Working with athletes is an art as well as a science. We don't just have to appreciate their movement, but also their motivation, attitudes and beliefs. We also need to understand the context and environment within which they work and very often the culture of the sport, its development and attitudes.

Integration of sports medicine principles into the coaching environment can be met with resistance if the sports medicine professional doesn't communicate in a way that is meaningful to the coach and the athlete. Taking time to understand the sport and its demands often saves time in the long run. The following list of observations regarding this work has been generated from many years of trouble shooting for athletes and sporting organisations.

- Assume nothing and therefore consider everything.

- Apply absolute attention to detail, both structurally and functionally.

- Technical problems are not "personal style" just because the athlete is a high flyer.

- The best performer is not necessarily the one with the least issues. He is the one who compensates most effectively for them. When his ability to compensate is exceeded by the demands on his body and mind, a cycle of injury often ensues. Assess accurately without prejudice.

- The issues which predispose to injury are usually the same as those which influence performance. Assess the movements and control that the athlete will require or encounter in his sport, even those which would seem too obvious to examine.

- In order to develop self-awareness and responsibility, actively engage the athlete by asking for direct feedback during exercises. The ability to give high quality feedback may never have been developed in the athlete but it can be learned. Acquiring this skill and providing opportunities to use it increases confidence and internal motivation.

- Keep it relevant. An athlete who has never been injured doesn't prioritise prevention, but if the programme might improve performance, he will more readily engage with it.

- The art of applying science to sport is in making potentially complex concepts seem simple and accessible. Know the rocket science but teach it as though it is simply common sense.

- A common error in athletic development is to randomly add variety and complexity without attending to quality. Adding variety to training drills can enhance motor skill acquisition, but will not automatically foster ideal movement habits if sound movement foundations are not already in place. The experience of this author is that talented athletes find a way to manage a task using their own particular patterns and attributes. These patterns may not however be the best strategies for continued improvement or injury resistance. Progress athletic development by building secure foundations and challenging them in a systematic manner.

- Perform everything with excellence, from the warm-up across the whole programme. The mind and body note every movement pattern whether it is good or bad, so feed only the most efficient messages into the nervous system.

- Performance plateaux and chronic injuries relate to training which only asks "how many?", "how much?", "how far?" and "how fast?" without insisting on "how well?".

- Aim for effortless control. It trims away inefficiency, facilitates balance and stimulates the most effective muscle patterns.

- Train for confidence, adaptability, and creativity. Athletes with these qualities work out how to solve problems and exploit opportunities.

- Communicate and integrate. The multidisciplinary team needs to be on board. Although individual priorities may be different between professional personnel, the overall goal should be the same. Gaps in the programme emerge if one professional's findings do not influence the planning of other team members.

- Keep the big picture in mind: long range planning creates the context for tomorrow's athlete, not just today's athlete.

- Professional athletes should enjoy their movement in training and performing, and should understand that the best of the best know how to make it look easy even when it isn't.

Treatment Pathways

The following outlines summarise the rehabilitation pathways taken for athletes with a variety of injuries. They are not intended to be comprehensive case studies. Their purpose is to illustrate the relevance of functional tests for these athletes and the application of the principles described earlier in the book to specific presentations. Each of the athletes listed had chronic or recurrent injuries. They had previously received standard local treatment for their pain. However, this approach had not permanently resolved the problem. For all of these athletes, there was a fundamental functional movement issue causing a structural breakdown.

The Tennis Player with Shin Pain

A 23-year-old tennis player presented to the clinic with bilateral medial shin pain of six months duration. She was palpably tender over her tibialis posterior but had no other musculo-skeletal pain.

Performance perspective
The player was relatively slow off the mark and unstable when trying to control her momentum on court.

The player had noticed that her knees tend to collapse inwards when training. She had been practising exercises in the gym and trying to gain knee control for five months.

This outline describes a 30-minute session aimed at changing her patterns. The player was observed with her shoes off during testing.

Main Findings for Function Related Testing

Basic balance testing
The entire leg rotated medially from the hip, turning the knee inwards and flattening the foot. This movement was amplified by adding a simple arm movement. The greater the balance challenge, the more deeply the leg would rotate. Several points should be considered from this result. The inability to maintain the femur in neutral indicates further investigation of hip control and GMax–GMed activity. The tendency to depend on the inner part of the foot for balance and control will lead us to investigate sensory awareness in the sole of the foot. The response to simple arm movements with eyes open implies dissociation problems.

Static lunge testing
The player's knee alignment collapsed inwards immediately in the movement. She moved her hips backwards instead of downwards indicating a lack of eccentric control in GMax.

Listening foot test
This test demonstrated to the athlete that she had very poor awareness of the central forefoot area, and very little control of her foot and ankle other than in the collapsed position where the medial border of her foot was contacting the floor. She was overusing tibialis anterior and posterior to control her foot pressure in a low weight-bearing position. She was unable to activate popliteus.

Likely mechanism of injury
The athlete would push off her stance limb with her foot and leg in an inwardly collapsed position, causing tibialis posterior to repetitively contract in a stretched position.

Treatment Approach

Proprioception-dissociation at the foot-ankle

The athlete first worked on her plantar surface connection with the listening foot exercise. After being shown how to feel how her fibula moved in response to her foot pressure, she was able to decrease her excessive peripheral muscle activity and increase the sensitivity of her foot control.

The same technique was applied in standing with the athlete feeling movement in her hip joint in response to changes in foot pressure. This helped her to make a sensory connection between her foot and her hip.

Activation

The Clam was used to establish basic activation of GMed and increase awareness in the area of the lateral hip.

The basic Bridge was used to establish activation of GMax and differentiate between hip extension and back extension. This was quickly progressed to Hip Swivels in the Bridge position to introduce alternating GMax contractions.

Some simple seated bouncing with arms stretched above the head increased the player's central tone and stimulated trunk stabiliser activation.

Balance

Having increased the plantar surface sensory connection and established activation of the gluteal group, basic balance was reintroduced, with the athlete focusing on the feeling under her foot. She was quickly able to recognise the feeling of her limb collapsing and was able to correct it.

Increasing functional loading

The athlete was taught a basic wall squat with the Swiss Ball in order to develop an awareness of her spinal position, knee and foot position and eccentric control of her GMax. In testing we learned that this athlete shifted her pelvis backwards when performing the lunge to compensate for inadequate eccentric GMax control. Using the ball decreases the complexity of the movement compared to a standard squat by limiting the number of possible compensations in the kinetic chain from foot to spine. By maintaining a consistent trunk and ankle position, it was easy for the athlete to detect errors in her hip movement.

Once the athlete felt secure in her hip, foot and knee control, she was progressed to a ball lunge. The ball version slightly decreases the loading on the limb, making it an ideal intermediate step towards full body weight control.

Re-testing at the End of Session 1

The basic lunge was re-tested. Foot, knee and hip control was achieved to 95 degrees of knee flexion. On basic balance testing, the athlete could detect control problems early and correct them.

A foundation like this can then be built upon at increasing functional levels. The key was establishing awareness links between the foot and the hip, and increasing sensory awareness around the foot and ankle. With this in place the positive support reflex could be accessed to improve hip, knee and pelvic control.

The Rower with Lower Back Pain

This athlete presented with severe recurrent episodes of lower back pain which failed to respond to standard treatment regimens, and he was unable to continue with his sport due to this problem.

Main Findings for Function Related Testing

- **Lumbo-pelvic mobility:** poor mobility and dissociation.
- **Hamstring length in sitting:** poor trunk proprioception and postural control.
- **Supine hip flexion:** pelvis rotated posteriorly at 80 degrees of hip flexion.
- **Seated forward tilt test:** trunk folded into flexion early in the motion.
- **Lunge:** poor lateral pelvic control, overuse of latissimus dorsi.
- **Minisquat:** loss of normal hip flexion.
- **Balance:** poor trunk orientation over each foot.

Likely mechanism of injury

This athlete was relatively more flexible in his spine than in his hips, and had poor awareness and control of his lumbo-pelvic region. In the recovery phase of his stroke, his spine bent into flexion very early, partly because he had greater "give" in it than in his hips, and partly because he lacked the proprioception and stability in his spine to prevent it. This placed him in a poor position for engaging the water resistance on his catch and placed maximum stress on his back at the beginning of his pull.

Treatment Approach

Proprioception and activation were high priorities for this athlete. He started with some gentle seated bouncing on the Swiss Ball, trying to land accurately in the same place each time. This addressed several issues: trunk orientation, trunk stabiliser activation and proprioception.

Following this, he practised basic lumbo-pelvic movements, recovering to his neutral position after each one. This combined mobility with control and proprioception. The same concept was progressed using only lateral pelvic tilts with recovery to neutral while bouncing.

For the hip to lumbar spine relationship, the supine hip flexion test position was used as a sustained positional hold to allow the athlete to improve his hip mobility and relax his back.

For basic TrA activation and integration, the athlete learned the Greyhound exercise and the Wall Press. He was accustomed to collapsing his trunk into a flexed position, so these two exercises introduced the concept of activating stabilisers to maintain a neutral trunk position. Once he could achieve this, he performed the seated trunk tilt to combine the neutral trunk control with hip flexion.

Bridge was introduced to activate the rower's GMax and this activation was applied to the Swiss Ball wall squat. This movement had several purposes. The rower had a primary movement dysfunction involving his hips and lumbar spine. He would flex his lumbar spine rather than flex his hips. The wall squat altered his movement pattern by teaching him how to flex his hips and knees while maintaining a consistent spinal position. In this manner it worked on kinaesthetic, proprioceptive and stabilising elements, while also training eccentric and concentric GMax activity.

Once these Phase 1 elements were established, the rower was able to progress to OTT. The basic OTT increased trunk stability in the neutral position, and then the Squat Thrust was added in this position to further train the relationship between the neutral trunk and the flexing hip.

The seated side tilts while bouncing were progressed to the single leg position sitting on the ball. This required higher level movement control and dynamic lumbopelvic stability.

Titanic was added to coordinate sustained hip and back extensor activity with neutral trunk control. To coordinate dynamic hip and trunk stability, Medicine ball cleans and lunges were introduced, with rotation added when the basic movement was achieved.

For low load dynamic trunk control and endurance, the rower was asked to sit on the ergo with his hands on his head and a neutral trunk. He was asked to maintain his trunk position as he moved forward and backwards on the ergo. Pulley exercises and general gym exercises were finally added to restore confidence in a training environment.

Eventual Outcome

Increased confidence, decreased pain and return to sporting activity.

The Sprinter with Recurrent Groin and Hamstring Strains

This athlete had a two year history of recurrent injury. He complained of chronic tightness around his hips, a loss of technical proficiency, and restricted movement in his right shoulder. Prior to these problems emerging he had sustained a minor right knee injury.

Main Findings for Function Related Testing

- **Walking drills:** Loss of CLA when stepping onto the left foot. Trunk collapsed to the right.
- **Basic balance:** Extremely poor balance on both legs with the right leg slightly worse. Foot rigidity evident on the right foot.
- **Standing leg swing:** The athlete was unable to perform a standing leg swing on either leg. He lacked sufficient balance and pelvic stability to achieve the movement.
- **Knee raise in standing:** The athlete pulled down with his right latissimus dorsi if asked to lift his right knee.
- **Basic lunge**: Pelvis tipped laterally and anteriorly. Lumbar spine collapsed into extension. His right knee deviated medially.

Likely mechanism of injury

This athlete was unable to maintain a vertical CLA . When stepping onto his left foot, his trunk would collapse to the right, which biased his left adductors to increase their role in extending his hip and maintaining balance. His GMax did not activate spontaneously in any position or movement, so his adductor group and his hamstrings were overloaded to compensate. By pulling his right shoulder down, the athlete was unable to move his elbow backwards, giving him the perception of shoulder stiffness where there was none actually present.

This athlete was highly dominant in his hamstrings and erector spinae. He also lacked the awareness to detect that he consistently moved his lumbar spine instead of his hip. His poor trunk stabilising strategy depended upon his erector spinae and his hip flexors, as his TrA was not active, and this amplified his feelings of hip stiffness. The absence of a listening foot on the right was linked to poor pelvic control on the right side, again causing overuse of his hamstrings.

Because the athlete could not productively move his hips up and forward with hip extension, he ran in a "sitting down" position, pulling his body over his fixed foot with his hamstrings instead of pushing his hips forward over his fixed foot.

Treatment Approach

This athlete required a classic progression through the four Phases. In Phase 1, all the exercises were used to activate the athlete's GMax, GMed and TrA. The listening foot exercise was critical in improving his balance and encouraging normal stabilising mechanisms in his right leg. Seated lumbo-pelvic movements and bouncing were used to increase the athlete's awareness and control of his pelvic position. Wall Press worked on symmetry and trunk stability in a position which established a secure CLA. Superman worked on dissociation of lower limb movement from the trunk by requiring the athlete to flex and extend his hip with consistent control of his spine.

The athlete smoothly worked through Phase 2, aiming for a long body shape with low effort. Lunges and Titanics developed posterior chain coordination with trunk control, and single leg bouncing challenged his body orientation over the fixed foot. His OTT was eventually progressed through to single leg squat thrusts for high level hip flexion patterning, as he had a tendency to let his right knee drift medially on flexion.

Phase 3 was important in establishing correct timing between the athlete's knees and hips. The Medicine ball cleans and sweeps trained full range coordinated extension of the lower limbs from the floor and continued to train the CLA at a higher level. Because the athlete needed to resume a strength training programme in the gym, this pattern needed to be firmly established. Pulley exercises trained global control with a lengthened trunk position. The standing stretch band knee drive focused the athlete on actively moving his body over his stance hip.

Phase 4 introduced speed and load demands to the athlete's control, as well as adding variability to his stability challenges. Stair bounding ensured that full power was generated from the athlete's lower body without the trunk posture being affected.

Once this athlete achieved a secure CLA, the strain on his groin decreased. Previous treatment had tried to activate the major stabilising groups, but in order to be successful they had to be combined with proprioceptive and kinaesthetic awareness work. This tied in nicely with the athlete's technical work on the track, as it made sense of his movement problems and increased his motivation to comply with the programme.

The Golfer with Lower Back Pain

This athlete presented with a history of increasing lower back problems and a persistent barrier to technical improvement. She was attempting to increase her power with a gym-based resistance programme but was seeing no improvement.

Main Findings for Function Related Testing

- **Basic standing position:** The athlete displayed excessive muscle activity in her tibialis anterior and quadriceps in quiet standing. She had poor tone in her lower abdominal region and high tone in her upper abdominal region.
- **Balance:** Extremely poor, with particular rigidity in the right foot and ankle.
- **Pelvic rotation in standing:** Poor, with a tendency to over rotate the upper trunk to compensate.
- **Seated forward trunk tilt:** This position provoked strong erector spinae activity.

Likely mechanism of injury

There were several contributing factors. The player's address position placed her in lumbar extension which was sustained with high erector spinae use. As she moved into her back swing, her poor pelvic rotation caused her to shift her hips excessively sideways and disengage her upper trunk from her lower trunk. As she began her swing from this position, her right lower leg was unable to rotate adequately, causing her to try to force her pelvis into a poorly timed rotation. Her spine was forced into excessive extension and side bending, causing a compression force through her lumbar facet joints.

Treatment Approach

Stability, mobility and awareness needed to be worked on simultaneously. The first step was achieving a listening foot on the right side, which would permit the lower leg to rotate normally in the swing. This was combined with standing pelvic rotation awareness to reduce the excessive sideways weight shift in her backswing and provide a basis for maintaining the tensile relationship between the upper and lower trunk that would allow her to generate more power.

As this movement vocabulary was being developed, the player was taught Greyhound, Wall Press and Seated Bouncing to activate TvA and train a neutral trunk position. She was also taught Wall Squat to learn how to activate GMax without using her back extensors, and to increase the proportion of control coming from her hip region rather than her back and lower legs.

Once these elements were in place, it was possible to progress into Phase 2 and 3 exercises such as Titanic, Over the Top and Body Spin as well as integrating the yoga-based mobility sequences for strength and flexibility.

As with the sprinter, the player's rehabilitation was strongly connected to analysis of her stroke problems. Addressing the movement barriers in addition to the stability problems increased the specificity of the treatment and targeted prevention of further problems. She was able to resume play at a professional level with an increase in technical proficiency and minimal discomfort.

The Tennis Player with Shoulder Pain

This left-handed player presented with increasing anterior shoulder pain, particularly on open forehands and slice backhands. Her playing tolerance had dropped to thirty minutes before pain stopped her.

Main Findings for Function Related Testing

- **Postural observation:** The player had an over developed upper trapezius and pectoralis major on her left side.
- On normal gait, the player did not rotate her upper trunk effectively.
- **Lunge:** The player showed a tendency to tip forward on the lunge and an unwillingness to move into full range of motion.
- **Shoulder rotation test:** The player's head of humerus would slide forward as the player rotated her arm.
- **Trunk rotation test:** The player rated poorly in both directions.
- Scapular and trunk stability was normal on formal testing.

Likely mechanism of injury
When playing a forehand, the player rotated herself as a block rather than separating her pelvic and thoracic rotation. Without this rotation dissociation, she did not weight transfer effectively during the stroke and did not access potential elastic energy in her trunk to generate power. This caused her to overuse her arm to deliver power in her stroke.

On the slice backhand, the player kept her front knee relatively straight and tipped her body forward, causing her to poorly position her shoulder. As she played the stroke in this position, the head of her humerus drifted forward, and her perception of muscular effort was on the anterior surface of the shoulder instead of the posterior surface.

Treatment Approach

In standing, the player was introduced to the Total Body Rotation exercise in order to increase her awareness of pelvic and thoracic rotation as well as her available mobility.

This was progressed onto pelvic rotation over the fixed foot, focusing on initiating the movement with the pelvis and allowing the shoulders to follow. This movement was progressed into a forehand movement, integrating the arm into the movement.

The scapula awareness exercise from Phase 1 was performed to increase the player's appreciation of scapular protraction and retraction. Although her scapular control was quite good in overhead positions, her scapular mobility at lower arm positions was poor.

This entire session took place on court so that the new movement awareness could immediately be integrated into the tennis stroke. The player regularly performed stability exercises, so her trunk, pelvic and scapular stability were sound. Her problem was functional mobility. Once the mobility awareness had been restored and assimilated into her movement, the shoulder loading was reduced. The player continued to play for two hours with no onset of pain.

The Footballer with Knee Pain

This player had undergone reconstructive surgery for the anterior cruciate ligament in his right knee one year previously. He continued to experience increasing pain and a feeling of instability in his knee, despite the ligament showing no signs of insufficiency on testing. The player had undergone standard rehabilitation for his knee, but he was now no longer able to train or play.

Main Findings for Function Related Testing

- **Basic balance:** Extremely poor on the right leg with visible rigidity in the foot and ankle.
- **Standing knee lift:** The player tipped his trunk to the right when lifting his left knee, and collapsed his trunk to the right when he lifted his right knee.
- **Basic lunge:** The pelvis tipped laterally and tilted forward, with loss of knee alignment on both left and right knees.
- **Landing from a basic jump:** Loss of normal shock absorbing motion in the knee and hip. The player landed with stiff joints, causing more pain than was necessary.

Mechanism of continuing pain

The rigidity observed in the right foot was confirmed with the listening foot exercise. The player had no available tibial rotation, which affected the self-locking mechanism of the knee.

With a faulty positive support mechanism, the player's quadricep and gluteal muscle activity was impaired. Without this control, he used maladaptive strategies like stiffening his joints to cope with impact as well as checking forward momentum. With poor GMed and GMax, the player's pelvic stability was inadequate to cope with change of direction activities. The poor pelvic platform led to loss of trunk control and stability, which increased the forces acting on his knee.

Treatment Approach

All of the Phase 1 exercises were used, as this player was initially unable to activate trunk or pelvic stabilisers. The tibial rotation and sensory feedback from the right foot needed to be established to enable the pelvic stabilisers to activate. The player performed active listening foot exercises to improve this. This was backed up with Clam and Bridge exercises to encourage activation of the pelvic stabilisers. Superman trained the player not to collapse his hip when it was weight bearing, and to improve the symmetry of his trunk. The Phase 2 exercises were added to the programme, with emphasis on maintaining a vertical CLA, as the player tended to support his trunk tipped to the right through habit. The Step-up and Lunge were priority movements. Space Invaders developed strength in the player's hip abductors, but he needed to focus on bending his hips to avoid tipping his trunk excessively forward.

In Phase 3, most of the exercises were used in order to coordinate and sequence the hip and knee movement. In addition to the listed Phase 4 exercises, the player's strategies for controlling momentum were addressed, as he took up to six steps to check momentum where only two steps were necessary. This was the result of failing to drop his centre of gravity effectively to check his speed. Particular care was taken to address landings from jumps, especially if contacted in the air. Having taken an approach which restored neurosensory elements as well as stability and strength, the player reported feeling stronger, his pain diminished and his speed and agility improved. He was able to return to Premier League play.

The Dressage Rider with Lower Back Aching and Performance Problems

This rider presented with ongoing spinal pain as well as persistent performance barriers. When observed, she rode with her weight predominantly down her right side. As with many riders, she had a history of falls from horses since childhood.

Main Findings for Function Related Testing

- **Seated lumbo-pelvic lateral tilting:** Poor to the left.
- **Standing knee raise:** Poor when lifting the right knee.
- **Seated knee raise on the ball:** Poor when lifting the right knee.
- **Basic balance:** Poor on the left leg.
- **Listening foot:** poor on left side.

Likely mechanism of injury

The relationship between this rider's left foot, left side of the body, sense of body orientation and balance mechanisms was impaired. Her testing results are common in riders, who sustain blows to the pelvis and back through falls and sometimes being kicked by horses. These blows can interrupt normal pelvic mechanics and the effect can continue to influence a rider's movement and control despite the original pain of injury subsiding. The rider's sensory feedback was most consistent through her right side. She was unable to evenly weight bear in the saddle, not due to pain but because she perceived that her weight was evenly distributed when her CLA collapsed over her right side. This was her "normal" position.

Treatment Approach

The main aim for this rider was to achieve symmetry in order to relieve the stress on her spine, restore normal lumbo-pelvic mobility and allow her to use weight and leg aids effectively. To enable the rider to start establishing a firm CLA, the left foot was stimulated with the listening foot exercise, followed by lateral pelvic tilting in a seated position to release her left side. Once she could sit with weight through both sides of her pelvis, she was introduced to seated bouncing with her arms stretched above her head in order to practice a neutral centred trunk position. Placing a broomstick in her hands as she sat with her arms above her head, she practised bouncing with lateral pelvic tilt, landing on one side of the pelvis, bouncing in the centre and then bouncing on the other side while keeping the broomstick horizontal.

The Greyhound exercise and the Wall Press further encouraged trunk symmetry and TrA activation. Basic bridging with hip swivels started to establish GMax activity and lumbo-pelvic mobility. The rider practised standing balance exercises to encourage pelvic stability, stable, central body orientation over both sides of the body and increased sensory feedback from her left side. Once she was able to sit evenly, forward and backward lumbo-pelvic tilting and thigh slides for pelvic rotation were introduced to enable better movement in response to the horse's motion. The rider could progress into Phase 2 with Over the Top, Lunge and Titanic to increase anterior and posterior chain balance and stability. Sitting on the ball to perform bouncing and mobility exercises proved to be very effective in assisting the rider to find a new position when on her horse. She imagined the feeling of sitting on the ball as she rode, and she found that this helped her to find a central position. The horse was able to strike off into canter equally on both sides as a result. A central, balanced position decreased the stress on the rider's spine and allowed it to respond to the horse's movement, improving the security of her seat.

The Triathlete with Chronic Achilles Tendonitis

This athlete had been struggling with left Achilles tendon pain for three months. She had undergone an eccentric loading programme and conservative treatment including electrotherapy and soft tissue massage which did not help and she was unable to continue running.

Main Findings for Function Related Testing

- Looking at gait, the athlete demonstrated asymmetry in pelvic rotation. She did not advance the right side of her pelvis as she pushed off her left foot, causing her to push harder with her left calf.

- **Standing knee lift:** The athlete was unable to maintain a straight supporting left hip as she raised her right knee.

- **Lunge:** Poor pelvic control and unwillingness to adequately bend the left hip was observed.

- **Listening foot:** The athlete was unable to alter her foot pressure on the floor. Both feet were functionally rigid and unable to provide accurate sensory feedback.

- **Basic balance:** The athlete's body rotated to the left when standing on her left leg.

Likely mechanism of injury

This athlete had a combination of stability and mobility issues. Her poor GMed and GMax activation caused her pelvis to collapse on impact with the ground, increasing foot contact times and lower limb loading. She also had a fundamental locomotion dysfunction in that she lacked symmetry of pelvic rotation as she ran, causing her to over push with her calf muscle.

Treatment Approach

In order to directly address the biomechanical aspects of the problem, the athlete was taught counter body rotation while lying on her side. She was surprised to find the marked difference in her mobility from one side to the other. Once she had experienced this, she was asked to apply the feeling to her normal walking, simply noticing pelvic rotation as she moved.

Basic Phase 1 GMax and GMed exercises were learned in order to experience activation. This was progressed into weight bearing with the Lunge and Step-up to gain hip control through outer, mid and inner ranges. The standing Stretch Band Drive from the lunge position was used to give the athlete the feeling of moving her hip forward over her fixed foot using GMax instead of overusing her calf.

The Step-up was progressed by adding a high knee lift from the trail leg, aiming to increase the speed of hip extension on the supporting leg.

Once the athlete could control an inner range GMax contraction in standing, calf raises were added, ensuring that the athlete's body could maintain its alignment.

The biggest factor in this athlete's recovery was treatment of her faulty movement patterns rather than focusing exclusively on regimens for the Achilles tendon. Once the counter body rotation was re-established along with an ability to support her body weight on impact with the ground and then to extend her hip, the athlete's symptoms began to diminish. She was able to return to running without further problems.

The Golfer with Shoulder Pain

This athlete had a two-year history of pain across his right upper trapezius, right scapula, and right thoracolumbar area. He had invested a great deal of money on treatment, with no improvement in his symptoms. Despite the amount of treatment this athlete had received, no one had ever looked at his swing. All of his prior treatment had been directed to the area of pain, not the cause of the tissue stress.

Main Findings for Function Related Testing

- **Total body rotation:** extremely poor to the right.
- **Total body rotation with hips and knees bent:** provoked the right hip to shoot backwards, dropping the left shoulder.
- **Thoracic rotation:** normal.
- **Cervical rotation:** normal.
- **External rotation of the right shoulder:** moderately restricted.

Performance perspective
Undesirable swing plane. The player tended to swing the club around his body on the back swing, disconnecting the arm motion from his body.

Likely mechanism of injury
Due to pelvic rotation restrictions, the player was shifting his right hip backwards. This caused him to drop his left shoulder as he swung the club backwards, making it necessary for him to over pull with the muscles of his neck and posterior shoulder on the right side.

Treatment Approach

The main priority for this athlete was to restore the pelvic rotation necessary to correct his swing. He performed the Total Body Rotation exercise to start restoring motion in his hip, followed by Pelvic Rotation over the Fixed Foot to raise his awareness of the pelvic rotation movement and establish it as part of his movement vocabulary. The athlete was also taught piriformis stretching.

At the end of session 1, the athlete re-evaluated his swing, and found that he could swing without discomfort and with an increased sensation of free rotation.

The athlete's programme was expanded to include the Phase 1 exercises Greyhound, Basic Bridge, Hip Pops and Clam as well as Diamonds. He added Phase 2 exercises Titanic, Over the Top, and Suspension Bridge. Finally, the yoga-based mobility sequences from Phases 2 and 3 were added.

Eventual Outcome

After several months on the programme, the athlete was able to report greatly improved performance with minimal discomfort.

The Footballer with Lower Back Pain and Groin Pain

The player was referred by his professional club with a history of lower back pain and acute right groin pain which stopped him playing. Hernia had been eliminated as a possible diagnosis.

Main Findings for Function Related Testing

- **Static lunge:** very poor control of pelvis, knee and trunk, decreased hip flexion, forward inclined trunk.
- **Double arm raise:** poor trunk control, no evidence of abdominal activity in response to arm raise, forward pelvic shift.
- **Single knee raise:** loss of control over the right stance leg, dependence on right latissimus dorsi, right side bending of the trunk on lifting the right knee, overactive feet.
- Palpable insufficiency of multifidus at L4–L5 levels.

Likely mechanism of injury
Primary instability of trunk and pelvis.

Treatment Approach

After manual therapy treatment to the pelvis, the player was taught counter body rotation in side lying to establish better muscle patterns around his lumbar spine. He performed these along with Greyhound, Basic Bridging and Superman as his first programme.

Initially the player had problems with very simple movements. He was unable to sit on a Swiss Ball with his arms above his head and then move his right arm down to his side without losing control of his trunk. He was also unable to perform a simple Wall Press. This underlines the importance of assessment without prejudice: international-level athletes would be expected to be able to perform such simple movements but they are seldom evaluated.

To overcome these problems, the player needed to be taught correct breathing patterns. He was unable to stabilise his trunk using an efficient muscle pattern, and his over dependence upon his oblique abdominals had forced him to use an upper chest breathing pattern. Once he learned how to breathe and how to use the Balloon cue to correct his posture, his stability pattern changed and his progress was swift.

Once the basic TrA contraction was established and integrated with OTT, hip flexion was added with the Squat Thrust, and eventually the single leg Squat Thrust. Spinal rotation control was added by twisting the squat thrust.

The collapse of the player's trunk and problems with maintaining a strong vertical axis was addressed with seated bouncing with pelvic tilts, progressing to single leg seated bouncing with pelvic tilts.

The semi-supported lunge with the Swiss Ball helped the player to deepen his hip movement with control, which then transferred over onto normal body weight lunges. The player's lower back pain was resolved in one session and the groin pain resolved in three sessions. Recommendations were made for continued progression of the player's dynamic stability to develop it to an acceptable level for the demands of his sport.

The Long Jumper with Chronic Bilateral Anterior Compartment Syndrome

This athlete had struggled since her early teenage years with shin pain associated with running and jumping. This had eventually escalated into a compartment syndrome involving her tibialis anterior on both sides, for which she received a bilateral fasciotomy. This had failed to correct the problem and the athlete pursued physiotherapy. However, despite stabilising exercises being prescribed, there was no improvement in the athlete's symptoms. She had not been able to run for three years, and even walking could provoke her symptoms. She also suffered from pelvic and hip pain, and right shoulder pain.

Main Findings for Function Related Testing

- **Basic balance:** extremely poor, with a functionally rigid foot on both sides.
- **Static and dynamic lunges:** both poor, with tipping of the trunk to the right. The hips moved backwards rather than downwards indicating unwillingness to use GMax eccentrically.
- **Double arm raise:** pelvis drifted forward markedly, indicating poor trunk control and postural habits.
- **Standing knee raise:** over dependence upon latissimus dorsi on both left and right stance.

Likely mechanism of injury

This athlete's primary balance strategy was to overuse her tibialis anterior muscle. She also attempted to pull her tibia over her foot to move forward instead of using larger posterior leg muscles to push her body over the foot. In normal stance, she was unable to straighten her knees or hips, and stood with her pelvis shifted forward. Instead of running with her trunk supported by her pelvis, she collapsed her spine into a deep extension arch so that her pelvis was carried behind her spine with her hips very flexed. To counteract this, she tried to pull her shoulders back in an attempt to improve her posture as instructed by her coach. This combination put her pelvic muscles at a disadvantage and increased her dependence upon tibialis anterior. The area of the athlete's lower legs was congested, hard, and lacking in a normal pliable muscle quality.

Treatment Approach

In the initial stages, this athlete required myofascial release to the scarred areas of her shins, in addition to soft tissue mobilisation and manual lymphatic drainage. This was necessary to establish a healing environment through reducing congestion and increasing normal circulation. Retraining of movement patterns was the key element to recovery for the athlete however, as her natural pattern of locomotion would continue to aggravate the area of her pain.

Step 1 was activation of the pelvic and trunk stabilisers. Although the athlete had been performing stabilising exercises, she was not using the muscles that they were designed to address. She started with Basic Bridging, Hip Pops and Hip Swivels, as well as Clams and Standing Knee Press. She performed Greyhound exercises, Superman and Wall Press to learn to control a neutral trunk and coordinate limb movement with trunk stability. In order to prepare for weight-bearing exercise, she performed Listening Foot exercises, followed by Basic Balance.

Step 2 established restoration of Counter Body Rotation and increased the stabiliser loading by adding Over the Top, Titanic, Suspension Bridge and the Supported Lunge.

Step 3 focused on teaching the athlete to drive her hip forward over the supporting foot, so the Standing Knee Lift Drive and Pulley Pull Drive were added. A static lunge with lateral elastic resistance to the ribs proved to be extremely effective in coordinating the trunk with the pelvis.

Eventual Outcome

This was not a "quick fix". It took some time for the tissues in the local area to normalise; however, the athlete was able to return to running several times a week.

Appendix 1: Commonly Used Terms

Positional Relationships

Anterior (or ventral)

The front surface of the body or structure within the body. It can also describe a relationship between body parts, e.g. the sternum is *anterior* to the lungs so anterior also means *towards* the front. The lungs as a structure will have an anterior surface.

Posterior (or dorsal)

The back surface of the body or structure within the body, e.g. your back is your posterior surface, and your spine is posterior to your lungs.

Superior

The structure is higher on the body with respect to another structure, e.g. you head is superior to your shoulders.

Inferior

The structure is lower on the body with respect to another structure, e.g. your feet are inferior to your knees.

Proximal

The part of a body structure that is closest to your body's centre, e.g. your femur is more proximal than your tibia.

Distal

The part of a body structure which is furthest from your body's centre, e.g. your hand is more distal than your elbow.

Movement Terms

Spine

Flexion: bending forward.
Extension: bending backward.
Lateral flexion: side bending.

Knee

Flexion: bending the knee.
Extension: straightening the knee.

Hip

Flexion: moving the thigh forwards to bend the hip.
Extension: moving the thigh backwards to straighten the hip.
Abduction: moving the thigh away from the midline of the body.
Adduction: moving the thigh towards or across the midline of the body.
Lateral rotation: the thigh turns outwards.
Medial rotation: the thigh turns inwards.

Shoulder

Flexion: moving the arm forward and up in a straight line.
Extension: moving the arm back in a straight line.
Abduction: moving the arm away from the body.
Adduction: moving the arm in the direction of or across the midline of the body.
Lateral rotation: moving the arm so that the inside surface faces relatively forwards.
Medial rotation: the inside surface of the arm faces relatively backwards.

Planes of Movement

Sagittal

The plane of flexion and extension, or forward and backward motion, eg. cycling.

Coronal

Sideways motions the plane of abduction and adduction, e.g. performing a cartwheel.

Transverse

The plane of rotation within the body, e.g. striking a baseball.

Muscle Contraction Terms

Inner range

The muscle is acting when it is shortest, e.g. if your elbow is fully bent and you try to actively bend it further, the bicep is contracting at its shortest.

Outer range

The muscle is contracting at its longest, e.g. in a pull up, starting with your elbows straight would be starting in the outer range as the bicep is at its longest.

Mid range

The point between these two extremes, and usually the strongest position for a muscle, e.g. the pull up is easier if you start with your elbows bent.

Concentric

As the muscle generates force, it shortens, e.g. the biceps in a bicep curl.

Eccentric

As the muscle contracts, it lengthens, e.g. the quadriceps as you move into a deep squat.

Isometric

The muscle does not change length as it contracts, e.g. the weight lifter holding a bar over her head is clearly working her muscles, but they are sustaining a position and therefore not changing length.

Motor Control Terms

Base of support

The total area contained between surface contact points of the body, e.g. standing on one foot offers a small base of support. Supporting your body on hands and knees offers a large base of support. A larger base is generally more stable.

Postural control

The body's ability to act automatically to control its equilibrium in response to *feedback* from visual, vestibular (inner ear) and somatosensory (muscles, tendons, skin and ligaments) sources. It is also the body's ability to prepare for movement in response to the impulse or idea to move, a response which triggers weight shift and stabiliser activity to produce a foundation for movement. This preparation is called a *feedforward* response.

Dissociation

The ability to move a body part smoothly and independently of other parts. If you "fix" with global muscle groups, it will make it difficult to move freely due to excessive muscle tension.

Proprioception

Awareness of joint position or joint motion generated from sensory feedback from the body.

Positive support response

The response of hip and knee extensors to stimulation to the sole of the foot, usually weight bearing.

Open chain

Movement where the distal end of the movement segment is not fixed, e.g. throwing a ball.

Closed chain

Movement where the distal movement segment is fixed, e.g. leg press.

Motor Learning Terms

Explicit learning

Learning that occurs as a result of acquiring an understanding of rules or processes, concepts or problem-solving strategies; the result of being taught "how to do" something.

Implicit learning

Learning that occurs unconsciously, without awareness that learning is occurring. It is usually difficult to express knowledge acquired in this way.

Appendix 2: List of Common Patterns

Throughout this book, many muscle action relationships have been discussed. This table summarises these relationships. The directional relationship simply refers to the position of the overactive groups with respect to the underactive groups.

Directional relationship	Anatomical relationship	Overactive muscles	Action of overactive muscles	Underactive/poorly timed muscles
Vertical	Proportion of upper to lower body used for force production. Overuse of arms	Pectoralis major Pectoralis minor Anterior deltoid	Creating and controlling force	TrA, multifidus, internal obliques. Poor force transfer through trunk to pelvis
Vertical	Lower leg activity with respect to hip activity	Tibialis anterior	Pulling leg forward over fixed foot	GMax/hamstrings failing to push hip forward over fixed foot
Vertical	Lower leg activity with respect to pelvis-hip control	Gastrocnemius/ soleus/flexor hallucis	Stabilising the leg peripherally	Poor GMed, GMax, unstable CLA
Vertical posterior	Lumbo-pelvic region to hip	Hamstrings Erector spinae	Controlling extensor forces at lumbo-pelvic-hip region	GMax, multifidus
Vertical anterior	Pelvis to hip	Superficial abdominals (rectus abdominis, external obliques) and hip flexors (iliopsoas and rectus femoris)	Controlling the pelvic-hip relationship	Transversus abdominis
Diagonal	Pelvis to contralateral shoulder	Latissimus dorsi	Maintaining the posterior oblique sling	GMax opposite side
Lateral	Trunk to unilateral pelvis	Quadratus lumborum	Managing the position of the trunk on the pelvis	GMed
Lateral	Medial to lateral hip	Adductor group	Controlling the hip	GMax/Gmed/deep rotators of the hip
Anteroposterior	Upper limb to trunk	Pectoralis major Pectoralis minor Anterior deltoid	Supporting and transferring load between the upper limb and trunk	Serratus anterior, lower trapezius, rotator cuff
Anteroposterior cross pattern	Lumbar spine to pelvis	Hip flexors Erector spinae	Stabilising the lumbo-pelvic relationship	Transversus abdominis, GMax

Appendix 3: Scoring Charts for the Basic Functional Assessment

The Basic Functional Assessment is a general array of tests which can be applied to anyone involved in sport. It is not intended to be sports specific, but covers the main areas involved in basic control. For more information on sports specific testing, refer to Chapter 11 of the book.

The following charts can be used to record a baseline impression of physical competence. Functional movements are difficult to measure objectively as there are many variables to consider throughout the kinetic chain. The intention of this test procedure is to quickly and simply highlight control problems which should be considered when planning training programmes.

If any of the tests scores 2 or more, it qualifies as a High Priority area.

If the sum of all the totals in the Basic Functional Assessment exceeds 5, the overall rating for the athlete is Remedial High Priority (RHP). If the score is between 3 and 5, the rating will be Remedial Priority (RP). If the score is 0–2, the athlete is rated as Competent (C).

Once you have done this, formulate an **action plan.** Work out your priority areas, and refer to the book for a plan to address them. Look at your training programme: make sure that it addresses your priority areas. For example, if you have poor lower and central control, hopping and bounding will increase your risk of injury. Prioritise improvement in your control while working on explosive power off both legs instead of alternate legs in order to satisfy training goals while developing the movement patterns to support them.

Finally, work out whether your findings can be linked to your technique. The concepts presented in Chapters 1 and 2 can help you to link test findings to movement issues.

Basic Functional Assessment Charts

Name: _____

Date of birth: _____

Date of testing: _____

1. Balance

Scoring: Select only the highest scoring error that you observe, i.e. select only one of the first three options. Add a point each if foot or face fixing are observed.

Balance		Eyes open balance		Eyes closed balance	
		R	L	R	L
Wobbles	1				
Foot shifts	2				
Toe touch	3				
Foot rigid	1				
Face fix	1				
Total:					

Balance subtotal: _____

2. Mobility Relationships

Scoring: Circle the relevant score.

Double arm raise		Seated hamstring test	R	L	Total body rotation	R	L
Pelvis rotated forward/ spinal curve deepened	1	Spinal neutral is lost	1	1	Turn limit is 1/3 of semicircle	2	2
Pelvis/weight shifted forward	1	Knee does not fully straighten	1	1	Turn limit is 2/3 of semicircle	1	1
Shoulders less than 180 degrees	1				Incorrect foot pressure response	1	1
Total:		**Total:**			**Total:**		

Mobility relationships subtotal: _____

3. Lower and Central Zone Stability

a)

Static Lunge	R leg forward	L leg forward	Eyes closed static lunge	R leg forward	L leg forward	Dynamic lunge	R leg forward	L leg forward
Knee moves inwards	1		Knee moves inwards	1		Knee moves inwards	1	
Pelvis tips sideways	1		Pelvis tips sideways	1		Pelvis tips sideways	1	
Hips move backward (lumbar curve deepens)	1		Hips move backward (lumbar curve deepens)	1		Hips move backward (lumbar curve deepens)	1	
Trunk tips sideways	1		Trunk tips sideways	1		Trunk tips sideways	1	
One arm drops lower than the other	1		One arm drops lower than the other	1		Trunk collapses forwards	1	
Lip biting or facial fixing	1		Lip biting or facial fixing	1		Moving shoulders back initiates return to start position	1	
Rigid front foot	1		Rigid front foot	1		Lip biting or facial fixing	1	
						Rigid front foot	1	
Total:			**Total:**			**Total:**		

b)

Standing knee lift		R Lift	L Lift	Seated knee lift		R Lift	L Lift
Hip hitches up on the lifting side-trunk shortens on that side	1			Hip hitches up on the lifting side-trunk shortens on that side	1		
Stance hip moves out to side	1			Pelvis moves out to side	1		
One arm moves lower	1			One arm moves lower	1		
Trunk tips sideways	1			Trunk tips sideways	1		
Leg does not lift straight	1			Leg does not lift straight	1		
Facial fixing	1			Facial fixing	1		
Foot fixing	1			Foot fixing	1		
Total:				**Total:**			

Lower and central zone control subtotal: _____

4. Upper Zone Control

Diamonds		R	L	Seated knee lift	
Shoulders move towards ears	1			Head rotates backward	1
Forearms lift < 10cm	1			Shoulders move up, or scapula wings off rib cage	1
				Pelvis drifts forwards	1
				Stomach protrudes	1
Total:				**Total:**	

Upper control zone subtotal: _____

5. Basic Global Control

Superman		R arm/L leg raised	L arm/R leg raised
Head rotates backward	1		
Shoulders move up, or scapula wings off rib cage	1		
Chest drops on unsupported side	1		
Pelvis rotates upwards or downwards on unsupported side	1		
Stomach protrudes-spinal curve deepens	1		
Total:			

Score summary:

Balance	
Mobility relationships	
Lower and central control	
Upper zone control	
Global relationships	

Overall total score: _____

Action plan:

1 Priority areas: _____

_____

2 Strength and conditioning programme implications: _____

_____

3 Technique implications: _____

_____

Bibliography and References

1   Abt, J.P., Smoglia, J.M., Bricj, M.J., Jolly, J., Lephart, S., & Fu, F.: 2007. Relationship between cycling mechanics and core stability. *Journal of Strength and Conditioning Research,* **21**(4): 1300–1304.

2   Alon, R.: 1996. *Mindful Spontaneity: Returning to Natural Movement.* North Atlantic Books, Berkeley, CA.

3   Anderson, T.: 1996. Biomechanics and running economy. *Sports Medicine,* 22(2): 76–89.

4   Barlow, W.: 1973. *The Alexander Principle: How to Use Your Body Without Stress.* Victor Gollancz, London.

5   Bergmark, A.: 1989. Stability of the lumbar spine: a study in mechanical engineering. *Acta Orthopedica Scandinavica,* **230**: 20–24.

6   Besier, T.F., Lloyd, D.G., Ackland, T.R. & Cochrane, J.L.: 2001. Anticipatory effects on knee joint loading during running and cutting manoeuvres. *Medicine and Science in Sports and Exercise,* **33**(7): 1176–81.

7   Bolgla, L.A. & Keskula, D.R.: 2000. A review of the relationship among knee effusion, quadriceps inhibition and knee function. *Journal of Sport Rehabilitation,* **9**(2): 160–168.

8   Bullock-Saxton, J.E., Janda, V. & Bullock, M.I.: 1994. The influence of ankle sprain injury on muscle activation during hip extension. *International Journal of Sports Medicine,* **15**(6): 330–334.

9   Burden, A.M., Grimshaw, P.N. & Wallace, E.S.: 1998. Hip and shoulder rotations during the golf swing of sub-10 handicap players. *J. Sports Sci.,* **16**(2):165–76.

10   Burnett, A., Cornelius, M., Dankaerts, W. & O'Sullivan, P.: 2004. Spinal kinematics and trunk muscle activity in cyclists: a comparison between healthy controls and non-specific chronic low back pain subjects: a pilot investigation. *Manual Therapy,* **9**(4): 211–219.

11   Cairns, M.C., Foster, N.E., & Wright, C.: 2006. Randomized controlled trial of specific spinal stabilization exercises and conventional physiotherapy for recurrent low back pain. *Spine,* **1**:31(19): E670–81.

12   Chappell, J.D., Yu, B., Kirkendall, D.T. & Garrett, W.E.: 2002. A comparison of knee kinetics between male and female recreational athletes in stop-jump tasks. *American Journal of Sports Medicine,* **30**(2): 261–267.

13   Christina, R.W.: 1996. Major determinants of the transfer of training: Implications for enhancing sport performance. In: Kim, K.W. (ed.) *Human Performance Determinants in Sport.* Korean Society of Sport Psychology, Seoul, pp. 25–52.

14   Comerford, M.J. & Mottram, S.L.: 2001. Movement and stability dysfunction: contemporary developments. *Manual Therapy,* **6**(1): 15–26.

15   Cowan, S.M., Hodges, P.W., Bennell, K.L., & Crossley, K.M.: 2002. Altered vastii recruitment when people with patellofemoral pain syndrome complete a postural task. *Arch. Phys. Med. Rehabil.,* **83**(7): 989–995.

16   Cowan, S.M., Schache, A.G., Brukner, P., Bennell, K.L., Hodges, P.W., Coburn, P. & Crossley, K.M.: 2004. Delayed onset of transversus abdominus in long-standing groin pain. *Med. Sci. Sports Exerc.,* **36**(12): 2040–2045.

17   Decker, M., Torry, M., Noonan, T., Riviere, A. & Strerett, W.: 2002. Landing adaptations after ACL reconstruction. *Medicine and Science in Sport and Exercise,* **34**(9): 1408–1413.

18   De Luca, L., Di Giorgio, P., Signoriello, G., Sorrentino, E., Rivellini, G., D'Amore, E., De Luca, B. & Murray, J.A.: 2004. Relationship between hiatal hernia and inguinal hernia. *Digestive Diseases and Sciences,* **49**(2): 243–247.

19   Diallo, O., Dore, E., Duche, P. & Van Praagh, E.: 2001. Effects of plyometric training followed by a reduced training programme on physical performance in prepubescent soccer players. *Journal of Sports Medicine and Physical Fitness,* **4**(3): 342–348.

20   Dickerman, R.D., Smith, A. & Stevens, Q.E.: 2004. Umbilical and bilateral inguinal hernias in a veteran powerlifter: is it a pressure-overload syndrome? Clinical Journal of Sport Medicine, 14(2): 95–96.

21   Don Tigny, R.: 2005. Critical analysis of the functional dynamics of the sacroiliac joints as they pertain to normal gait. *Journal of Orthopaedic Medicine,* **27**(1): 3–10.

22   Dufek, J. & Bates, B.: 1990. The evaluation and prediction of impact forces during landings. *Medicine and Science in Sports and Exercise,* **22**(2): 370–377.

23   Ellenbecker, T.S., Roetert, E.P., Piorkowski, P.A. & Schulz, D.A.: 1996. Glenohumeral joint internal and external rotation range of motion in elite junior tennis players. *Journal of Orthopaedic and Sports Physical Therapy,* **24**(6): 336–341.

24   Elphinston, J. & Pook, P.: 2000. *The Core Workout: The Definitive Guide To Swiss Ball Training for Athletes, Coaches and Fitness Professionals.* Lotus Publishing, Chichester.

25   Elphinston, J. & Hardman, S.L.: 2006. Effect of an integrated functional stability program on injury rates in an international netball squad. *J. Sci. Med. Sport,* **9**(1–2): 169–176.

26   Elphinston, J.: 2006. *Total Stabilitets-Traning: Prestationsutvecklande, Skadeforebyggande, Ovingar Och Teori.* SISU Idrottsbocker, Stockholm.

27   Escorsell, A., Gines, A., Llach, J., Garcia-Pagan, J.C., Bordas, J.M., Bosch, J. & Rodes, J.: 2002. Increasing intra-abdominal pressure increases pressure, volume, and wall tension in esophageal varices. *Hepatology,* **36**(4): 936–940.

28   Feldenkrais, M.: 1972. *Awareness Through Movement.* Harper and Row, New York.

29   Fleisig, G.S., Barrentine, S.W., Escamilla, R.F. & Andrews, J.R.: 1996. Biomechanics of overhand throwing with implications for injuries. *Sports Medicine,* **21**(6): 421–437.

30   Garrick, J.G. & Requa, R.: 2005. Structured exercises to prevent lower limb injuries in young handball players. *Clinical Journal of Sport Medicine,* **15**(5): 398.

31   Gibbons, S.: 2001. Biomechanics and stability mechanisms of psoas major. In: *Conference Proceedings 4th Interdisciplinary World Congress on Low Back and Pelvic Pain,* pp. 246–247.

32   Gracovetsky, S.A.: 1997. Linking the spinal engine with the legs: a theory of human gait. In: Vleeming, A., Mooney, V., Dorman, T., Snijders, C. & Stoeckart, R. (eds.). *Movement, Stability and Low Back Pain. The Essential Role of the Pelvis.* Churchill Livingstone, Edinburgh, pp. 243–251.

33   Grenier, S.G. & McGill, S.M.: 2007. Quantification of lumbar stability by using two different abdominal activation strategies. *Arch. Phys. Med. Rehabil.,* **88**(1): 54–62.

34   Grimstone, S.K. & Hodges, P.W.: 2003. Impaired postural compensation for respiration in people with recurrent low back pain. *Experimental Brain Research,* **151**(2): 218–224.

35   Hagins, M. & Lamberg, E.M.: 2006. Natural breath control during lifting tasks: effect of load. European Journal of Applied Physiology, **96**(4): 453–458.

36   Hall, K.G., Domingues, D.A. & Cavazos, R.: 1994. Contextual interference effects with skilled baseball players. *Perceptual and Motor Skills,* **78**(3): 835–841.

37   Hamlyn, N., Behm, D.G. & Young, W.B.: 2007. Trunk muscle activation during dynamic weight training exercises and isometric instability exercises. *Journal of Strength and Conditioning Research,* **21**(4): 1108–1112.

38   Hewett, T.E., Myer, G.D., Ford, K.R., Heidt, R.S. Jr., Colosimo, A.J., McLean, S.G., van den Bogert, A.J., Paterno, M.V. & Succop, P.: 2005. Biomechanical measures of neuromuscular control and valgus loading of the knee predict anterior cruciate ligament injury risk in female athletes: a prospective study. *American Journal of Sports Medicine,* **33**(4): 492–501.

39   Hides, J.A., Richardson, C.A. & Jull, G.A.: 1996. Multifidus recovery is not automatic following resolution of acute first-episode low back pain. *Spine,* **21**(23): 2763–2769.

40   Hintermeister, R.A., O'Connor, D.D., Lange, G.W., Dillman, C.J. & Steadman, J.R.: 1997. Muscle activity in wedge, parallel, and giant slalom skiing. *Medicine and Science in Sports and Exercise,* **29**(4): 548–553.

41   Hodges, P. & Richardson, C.A.: 1997. Feedforward contraction of transversus abdominis is not influenced by the direction of arm movement. *Experimental Brain Research,* **114**(2): 362–370.

42   Hodges, P. & Gandieva, S.C.: 2000. Changes in intra-abdominal pressure during postural and respiratory activation of the human diaphragm. J. Appl. Physiol., Sept. **89**(3): 967–976.

43   Hodges, P.: 2001. Changes in motor planning of feedforward postural responses of the trunk muscles in low back pain. *Experimental Brain Research,* **141**(2): 261–266.

44   Hodges, P.W., Heijnen, I. & Gandevia, S.C.: 2001. Postural activity of the diaphragm is reduced in humans when respiratory demand increases. *Journal of Physiology,* **537**(3): 999–1008.

45   Hodges, P.W., Gurfinkel, V.S., Brumagne, S., Smith, T.C. & Cordo, P.C.: 2002. Coexistence of stability and mobility in postural control: evidence from postural compensation for respiration. *Experimental Brain Research,* **144**(3): 293–302.

46   Hodges, P.W., Eriksson, A.E., Shirley, D. & Gandevia, S.C.: 2005. Intra-abdominal pressure increases stiffness of the lumbar spine. *Journal of Biomechanics,* **38**(9): 1873–1880.

47   Hodges, P.W., Sapsford, R., & Pengel, L.H.: 2007. Postural and respiratory functions of the pelvic floor muscles. *Neurourol Urodyn.* **26**(3): 362–371.

48   Hudson, J.L.: 1986. Coordination of segments in the vertical jump. *Medicine and Science in Sports and Exercise,* **18**(2): 242–251.

49   Hungerford, B., Gilleard, W. & Hodges, P.W.: 2003. Evidence of altered lumbo-pelvic muscle recruitment in the presence of sacroiliac joint pain. *Spine,* **28**(14): 1593–1600.

50   Hurd, W.J., Chmielewski, T.L., Axe, M.J., Davis, I. & Snyder-Mackler, L.: 2004. Differences in normal and perturbed walking kinematics between male and female athletes. *Clinical Biomechanics,* **19**(5): 465–472.

51   Huxel, K.C., Swanik, C.B., Swanik, K.A., Bartolozzi, A.R., Hillstrom, H.J., Sitler, M.R. & Moffit, D.M.: 2008. Stiffness regulation and muscle-recruitment strategies of the shoulder in response to external rotation perturbations. *J. Bone Joint Surg. Am.,* **90**(1): 154–162.

52   Irmischer, B.S., Harris, C., Pfeiffer, R.P., DeBeliso, M.A., Adams, K.J. & Shea, K.G.: 2004. Effects of a knee ligament injury prevention exercise program on impact forces in women. *Journal of Strength and Conditioning Research,* **18**(4): 703–707.

53   Ishikawa, M., Komi, P.V., Grey, M.J., Lepola, V. & Bruggemann, G.P.: 2005. Muscle-tendon interaction and elastic energy usage in human walking. *Journal of Applied Physiology,* **99**(2): 603–608.

54   Itoi, E., Kuechle, D.K., Newman, S.R., Morrey, B.F., & An, K.N.: 1993. Stabilising function of the biceps in stable and unstable shoulders. *J. Bone Joint Surg. Br.,* **75**(4): 546–550.

55   Itoi, E., Newman, S.R., Kuechle, D.K., Morrey, B.F. & An, K.N.: 1994. Dynamic anterior stabilisers of the shoulder with the arm in abduction. *J. Bone Joint Surg. Br.,* **76**(5): 834–836.

56   Jackson, O.: 1999. *Neuro-orthopaedics and geriatric rehabilitation: balance, flexibility, coordination: improving function for older persons, using the Feldenkrais method.* Northeast Seminars, East Hampstead, NH.

57   Janda, V.: 1983. On the concept of postural muscles and posture in man. *Aus. J. Physioth.,* **29**(3): 83–84.

58   Jull, G., Kristjansson, E. & Dall'Alba, P.: 2004. Impairment in the cervical flexors: a comparison of whiplash and insidious onset neck pain patients. *Manual Therapy,* **9**(2): 89–94.

59   Jung, A.P.: 2003. The impact of resistance training on distance running performance. *Sports Med.,* **33**(7): 539–552.

60   Karlson, K.: 2000. Rowing injuries. Identifying and treating musculo-skeletal and nonmusculo-skeletal conditions. *The Physician and Sports Medicine,* **28**(4): 40–50.

61   Kibler, W.B., McMullen, J. & Uhl, T.: 2001. Shoulder rehabilitation strategies, guidelines and practice. *Orthopedic Clinics of North America,* **32**(3): 527–538.

62   Kolar, P.: 1999. The sensomotor nature of postural functions: its fundamental role in rehabilitation of the motor system. *Journal of Orthopaedic Medicine,* **21**(2): 40–45.

63   Kornecki, S.: 1992. Mechanism of muscular stabilisation process in joints. *Journal of Biomechanics,* **25**(3): 235–245.

64   Kristjansson, E.: 2004. Reliability of ultrasonography for the cervical multifidus muscle in asymptomatic and symptomatic patients. *Manual Therapy,* **9**(2): 83–88.

65   Lee, D.G.: 2005. The thorax: an integrated approach for restoring function, relieving pain. *Physiotherapist Corporation,* Canada.

66   Lee, D. & Vleeming, A.: 2000. Diagnostic tools for the impaired pelvis. American Back Society Annual Meeting, December 7-9, Vancouver, Canada.

67   Leetun, D.T., Ireland, M.L., Willson, J.D., Ballantyne, B.T., & Davis, I.M.: 2004. Core stability measures as risk factors for lower extremity injury in athletes. *Med Sci Sports Exerc.* **36**(6):926–34.

68   Lephart, S.: 2003. Sensorimotor system: performance and protection. Paper presented at the *Seventh Olympic Conference in Sports Sciences, Athens,* 7-11 October.

69   Lewit, K.: 1999. Chain reactions in the locomotor system in the light of coactivation patterns based on developmental neurology. *Journal of Orthopaedic Medicine,* **21**(2): 52-57.

70   Li, L. & Caldwell, G.E.: 1998. Muscle coordination in cycling: effect of surface incline and posture. *Journal of Applied Physiology,* **85**(3): 927–934.

71   Louw, Q., Grimmer, K. & Vaughan, C.: 2006. Biomechanical outcomes of a knee neuromuscular exercise programme among adolescent basketball players: a pilot study. *Physical Therapy in Sport,* **7**: 65–73.

72   Magarey, M.E. & Jones, M.A.: 2003. Dynamic evaluation and early management of altered motor control around the shoulder complex. *Manual Therapy,* **8**(4): 195–206.

73   Malinzak, R.A, Colby, S.M., Kirkendall, D.T., Yu, B. & Garrett, W.E.: 2001. A comparison of knee joint motion patterns between men and women in selected athletic tasks. *Clinical Biomechanics,* **16**(5): 438–445.

74   Mascal, C.L., Landel, R. & Powers, C.: 2003. Management of patellofemoral pain targeting hip, pelvis, and trunk muscle function: two case reports. *Journal of Orthopaedic and Sports Physical Therapy,* **33**(11): 647–660.

75   McLean, S.G., Felin, R.E., Suedekum, N., Calabrese, G., Passerallo, A., & Joy, S.: 2007. Impact of fatigue on gender-based high-risk landing strategies. *Med. Sci. Sports Exerc.,* **39**(3): 502–514.

76   McNair, P.J., Prapavessis, H. & Callender, K.: 2000. Decreasing landing forces: effect of instruction. *British Journal of Sports Medicine,* **34**(4): 293–296.

77   McNitt-Gray, J.L., Hester, D.M., Mathiyakom, W. & Munkasy, B.A.: 2001. Mechanical demand and multijoint control during landing depend on orientation of the body segments relative to the reaction force. *Journal of Biomechanics,* **34**(11): 1471–1482.

78   Mellor, R., & Hodges, P.W.: 2006. Effect of knee joint angle on motor unit synchronization. *J. Orthop. Res.,* **24**(7): 1420–1426.

79   Mens, J., Inklaar, H., Koes, B.W., & Stam, H.J.: 2006. A new view on adduction-related groin pain. *Clin. J. Sport Med.* **16**(1): 15–19.

80   Mok, N.W., Brauer, S.G. & Hodges, P.W.: 2004. Hip strategy for balance control in quiet standing is reduced in people with low back pain. *Spine,* **29**(6): E107–112.

81   Moraes, G.F., Faria, C.D. & Teixeira-Salmela, L.F.: 2008. Scapular muscle recruitment patterns and isokinetic strength ratios of the shoulder rotator muscles in individuals with and without impingement syndrome. *J. Shoulder Elbow Sur.,* **17**(1): 48S–53S.

82   Moseley, G.L., Nicholas, M.K. & Hodges, P.W.: 2004. Pain differs from non-painful attention-demanding or stressful tasks in its effect on postural control patterns of trunk muscles. *Experimental Brain Research,* **156**(1): 64–71.

83   Moseley, G.L., Nicholas, M.K. & Hodges, P.W.: 2004. Does anticipation of back pain predispose to back trouble? *Brain,* 127(10): 2339–2347.

84   Mottram, S. & Comerford, M.: 1998. Stability dysfunction and low back pain. *Journal of Orthopaedic Medicine,* **20**(2): 13–19.

85   Myer, G.D., Ford, K.R., Brent, J.L. & Hewett, T.E.: 2006. The effects of plyometric vs. dynamic stabilization and balance training on power, balance, and landing force in female athletes. *J. Strength Cond. Res.,* **20**(2): 345–353.

86   Myer, G.D., Ford, K.R., McLean, S.G. & Hewett, T.E.: 2006. The effects of plyometric versus dynamic stabilization and balance training on lower extremity biomechanics. *Am. J. Sports Med.,* **34**(3): 445–455.

87   Myklebust, G., Engebretsen, L., Braekken, I.H., Skjolberg, A, Olsen, O.E. & Bahr, R.: 2007. Prevention of noncontact anterior cruciate ligament injuries in elite and adolescent female team handball athletes. *Instr. Course Lect.* **3**:56: 407–418.

88   Neptune, R.R., Zajac, F.E. & Kautz, S.A.: 2004. Muscle force redistributes segmental power for body progression during walking. *Gait and Posture,* **19**(2): 194–205.

89   Newcomer, K.L., Laskowski, E.R., Yu, B., Johnson, J.C. & An, K.N.: 2000. Differences in repositioning error among patients with low back pain compared with control subjects. *Spine,* **25**(19): 2488–2493.

90   Nuzzo, J.L., McCaulley, G.O., Cormie, P. & Cavill, M.J.: 2008. Trunk muscle activity during stability ball and free weight exercises. *Journal of Strength and Conditioning Research,* **22**(1): 95–102.

91   Olsen, O.E., Myklebust, G., Engebretsen, L., Holme, I. & Bahr, R.: 2005. Exercises to prevent lower limb injuries in youth sports: cluster randomised controlled trial. *British Medical Journal,* **330**(7489): 449.

92   Onate, J.A., Guskiewicz, K.M. & Sullivan, R.J.: 2001. Augmented feedback reduces jump-landing forces. *Journal of Orthopaedic and Sports Physical Therapy,* **31**(9): 511–517.

93   O'Sullivan, P.B., Burnett, A., Floyd, A.N., Gadson, K., Logiudice, J., Miller, D. & Quirke, H.: 2003. Lumbar repositioning deficit in a specific low back pain population. *Spine,* **28**(10): 1074–1079.

94   O'Sullivan, P.B., Phyty, G.D., Twomey, L.T. & Allison, G.T.: 1997. Evaluation of specific stabilizing exercise in the treatment of chronic low back pain with radiologic diagnosis of spondylolysis or spondylolisthesis. *Spine.* Dec. 15, **22**(24): 2959–2967.

95   Pfeiffer, R.P., Shea, K.G., Roberts, D., Grandstrand, S., & Bond, L.: 2006. Lack of effect of a knee ligament injury prevention program on the incidence of non-contact anterior cruciate ligament injury. *J. Bone Joint Surg. Am.,* **88**(8): 1769–1774.

96   Pirouzi, S., Hides, J., Richardson, C., Darnell, R. & Toppenberg, R.: 2006. Low back pain patients demonstrate increased hip extensor muscle activity during submaximal rotation efforts. *Spine,* **15**:31(26): E999–E1005.

97   Renkawitz, T., Boluki, D. & Grifka, J.: 2006. The association of low back pain, neuromuscular imbalance, and trunk extension strength in athletes. *Spine,* **6**(6): 673–683.

98   Roll, R., Kavounoudias, A. & Roll, J.P.: 2002. Cutaneous afferents from human plantar sole contribute to body posture awareness. *Neuroreport,* **13**(15): 1957–1961.

99   Rose, D.J.: 2003. *Fallproof! A Comprehensive Balance and Mobility Training Programme.* Human Kinetics, Champaign, IL.

100   Ross, A.L. & Hudson, J.L.: 1997. Efficacy of a mini-trampoline program for improving the vertical jump. In: Wilkerson, J.D., Ludwig, K.M. & Zimmermann, W.J. (eds.) *Biomechanics in Sports XV,* Texas Women's University, Denton, pp. 63–69.

101   Sahrmann, S.: 2002. *Diagnosis and Treatment of Movement Impairment Syndromes.* Moseby, St. Louis, pp.30–31.

102   Santello, M., McDonagh, M.J. & Challis, J.H.: 2001. Visual and non-visual control of landing movements in humans. *Journal of Physiology*, **537**(1): 313–327.

103   Saunders, S.W., Rath, D., & Hodges, P.W.: 2004. Postural and respiratory activation of the trunk muscles changes with mode and speed of locomotion. *Gait Posture.* **20**(3): 280–290.

104   Sell, T., Tsai, Y., Smoglia, J., Myers, J. & Lephart, S.: 2007. Strength, flexibility and balance characteristics of highly proficient golfers. *J. Strength and Conditioning Research,* **21**(4): 1166–1171.

105   So, R.C.H., Ng, J.K.F. & Ng, G.Y.F.: 2005. Muscle recruitment pattern in cycling: a review. *Physical Therapy in Sport,* **6**(2): 89–96.

106   Stanton, R., Reaburn, P.R., & Humphries, B.: 2004. The effect of short-term Swiss ball training on core stability and running economy. *J. Strength Cond. Res.*, **18**(3):522–8.

107   Thompson, C.J., Cobb, K.M., & Blackwell, J.: 2007. Functional training improves club head speed and functional fitness in older golfers. *J. Strength Cond. Res.*, **21**(1):131–7.

108   Umphred, D.A.: 2001. The limbic system: influence over motor control and learning. In: *Neurological Rehabilitation 4th Ed.*, Mosby, St Louis, pp. 148–177.

109   Urquhart, D.M., Hodges, P.W. & Story, I.H.: 2005. Postural activity of the abdominal muscles varies between regions of these muscles and between body positions. *Gait Posture,* **22**(4): 295–301.

110   Vad, V., Gebeth, A., Dinas, D., Altcheck, D. & Norris, B.: 2003. Hip and shoulder rotation range of motion deficits in professional tennis players. *Journal of Science and Medicine in Sport,* **6**(1): 71–75.

111   Van Wingerden, J.P., Vleeming, A., Buyruk, H.M. & Raissadat, K.: 2004. Stabilization of the sacroiliac joint in vivo: verification of muscular contribution to force closure of the pelvis. *European Spine Journal,* **13**(3): 199–205.

112   Vleeming, A., Pool-Goudzwaard, A.L., Stoeckart, R., van Wingerden, J.P. & Snijders, C.J.: 1995. The posterior layer of the thoracolumbar fascia. Its function in load transfer from spine to legs. *Spine,* **20**(7): 753–758.

113   Vleeming, A., Mooney, V., Snidjers, C. & Dorman, T. (eds.): 1997. *Movement, Stability and Low Back Pain: the Essential Role of the Pelvis.* Churchill Livingstone, Edinburgh.

114   Walker, M., Rothstein, J., Finucare, S. & Lamb, R.: 1987. Relationship between lumbar lordosis, pelvic tilt and abdominal performance. *Physical Therapy,* **67**(4): 512–516.

115   Young, W.B. & Behm, D.G.: 2003. Effect of running, static stretching and practice jumps on explosive force production and jumping performance. *Journal of Sports Medicine and Physical Fitness,* **43**(1): 21–27.

116   Zazulak, B.T., Hewett, T.E., Reeves, N.P., Goldberg, B., & Cholewicki, J.: 2007. Deficits in neuromuscular control of the trunk predict knee injury risk: a prospective biomechanical-epidemiologic study. *Am. J. Sports Med.* **35**(7):1123–30.

Index of Exercises

Chapter 7

Chapter 8

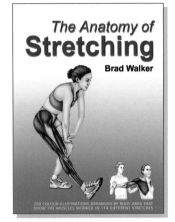

The Anatomy of Stretching

Brad Walker

978 1 905367 03 0 (UK)/978 1 55643 596 (US); **£14.99/$24.95**; 176 pages; 265 mm x 194 mm; 320 colour illustrations; paperback

Books on stretching are common, but *The Anatomy of Stretching* takes a more fundamental approach than the others, taking the reader inside the body to show exactly what is happening during a stretch. At the heart of the book are 300 full-colour illustrations that show the primary and secondary muscles worked in 114 key stretches arranged by body area. Author Brad Walker brings years of expertise – he works with elite-level and world-champion athletes, and lectures on injury prevention – to this how-to guide. He looks at stretching from every angle, including physiology and flexibility; the benefits of stretching; the different types of stretching; rules for safe stretching; and how to stretch properly. Aimed at fitness enthusiasts of any level, as well as at fitness pros, *The Anatomy of Stretching* also focuses on which stretches are useful for the alleviation or rehabilitation of specific sports injuries.

Brad Walker, B.Sc. Health Sciences, is a prominent Australian sports trainer with more than 20 years experience in the health and fitness industry. He graduated from the University of New England, and has postgraduate accreditations in athletics, swimming, and triathlon coaching.

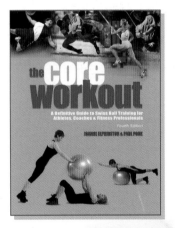

The Core Workout NEW EDITION

Joanne Elphinston & Paul Pook

978 1905367 10 8; **£14.95**, 144 pages; 250 mm x 212 mm; 120 black and white photographs; paperback

The Core Workout is your expert guide to Swiss ball training for core stability. Used by top athletes and fitness professionals across a wide range of sports, Swiss ball training can enhance essential stability and control for your sport. With over 30,000 copies sold worldwide and used by international and national elite sports organisations, including Premier Training, the leading personal trainer establishment in the UK, *The Core Workout* features: more than 85 drills with clear progressions, techniques to recruit your core muscles, common errors, partner and two ball drills, weight training and stretching on your ball, and sample sport specific programmes.

Joanne Elphinston is a Performance Consultant, international lecturer and physiotherapist working with elite and professional athletes including Olympic, Commonwealth and World Championship medallists, Premiership footballers and professional golfers.

Paul Pook is the National Fitness Coach for the Irish Rugby Football Union and has worked with elite athletes in a wide variety of sports.